Lily Briscoe: A Self-Portrait

Lily Briscoe
A Self-Portrait

an autobiography by
Mary Meigs

Talonbooks · Vancouver · 1981

copyright © 1981 Mary Meigs

published with assistance from the Canada Council

Talonbooks
201 1019 East Cordova
Vancouver
British Columbia V6A 1M8
Canada

Excerpts from this book have appeared in *Exile, Fireweed, Room of One's Own* and *Broadside*.

This book was typeset by Mary Schendlinger, designed by David Robinson and printed in Canada by Hignell for Talonbooks.

Second printing: April 1982

Canadian Cataloguing in Publication Data

    Meigs, Mary.
       Lily Briscoe, a self-portrait

    ISBN 0-88922-195-2

    1. Meigs, Mary. 2. Painters - Canada - Biography.
I. Title.
ND249.M43A2 1981   759.11   C81-091328-3

to
Barbara Deming
and
Marie-Claire Blais

Except thyself may be
Thine enemy.
Captivity is consciousness;
So's liberty.

Emily Dickinson

Part One
Beginnings

Chapter One

Does every life deserve an autobiography? Does mine? I belong to an endangered species which in the eyes of many deserves to be extinct: the gently born, the monied, the sheltered, many of us squeamish about the things that make up the substance of life, its dark truth composed of everything we deny or refuse to think about. If we are lucky, as I have been, we have made friends of the witnesses of life, and have been humbled by them. I, who have never suffered from want, have known only the exigence of my own character, which has demanded that I rebel against my respectable and conservative family genes, though one scarcely knows for what reasons one branches off from the path that seems ordained by one's inheritance. I carried the baggage of that inheritance for a long time, though I gradually made decisions that made it imperative to get rid of it — decisions not to marry, to be an artist, to listen to my own voices. It was easy for me not to marry, for I was never seriously tempted; to be an artist was harder, for how could I know how much painful ground there was to cover between the wish and the becoming? I remember after World War II, when I had decided once and for all to become a painter, a friend of mine looked at some of my paintings and said, "Don't you want to marry and have babies?" I said that my paintings were my babies, a reply which made him look extremely dubious. "Babies are more important than pictures," he said. But, protected as I was by a beginner's blindness, a beginner's ignorance, I stubbornly continued to think that paintings were more important. What had taken place in me was a coalescing of this stubbornness and a kind of pride like vanity, but stronger than humiliation, united with the conviction that there was something there in my depths. (I thought I had depths.) The fact that this something was invisible to others was a goad which, again and again, produced the defiant thought, "I'll show you!" It required years of false starts, of failures, of periods of doubt and despair, for me to show anyone anything, or even to understand that one is not necessarily an artist by wanting to be one. In the course of those years, it was my good fortune, gradually, to acquire friends whose lives were wholly dedicated to their work as painters or writers or poets. They were, or are, the "witnesses of life," in a sense that I had never been. I had to learn, even if it was chiefly through these friends, that an artist must above all *see,* not a sterilized fragment of life, but its ugly paradoxes and "terrible beauty." I had to learn to get over some of my squeamishness about sex, for part of my inheritance was a belief in the life of the mind and the Christian soul at the expense of the life of the body. In my family, the body was unmentionable and sex was a secret subject, taboo, along with its vocabulary, including innocent words that might suggest it. Much great art has come from the sublimation of sex; I think not only of women writers like the Brontës or Emily Dickinson, whose passion was distilled in their art, but also of men such as Hopkins or George Herbert. Two of my friends, Hortense Flexner and Marianne Moore, were poets who belonged to this race. In my case, my upbringing prevented me from accepting my sexual nature by making me ashamed of it, doubly ashamed, because I belong to a despised sexual minority. The two chief tasks of my life have been to become an artist and to overcome my shame, and, at the age of sixty-one, I am only just beginning to feel that I have accomplished them.

We are formed, I suppose, by everybody we meet, out of resistance or emulation, but our choice of friends often seems to come from the pressure of whatever in us wants to grow, or refuses to grow. My meetings with Barbara Deming and Marie-Claire Blais came about because I recognized in their work a beauty which I wished for in my own work, but felt I hadn't attained, because they were beings somewhat like myself, but further advanced on their paths as artists. I was introduced to Marie-Claire by Edmund Wilson, but my meeting with him was pure chance (though I believe that chance is destined), which grew from a parent chance—that I had bought a house in Wellfleet and lived there with Barbara. Edmund's first paralyzing question to me had been, "Are you related to the Meigs of the Hill School?" a question I was unable to answer, except to mumble that all Meigses are, willy-nilly, related, there being so few of us. Later, he had become our friend and reigned over our winter life in Wellfleet, in which good friends were scarce and life so austere that many Wellfleetians took to drink or escaped in other ways. I have found a birthday sonnet (imitation Wordsworth) that I wrote from Pamet Point Road (where Barbara and I lived) on May 8, 1966, which gives an idea of our humourous and humble relation to Edmund:

EDMUND! Thank heaven thou livest at this hour!
Pamet hath need of thee; she is a fen
Of turbid waters: paintbrush, pencil, fren-
Etically struggle to preserve our dower
Of peace of mind and hope beyond our ken.
Oh! Cheer us up and read Verlaine again
To us, who tremble in our ivory tower.
Your soul is like the Sun and dwells on high,
You have a voice whose sound is like the ocean.
When in a happy mood, you set in motion
Our satellite thoughts that orbit all you say.
O indefatigable planet, I
Bring myriad wishes on your natal day.

My friendship with Edmund created in me a mixture of fear, shyness, humility, anger, uneasy love, pride, and a terrible anxiety that, through my unworthiness, I would lose his friendship.

13

Our friendship was complicated (for me, at least) by the fact that, for several years, he believed himself to be in love with me. I was, in fact, one of a good many women he loved during this time, but I was close at hand, whereas they (except for Elena, his wife) were far away. I did not want Edmund to be in love with me; I could not believe he really was, yet I was afraid he would cease to be, knowing the indifference that follows on the heels of love. "We belong to the same generation," he used to say, though he was old enough to be my father. He meant that we both belonged to the time of "ladies" and "gentlemen"; that we both had authentic good manners and impressive pedigrees. He had all the courtliness and gallantry of an old-fashioned gentleman, but at the same time, he belonged to the world of brutal maleness, of the Minotaur, that still frightens me; the world that accepts sex and its violence as a matter of course. How could he know not only that I was profoundly ignorant of this world, but also that I had yet to come to terms with myself, that the question, which seemed inexcusable to me when he asked it, was probably for him quite ordinary? "You're really a sort of Lesbian, aren't you?" He said this to me one evening when we were alone and I was in the state of slight apprehension I always felt with him. It was the first time in my life that anyone had associated the word "Lesbian" with me in my presence and the question made me feel faint and sick with terror. It was there, faceless, like the "Thing" that swelled and hummed in the dark when I was a child in bed at night, a black something, an extension of me that got bigger and bigger until it filled the whole room. I heard my stifled voice say, "I wouldn't say that," felt myself leave the house to go home where I spent a tormented and sleepless night. The next morning, Edmund called to apologize for having upset me, for mixed in with his blindness was a surprising delicacy, which made him, when I least expected it, protective of my feelings.

A "sort of." Perhaps all women artists are "sort of's"? The mitigating "sort of," lightly touching, without accusation, with an indulgent smile, all those women who wore pants before the time of pants, who inspired passions in other women, who, very often (fortunately for their biographers), had male lovers and husbands. They were bisexual, a respectable thing to be these days. Käthe Kollwitz, for instance, say her biographers, Mina and Arthur Klein, "though for her attraction for the masculine sex dominated...had found an inclination toward her own sex which she grew to understand only in her maturity. She came then to believe that such bisexuality is essential for the highest attainments in art. The masculine element within her, she felt, strengthened her own creative work." Facts like these about women artists, long hidden or glossed over, are now acceptable elements of their biographies, though in the eyes of the world, it is permissible for a woman to have "an inclination toward her own sex," only if she has married and produced at least one child. The marriage, the child, are the payment she must make to convention in order to have the freedom to love women. Käthe Kollwitz had the good fortune to be able to love her husband and children, to be an admirable mother and a toweringly great artist, and to love women without the pain and dislocation of her life that other androgynous women have suffered.

When Edmund asked if I wasn't really a "sort of Lesbian," I still lived in the shadowy world of denial and pretense, even though I was then living with another woman. How would I have felt if he had said, "You're really androgynous, aren't you?" Would I have been as terrified? Even then, the word "androgynous" did not carry a weight of opprobrium like the word "Lesbian"; on the other hand, "androgynous" which, unlike "hermaphrodite," seems to imply a spiritual and mental, rather than physical blending of the sexes, had not yet acquired its current dignity. "Androgyny," as the word is now used, has nothing to do with sex; it implies, rather, a new being, free of sexual stereotypes, a person who may be heterosexual, homosexual or bisexual. But a "sort of Lesbian," the "sort of" added for the sake of politeness, was something else again. No one had ever dared say to me *what* I was and I had not dared say it to myself with the proper conviction. Under pressure from a heterosexual friend, I had (before I knew Edmund) a week-long affair with a man in Italy, pleasant enough, but ending in recrimination on both sides. From the time I was very young, I fell in love with

15

men, women, heads, eyes and voices. I even fell in love, as I still do, with objects. I remember at six, being so enamoured of a jack-in-the-box for sale in a booth in the Tuileries that I howled all day long when my mother refused to buy it for me, and I believe the passion for things to be one of the many forms that sexual repression can take.

At the age of eleven, I had never heard of sex, did not know that people made love, and had never wondered where babies came from. On a voyage to Europe at this time, I wrote a poem about the sea beating against "Miss Porthole," which I found thirty years later and showed Edmund, who kept it for himself. "A sexual image," I could almost hear him thinking as he laughed delightedly over it, but couldn't Miss Porthole really have been a porthole, and the sea, the sea? For anyone who has read Freud, everything in nature contains a sexual overtone, and a little girl who has never seen a vagina, who does not know the meaning of the word "virgin," somehow achieves a prophetic use of sexual imagery. The fact was that for a long time my loves were purely visual and belonged to a realm where sex is non-existent. Perhaps they caused my childish heart to beat, but the physical reality, the coming close of any body with its every-day details, was invariably a shock to me. Objects and animals remained the same or were even more seductive if you looked closely at them, but men turned into the sum of their details: their huge feet, the hair that often covered their arms, legs, chests, or even sprouted from their ears, emphasizing their close cousinship with the apes, their mouths, their chins, like rough sandpaper, the friction of which, in those days of dancing cheek to cheek, left one's face sore for days. My fallings in love were a succession of failures, much more pronounced with men, but bedeviling even my relationships with women, as if a disgust of bodies had been planted in me like a curse. My interest in male bodies was purely plastic: I liked to look at men or boys who were clad in their skins like beautiful animals, with a rippling of hidden muscles when they moved, or when they posed negligently, with one hip bone thrown a little outward, with their hands on their hips, thumbs turned backwards, broad-shouldered and narrow-hipped like 6th Century Greek Kouroi, or like the walking Egyptian figures I have seen in the Louvre. Women, too, appear in those distant times to have had broad shoulders and narrow hips, or so one would infer from a 7th Century B.C. stone statue of an Egyptian woman in the Louvre, or from Hera of Samos (6th Century B.C.), herself the shape of a Kouros in her exquisite fine-fluted robe. These androgynous women seemed much more beautiful to me than the curvaceous and overly-modest Venus de Milo or the women with massive thighs and buttocks beloved by Rubens and Courbet. If I have never succeeded in liking Rubens, it is because of the sheer weight of all that well-fed female flesh — pink with what must have been the excellent circulation of the time. As for Courbet, whom I revere, the pallid and bloated bodies of his women suggest, not robust health, but the imminence of death — or perhaps a very cold studio.

My father and brothers did not take the unselfconscious poses of Greek statues, but had, nevertheless, much of their fineness of bone: beautiful wrists, ankles, feet and hands. Each was unhappy in his body, like an awkward adolescent, and hid it under clothes or droopy bathing suits (men had not yet begun to bare their torsos when I was little). The three men in our house had none of the redolence of men, the heaviness, the suggestion of sensuality. They had all been indoctrinated, like the female inhabitants of the house, with the idea that the body should, as far as possible, cease to exist. We were still encumbered by our bodies, which were like forbidden subjects, literally hidden by clothes and denied their physicality.

Later, I was both unconscious of my body and self-conscious, and my self-consciousness prevented me from putting the pagan energy into love-making that most people take for granted. My brief experience with a man gave me pleasure because I was scarcely aware of our bodies in the dark, just of a cool harmony with its terminal delight. Perhaps the reader will find it hard to believe that it is possible for a woman to make love with a man without ever setting eyes on his body, but such was my case. I remember how one afternoon Patricio and I walked to a lonely field on the heights of Anticoli (the little Italian village where we spent the summer) and how he sank down on me in the warm, dry grass with all the discretion of the swan over Leda. I must have kept my eyes closed, for only the agreeable sensation of his love-making remains in my memory. There was no single visual detail.

The time of my growing-up was long before the sexual revolution and it was not as peculiar as it would be now to maintain a Victorian distance between oneself and a man. For reasons which still puzzle me, there was an endless succession of men when I was in my twenties, who fell in love with me and who proposed marriage, which I invariably refused. Perhaps it was simply a response to my overwhelming properness, but none of these suitors ever proposed any living arrangement except marriage. A convenient psychological mechanism made every proposal a signal to fall *out* of love (for sometimes I believed that I was in love) or *not* to fall in love, a mechanism which still operated when I was in my forties and Edmund told me from time to time that he was in love with me. My reaction was my usual one of withdrawal and wariness, coupled with the certainty that it couldn't possibly be true, or, if it were true today, it wouldn't be tomorrow. And when Edmund said to me, "I don't know *why* I'm in love with you," I said, or rather shouted, since he was getting deaf, "I can't imagine!" It was just as I'd thought: there was no reason; it had nothing to do with *me.* I longed to think, but did not say so, that I was like those other women he had loved, remarkable in one way or another, but he never gave me the comfort of comparing me with them. Some of them were "sort of's," too, it was said. Did he love me not for myself, but because I didn't seem to care whether he loved me or not? How had the others been with him, not his wives, but the others he'd loved? Did *they* seem to care? Did he kiss them, striking his solid pose like a knotty-muscled acrobat about to swing someone up on his head? Did he make love to them? Did he appreciate my balancing act, walking the precarious wire between resistance and receptivity? Part of my "sort of" ethic was to conceal my fear—of bodies, of kisses, of passion—to protect our egos (his, the male's; and mine, the sort of's), to try, simultaneously, not to be prudish and not to be encouraging. His definition of me had stiffened my pride. But he, with his strange intuition, seemed to know exactly how far he could go without my fleeing. He would kiss me (I see him now, bearing down, striking the pose) without undue insistence, stand there heavily, or help me on with my coat. Even in his ancestral house, with my friend Barbara in the next room, after drunkenly prowling the corridor, he tottered into my room in his dressing gown and seated himself on my bed—even there, something gentlemanly in him (or was it the thin walls?) yielded to my refusal, stated calmly, loudly, to make him hear, though I was quaking inside. Instead, we went downstairs and talked about marriage. "What would you be like to be married to?" he asked, and I said, "I'd make a terrible wife." How could I explain that I couldn't be a wife to anyone, that I had never been tempted to sacrifice myself to anyone—to a man or a woman either. "I'm like Isabel Archer before she married Osmond," I said. "What? Oh, Isabel Archer. You're *not* like Isabel Archer," he said grumpily. Wanting to shout, "Can't you see that I have a sense of my own survival, that I don't want to be a slave?" I said, "It's because I'm too selfish," for in every man's mind is the conviction that nothing could possibly be more important to a woman than *he* is, than his love is. An odd kind of etiquette prevented me from reminding him of Elena, his wife, who had given herself to serving him in a graceful and beautiful way, who believed this to be the duty of a wife; it would have been to acknowledge that she was threatened by something real, when in fact, the "why" of his being in love with me and my absence of response, prevented it from being real. But perhaps he was playing with me, seeing how far a "sort of" would go, testing the depth of my vanity — or my gratitude? Edmund liked to set traps and play psychological games, but perhaps he was too genuinely humble to play this one. It seemed to me that he didn't even notice the effect he had on people—the tremors of excitement, the paralyzed timidity, the coquettishness, the discreet competition for his favour. Seismic waves ran round the living room when he said to the "Chosen One," "Come into my study, I want to talk to you." Hypnotized, she (it was almost always a woman) would rise from her chair and follow him, striking a little silence among the rest of us. She would emerge from his study twenty minutes later, flushed and proud. "What did he say?" I would ask if it was Barbara who was thus honoured. "Oh, we just talked about the non-payment of taxes," she would say. More wonderful than being called into his study was to be with him alone in a restaurant or at the theatre, to be part of the obeisance done to him, to shine like a full moon in the sun's light! It was then that I understood why women choose to be satellites, to reflect light rather than risk generating their own, in short, to be wives. How warm and comfortable I felt with Edmund; how nice everybody was to me! And how chilly it was to go back to my unprotected life as a non-wife, a "sort of," perpetually on the defensive.

"She is someone in her own right," I've heard it said admiringly of a wife who is more than just a satellite, as if a husband can legitimately ask his wife to be someone in *his* right. Isabel Archer. I loved her because she was born, evidently, with a sense of her own right (so were Charlotte Brontë's Jane Eyre and Shirley, Jane Austen's Elizabeth Bennett and Emma, and Virginia Woolf's Lily Briscoe). Henry James treated with perfect rectitude Isabel's determination to be herself, and allowed her to recognize all the marriage-traps: the suffocating prison of life with an English lord; the trap of Caspar Goodwood's passion —until the last, for poor Isabel, with her premonition of what women's liberation is all about, was punished by the man with whom she felt most free. James' genius lies in not seeming to have intervened. Still, he lets us know where he stands. Other women who go too far in the direction of liberation are mocked at, like old Miss Birdseye, a genuine feminist, or, like Olive Chancellor, pinned on a board, a perfect specimen of a repressed Lesbian. In real life, Henry James was shocked by Virginia Woolf (he would have been more shocked had he read Quentin Bell's biography) and all her untidy friends, a lot of them "buggers", as Bell puts it. Was James a snob? A persnickety old maid? Outwardly perhaps, but with an inward sensibility that was refined and refined, tortured by little dissonances, by noise, messiness, engaged with enormous cunning in the task of trying to hide the disorder in his inner self, lucky to die before the hounds ran his secret to earth. And Isabel? Does any man like Isabel? While I was thinking about Isabel, I got a letter from an old friend, the painter, Leonid, who had been reading *The Portrait of a Lady*. He was furious with Isabel for the same reasons that all men are furious with her. "De repousser un lord authentique, humain, anglais, pour s'amouracher de ce fake italien," and so on, to "sa vie aboutit à un mess." Leonid, who was no more like Lord Warburton than, say, Pissarro was, identified himself with Warburton and felt refused by Isabel, just as Edmund (I could swear) identified himself with Caspar, of the famous kiss like white lightning, who was also refused by Isabel, somewhat more ambiguously. And another painter friend (homosexual) ranted against Isabel, accused her of being a selfish monster, and turned all the virtues that I saw in her into vices. Some women are even angry with Isabel for refusing Lord Warburton (for some reason, no one remembers or cares about her refusal of her cousin Ralph, the only one with whom she might have been happy, but James has arranged for Ralph to have a fatal sickness), or with any heroine who refuses the hero—and not many do. I myself was vaguely irritated by Lily in Trollope's *The Small House at Allingham,* who adamantly turns down the likable Johnny, for even those of us who are happily unmarried have been conditioned to think of marriage as the only happy ending to a novel. But Isabel Archer is a real threat to the male ego, and for a woman to defend her, stirs up the little flame of jealousy at the bottom of every man's heart. Strange, because she is punished terribly, and what she sought was not real freedom, but a relative freedom within marriage. She would settle for this illusory freedom, just as they all did, the fighting women, the real ones and their fictional alter egos, except for Jane Austen. One would like to know, did any man ever propose marriage to her, and if he did, why did she refuse him? As for Charlotte Brontë, the fieriest of them all, finally she was submissive to her Arthur. She loved him, she said, but didn't she give up writing for his sake; couldn't she be said to have died for his sake? My heart bleeds for Charlotte, who, in *Jane Eyre,* had so perfectly described the ideal relationship with a man. One thinks of Jane and St. John, how she was dominated by him, petrified by his certainties, and how, after seeing him as he really was, after refusing to live his life, she suddenly discovered her

21

own. "I was with an equal," she says, "one with whom I might argue—one whom...I might resist." And of her life with Rochester, she says, "In his presence I thoroughly lived; and he lived in mine." One wants to take these phrases from *Jane Eyre* and broadcast them all over the world. "I know no medium between absolute submission and determined revolt," says the amazing Jane. But Charlotte, knowing this, chose submission. She married Arthur because she pitied him, emaciated and pale for love of her, and one feels that Arthur, after their marriage, putting on weight, becoming pink-cheeked and healthy, is feeding on the body and blood and will of Charlotte.

But to get back to Isabel, whose crime was to marry for her own sake—she who loved the company of beautiful forms, was had by appearances and by the art of the con man. If I feel less close to her than to Lily Briscoe, the painter in *To the Lighthouse,* one of the reasons is that her resignation at the end of *The Portrait of a Lady* is too much for me to stomach. "She had not known where to turn; but she knew now. There was a very straight path." Too straight! Back to Florence; in other words, back to hell. It is useless to hope that she will divorce Osmond; useless for Caspar to wait for her. She, the perfect lady, is going to stew in her own feelings of guilt. Oh Isabel, you had less courage than Ibsen's Nora, who, at the end, is where you began! I feel the twinge of disappointment I've felt so often in my life at the spectacle of this resignation, planted, it seems, deep in every woman's heart.

The wife of a great man. Finally, she is less in his light than in his shadow. Great men—with nothing to prevent them from soaring as high as they can, all those qualities of greatness (the selfishness, the iron will, the discipline that sets hours and refuses to be disturbed) coddled and encouraged and excused by the women around them, for every great man needs his slaves, even if one of them, his wife, is a great woman. She, with the same qualities perhaps, running into the stone wall of Him. Or perhaps, she is an almost artist, like Caitlin Thomas, who, eclipsed, went half-crazy in the effort to salvage her soul. Edmund, who gave me John Stuart Mill to read, put me down in my enthusiasm (his put-downs were part of his male arsenal) for, whatever his respect for individual women, he knew from experience that women *can't* be liberated. "They are the way they are, born that way, or they want to be that way," he would say impatiently. I had to agree that many women are, one might say, typically feminine, and proud of it, that they are superficial, irrational, catty, that they are all the things they are accused of being. But that they are born that way? Rather, don't they realize, very quickly, perhaps at birth, where their power lies, the perverted power that is allowed them? Anyway, that wasn't the point. The point, which Edmund was incapable of getting, because no one had ever effectively challenged *his* power, was his right to command, to shout orders to his wife, his children, like a master sergeant in the Marines. (At an early age, I challenged this right in my older brother. "Why?" I asked him, when he told me to do something. "Because I say so," he said, slapping me hard on the behind.) Where did this power come from, except from his own male assumption of it? Why was it that when he telephoned and said peremptorily, "Come over here around five, will you?" we trotted over like obedient dogs? To be sure, we grumbled; maybe we'd been in the middle of something, or ventured to give him some excuse for not coming. "Well, come if you can," he would say angrily and he would hang up. We went, torn between our doggy devotion to Edmund and our ferocious sense of ourselves as beings who couldn't, shouldn't, be ordered around. And, as usual, we fell under the spell of Edmund, triumphant, doing his card tricks, playing Authors, anagrams, Chinese checkers, *bouts rimés.* We would tiptoe into the bright house and shout above the deafening music that poured from the depths of his study and he would appear, his face pink and freshly-shaved, to greet us.

Thinking about Edmund's presence in my life, I make a distinction between the innocent prodigality of daytime and the nighttime Edmund who woke my anxieties. I described the daytime Edmund and his ancestral landscape in a letter to Anne Poor after our visit to him in July, 1964. "Upstate New York is...quite surprisingly like central Maine, with great elms, pastures, rolling hills and infinite green stretches under skies that generate thunderheads from nowhere, so there's a marvellous play of light à la Greco's 'Toledo.' One has more of a sense than in Maine of being on a frontier, even of something melancholy and sinister, but it's probably because so many houses are actually falling down, and if they aren't, they tend to be covered with hideous asbestos shingles or they consist of trailers that have been immobilized on cement blocks. There are very few really old houses and the towns are awful beyond words. Edmund's house is BEAUTIFUL, very sparsely and simply furnished and freezing cold. I shivered so hard that he finally lit a fire in the dining room fireplace and we sat as close to it as we could. It was obvious that it was the first fire of the season, and that E. isn't bothered by the cold. We spent almost all of the six days sightseeing—seeing natural wonders, ancestral mansions, Lake Ontario, Utica, Cooperstown. When there were a few minutes to spare, Bobbie [Barbara] and I would rush off to the underground river and the wonderful quarry, like Angkor Wat, but more ruined, or to some pasture where there were lovely cows (always Holsteins) and we'd run around to get warm.... Then we'd sightsee and Edmund would talk more or less continuously about the past, and, in the evenings, he would play records or read to us or even sing songs of the twenties. In six days, we met only one set of neighbours, so you can imagine that our powers of attention were stretched to the breaking point and we're still feeling rather limp."

The daytime Edmund was a marvellous companion, with his enthusiasm for everything under the sun, and my only fear was that the awful words he sometimes applied to others—"He or she is a bore"—might be applied to me if my responses were stupid or ignorant. But as I look over the letters, postcards and valentines from him that accumulated during my years in Wellfleet, I realize better now than when I first read them, that I needn't have worried, and I am moved by the courtly sweetness that permeates them, as if he needed the protective medium of the written word to express his most delicate feelings. He had a habit of sending small coloured engravings of fish with messages on them. I look at one of a pale blue fish resting dejectedly on an exotic shore. "I have missed you since you left—feel more and more like the picture on the other side," says Edmund. And a

24

little poem accompanies the Dolphin of the Ancients:

The Dolphin is extremely wise,
Turns rainbow colors when he dies;
But when the Dolphin thinks of you,
He turns a special lovely hue.

We shared a love for natural history and one of his presents to me was an Audubon engraving of an ocelot from the big folio edition. The munificence of this gift, and another of star-nosed moles, worried me, and I have a soothing letter from him, in which he says, "I didn't want to keep the ocelot. I was pleased to be able to give you something you liked. I think you need it to counterbalance the mole. I am sure you have an ocelot in your nature, too." Another of his psychological tests? For I had chosen, unconsciously, the opposites I harbour in me, timid and ferocious. Edmund's character, too, contained its opposites: on the one hand, the Minotaur; on the other hand, an animal as graceful, shy and tender as the Unicorn, who rests one hoof in the lap of the Lady, in the Cluny tapestry. His intuitions never failed to surprise me, for his spoken judgements were monolithic and unchangeable, and, in a sense, we only really communicated in letters, which gave him time, instead of immediately overpowering me, of listening to what I had to say. In my meetings with him, I was constantly frustrated by my inability to express myself, yet I come upon forgotten letters which show that, after all, he took me seriously. "I was very much interested in your ideas about *Edwin Drood*," he wrote in 1962. I cannot now remember what my ideas about *Edwin Drood* were, only that Edmund's enthusiasm for the book had kindled one in me and that I had read it with a sleuth's intensity, determined to solve its riddles. In the space of this one letter, which gives an idea of how he attempted to form my mind, he suggests that I read: "a long paper written on the probability that Dutchery is Bazzard," that, if I want to go seriously into *Edwin Drood*, I will "have to get Robertson Nicoll's book," and that I should "probably read *Love's Cross Currents*" by Swinburne, about whom he was writing then. He sometimes accused me of not reading anything he suggested, but I read as much as I could, and my anxiety to

25

please him made me read with particular attention. Perhaps only in the forgotten matter of *Edwin Drood* was I able to persuade him that I was right about anything. I wanted to convert him to my view of *The Turn of the Screw* (of which more later) and to bring up the as yet unaired subject of Henry James' homosexuality. He asserted on several occasions that Proust was not homosexual ("Proust wasn't anything," he said) and my heart would begin to beat with fear at the thought of discussing with him my theory about James.

I blurted out my theory after Edmund had written me one of his fish cards, in which he said, "I saw Leon Edel in New York and he has worked out the rest of Henry James' life in a way which I don't doubt is correct, but he has pledged me not to talk about it." It seemed to me that this could only refer to what I have already called James' secret (*i.e.,* his homosexual leanings), but in the fourth volume of his biography of James, Leon Edel produces both a young man to whom James wrote passionate letters and a woman friend who troubled him greatly by committing suicide. "I know what Leon Edel is going to say about Henry James," I said. "That he was homosexual." I was driving Edmund back to his house after he had had dinner with Barbara and me and there was such a long silence after the word "homosexual" that I thought he had not heard me. Then he said that James had suffered some kind of injury that prevented him from having a sexual life.

As long as it is thought disgraceful for a great man or woman to have been or to be homosexual, heterosexuals will use every means possible to deny it. Families destroy or conceal evidence or lock it away so that it is inaccessible; genders are changed in poems that have been written to someone of the same sex; biographers search for evidence that the great man loved a woman, or that the great woman loved a man. They consider it improper and shameless, an invasion of privacy, for homosexuals to keep insisting that so-and-so is one of their own, though it is not at all improper, for instance, to make public that Emily Dickinson sat on the lap of an eminent judge. Indeed, this piece of news is received with sentimental joy by all who care about Dickinson's reputation and are worried about her "excessive" feelings for certain women. When I knew Edmund, I hadn't thought much about this species of adamant denial which makes discussion impossible and conjecture indecent. But what if the intent of the biographer is an attempt to conceal something crucial to the understanding of a great man or woman, what if the view of him or her, as was the case of Walt Whitman, has been totally false? Is Virginia Woolf any less great a writer because it is now known that she fell in love with women?

Edmund was one of a host of people who accept homosexuals as friends, but for whom homosexuality is in contravention of some immutable law, people who, for the most part, have had a Christian upbringing. He loved Barbara and Marie-Claire and me, but he shared the community view that Lesbians are faintly ridiculous, that pairs of us are, in Gertrude Stein's words, "like two left-handed gloves." Because of our fear of men, we have settled, they think, for a half-life with its imperfect satisfactions. This view, which we cannot help but feel as a burden, made me uneasy in Wellfleet; it was always there—the unspoken mockery that attached itself to conventional problems, such as how to seat us at a dinner table or whether or not to invite us with heterosexual couples.

I will speak later of the period when Marie-Claire joined my life and my relation with Edmund became much more complicated and uneasy. Nevertheless, at the end of his life, he was still wistfully writing, "I miss you." I did not dare, during all those years, to accept his friendship with the joy it should have given me, but clung to it with secret pride and suffered torments when he was cold, angry or seemingly indifferent. When he died, I was living in France, but I felt his absence with a sense of desolation. He had enlarged my life with his myriad enthusiasms, with his programs for the improvement of my mind, with his brutal truths; it was enlarged even by my resistance to him and by the anxiety I felt.

> *This is a Valentine note for Mary,*
> *Of whom I am fond, and even very.*
> *I sometimes dream we are sitting astride*
> *A bicycle, taking a bicycle ride.*

Edmund sent me this in 1960, one of a series of valentines we all exchanged to lighten the winter cafard in Wellfleet. He and I dreamt about each other now and then (I dreamt after his death that he was seated at a round table wearing the mask of Queen Victoria), and sometimes, we even dreamt the same dream. It was about going into a house full of old things, going from room to room, seeing depressing changes. And then, the house was threatened—by a super-highway or by sinister people surrounding it, or by crumbling walls. It was our past, that house, what we cherished of the past—stolen, mutilated or decaying.

We belonged to the same generation, he had said. We shared the ability to be moved to tears or to feel a rush of joyful emotion in the presence of something beautiful. Edmund read Yeats to us (when he had begun to walk slowly, groaning, up the hill to our house), his voice becoming unsteady at, "Till the wreck of the body," and breaking at, "A bird's sleepy cry," unable to finish. Edmund was moved to tears by Yeats, who, bare as bleached bone at the end of his life, still used nature for his grandest image. "Like a long-legged fly upon the stream / His mind moves upon silence." These flies walk on water as blithely as Jesus, or a mind moving on insubstantial silence, where many minds drown; Edmund's mind must have moved easily upon silence.

Chapter Two

Edmund and I belonged to the same generation in the sense that I was brought up as a child of *his* generation and not of my own. My parents, in turn, belonged to a generation before their own, though my mother was born the same year as Virginia Woolf and my father the same year as her sister, Vanessa. If I place a photograph of my father at twenty next to the photographs of Vanessa and Thoby Stephen in Quentin Bell's biography, I see an extraordinary resemblance. My father might have been another Stephen brother, with his fine brow and clear blue eyes under curving, heavy eyelids, gazing at the camera with the guileless look people had at the turn of the century, like angels come down from heaven, the men dressed in high, stiff collars; the women, in angelic white, their dresses frilly at the neck. Not a single person in my family has inherited my father's eyes—of a blue so blue that one was struck dumb with amazement; eyes that could blaze or sparkle blueness, or emit the tranquil blue of a high summer day. Some of us have my father's eyebrows, or eyes, deep-set and heavy-lidded, but his bright blue eyes have been bleached or mixed with grey or green, have been reduced in me, at least (who am said to look like him), to several sizes smaller and to a less clear blue. Resemblances—the little things that emerge in children, grandchildren, nieces and nephews: an oblique look, the shadowy hollow between eyebrows, the flat cheekbones of the father wedded to the Roman nose of the mother, the elements of parents jumbled like anagrams to form the "word" of each of us. Hester, my twin sister was given the beautiful upper half of my father's head and the mouth of my mother's family; I was given a head like a cobblestone, his reduced eyes, set between a high forehead, and a wide square jaw like his, but out of all proportion to the top. One of the sorrows of my childhood was that I had not inherited my father's eyes, and I used to concentrate my whole being on willing my little eyes to be like his, hoping that someone would notice the resemblance. "She looks like her father." Once, in a sailboat, a grown-up said this to another grown-up at precisely the moment when I'd been gazing at the water, willing my eyes a dazzling blue. I was in love with my father's eyes. I see them now, a few weeks before he died of tuberculosis, at the moment of one of my great failures—my refusal to love *enough*. We were in the library of our big old house and my father was wearing rumpled pyjamas under a cream-coloured Chinese silk dressing gown. Stooped, emaciated, but with his eternally young face, high-coloured cheekbones and enormous eyes, an unbelievable blue, sparkling with happiness because, at last, we had been able to talk to each other—about Emerson, one of his gods. I had given my students *The American Scholar* to read and had written an ironic poem about the laws of compensation:

> *Wisdom goes in humble guise;*
> *He is ugly who is wise.*
> *Some are wise, the rest are dumb—*
> *Beautiful residuum!*

My father liked my poem and we laughed together. For the first time, we both felt that we were comrades, that this conversation was unlike those innumerable others we had had in which he had tried to instruct me, or I had tried to irritate him, or he had felt that I didn't understand him—and I hadn't tried to understand him. For most of my childhood, I had been in that hateful state of being where one does not get out of oneself

30

enough to feel the presence and reality of another person. When I was leaving the library, he held out his arms to me, and instead of embracing him, I blew him a kiss. That was the last time I saw him alive, except in dreams. I still dream about him and see his eyes; sometimes he is younger, not sick; sometimes he takes the form of a blue-eyed child, tiny and wise. I gaze at this child in silent admiration. He is myself perhaps, as I wanted to be — a small replica of my father.

Later, having learned nothing, it seemed, from this failure with my father, I was irritated by the question, "Do you love me?" "Love me!" "Help me!" To me, it was the same idea in different words: the sudden weight of the other on oneself, a trap (the obligation to love) and the wary reaction; something grim inside that says, "Did you love me? Did you help me when I needed it?" A different "you," who, long ago, had withheld love. "I give when I feel like giving," says a stingy little voice inside me. It is fatal when a giver in his own time is wedded to a person who needs, who insists on love; the needer makes the needed even stingier.

"Yes, yes, it's a matter of temperament, from the day of one's birth, one has chosen to refuse or accept." My parents were like the couple in Ionesco's *Jeux de Massacre*: the wife has chosen acceptance and love; the husband, refusal and anguish. But is it a choice? Rather, is it not something in each person that succumbs or not under the weight of evidence? It is as if each one of us were a jury member for a huge trial with the evidence spread out: one chooses to believe that the good outweighs the bad, that the human race is worthy of survival, or vice versa. My parents, except for their Puritan heritage, began quite gaily. They adored each other, and in photographs taken of them after their marriage, they looked wonderfully joyful. Yet I remember my mother telling me that she cried from homesickness all through their honeymoon. How did it happen, the slow sinking of my father into depression ("a nervous breakdown," they said), his yielding to it, dying of it (which came first, the depression or the tuberculosis?) while he was still quite young? "It was his mother's fault," said my mother. His father, a doctor, had died young, too, of a ruptured appendix; and his mother, a tiny

31

person with a high-bridged nose and my father's eyes, several shades paler and frostier, ruled her three sons, each twice as tall as she was. She would write my father at medical school: "Be sure to leave cards at the Eliots'. Be sure to call on your Aunt Emma." She was still interfering, fussing, bossing him around when she was eighty and my father was fifty. "Your grandmother is a remarkable woman," everybody said. Could it have been this little woman, so dogmatic and sure of herself, who ruined my father's life? She kept lists of "Things to Do." She travelled with at least fifteen watches and clocks, wore her yellow-white hair piled high, a velvet ribbon round her neck, and her skirt down to the ground. She reigned over her house in the country; over her Irish cook and maids, her Scottish chauffeur, her Italian gardener and her butler, Percy; over her garden full of peonies, roses, giant oriental poppies, larkspur, box hedges; the vegetable garden beyond; the cows with wildflowers' names (Buttercup, Primrose, Four O'Clock), the geese, ducks, sheep, donkeys; and her little dog, Balfour. And she reigned over my uncle, her irascible unmarried son, an architect, who, after her death, tore down the Poicile, the imitation Greek temple in the garden (but left the Sunset Tower and the Burning Pit), and turned the Garden Room into a pool room; de-Victorianized the entire house with silvery carpets and a suppression of all but the most elegant furniture.

My grandmother was snobbish, arrogant and prejudiced, but packed in with these qualities, there was something whimsical and artistic. She painted exact watercolours of rocks and flowers. And the house she lived in was an extension of her best self. My sister and I felt happy there the moment we began the walk upstairs on the red-flowered carpets with polished brass rods to our room on the third floor which had straw matting on the floor, brass beds, and a window on a level with the tops of the tulip poplars outside, where the robins sang in a great chorus every morning at dawn, and from which you could look down into the open poplar flowers and see raindrops shining. And I felt happy with the ceremony of meals there: the smell of the little gas flame under the egg-boiler; the pepper enclosed in a silver pug dog; and Percy, the butler, with his white face, lank black hair and sardonic mouth, who stood close to my grandmother's chair. We had hominy for breakfast. There was laughter because I thought Harmony, an erstwhile dog of my grandmother's, whom I'd seen in a photograph, was named Hominy. Laughter, because I thought the multiplication tables were real tables. My uncle, ever-superior, mystified the four children with: "Irks care the cropfull bird? / Frets doubt the maw-crammed beast?" No amount of explanation could ever make this clear to me.

I remember the joy of that house, yet there was something missing at its heart. My grandmother and my uncle were two identical contentious souls who never really tried to understand another soul, who imposed themselves on other people and then judged the person that resulted. "Why don't you talk?" my grandmother would ask my sister and me, striking terror and silence into us, making it impossible to talk, and then she would tease us for our shyness. We were called "The White Rabbits." My grandmother even bullied my mother, just after her marriage, made her feel, because she was born in a little town where her father ran the iron works, that she belonged to a lower social order, made her cry—and cry by herself. (I have inherited the bully in her, the nagger, but at least I hear myself doing it.) My mother was always amazed by the high-pitched arguments between Mater, as she called my grandmother, and Mater's sons, which became louder and louder at the dinner table. After Mater died, the arguments continued, between my father and my uncle, violent argument being as necessary to certain members of the family, it seems, as food and drink.

Pater, who had been dead for a long time, looked down on us from the wall of the dining room. A "distinguished physician" in a long, unbroken line of them, says the *Dictionary of American Biography*, as Edmund pointed out to me. Pater looked kind and intelligent. Mater told a joke about him: that he had been introduced to her as a person who was timid and silent. It turned out that he wasn't at all timid and talked all the time. Mater telling this story, which for some reason always made everybody laugh, seemed not to realize that she herself was as loquacious as a guinea hen. Talking, in fact, is something that has always run in every branch of my family. "We're not fighting, we're discussing," my uncle used to say, but I see now that in these so-called discussions every member of the family thought he was right, except for my mother, who was preternaturally humble and only thought herself right about questions of morality. About these, she was as inflexible as the Rock of Gibraltar. Sometimes they were all "right" about the same things (they agreed); sometimes the sense of rightness lay like a huge weight in a scale and dragged the scale down, while the little weight of the counter-argument flew upwards.

The case for the family was composed of pride, self-importance, duties, responsibilities — an inflated sense of what we were as a family, for we selected our most distinguished ancestors to be descended from: the one who had signed the Constitution, for instance; and felt less enthusiastic about the ancestor who made hats in Guilford, Connecticut. The family case was argued by Mater and my uncle against my father, a renegade, who had left the ancestral city of Philadelphia to work for the government in Washington, for something in him obviously had longed to be free of the crushing burden of family. "He was losing his roots," my uncle said, and his children would be rootless. In every discussion of "roots," I took the position that I preferred to be rootless, which made my uncle furious. But lurking in me was a silly little pride; I suffered when my mother said that someone was "not quite" or when my aunt said that Grace Kelly came "from the other side of the tracks" (the royal ascent of Grace Kelly had not the slightest effect on this judgement), but refused, for the most hypocritical reasons, to invite my college roommate to our "coming out" party. "She wouldn't like it," I told my mother. My roommate was different from me in unimportant ways, in the kind of shoes she wore and in her ankle socks. I judged people by these little differences and preened myself on the niceness of my taste. I was snobbish in a worse way than my mother, who had an intuitive sense of the real worth of someone and was more offended by vulgarity than by superficial details.

Looking at this notion of family, I try to decide what there was in it of positive good. My father's side was prosperous and tidy, with Roman virtues: scrupulously honest, disciplined, rational, law-abiding; my mother's side was full of people who embarrassed me by their eccentricities. (I was embarrassed then by anything unconventional.) They were prosperous too, but messy, with a little Irish and Welsh fantasy thrown in, much less rational, but just as rigorously Puritan. On both sides of the immediate family, not a single person was divorced, not one husband was unfaithful to his wife, or vice versa. There were no homosexuals, though my mother once murmured something about "your Uncle Len," something I interpreted much later as "that." Unlike his brothers, Uncle Len had not been in the Union Army in the Civil War. Could "that" really have been the reason? On my father's side, in the coal-mining part of the family, people drank, caroused and were divorced. My parents did not drink and were probably among the few people in the United States during Prohibition who refused to have even a bottle of homemade wine in their house.

These "virtues" have been transmitted to us, the four children: we only tell white lies in the name of politeness; we scarcely drink and do not smoke; three of us are faithful spouses who had no premarital sex and frown on divorce. In short, we are real "ladies" and "gentlemen." The reader will say that there are things about my siblings that I don't know (little infidelities, etc.), just as there are things about me that they don't know. We never discuss our lives with each other; in this sense, we are total strangers. Once, driving somewhere with me, my older brother looked at my bare knees while I drove. "Couldn't you pull your skirt down a little?" he said. "Isn't it a little immodest?" I answered by fiercely pulling the offending skirt higher and decided that no secret of mine would be safe in his keeping. Of the four children, my older brother was certainly the most tormented by sex, and perhaps he had *almost* yielded to its temptations. But if he had yielded, would he have been so disturbed by the sight of my sunburned knees? We were all haunted by the Puritan ideal of chastity, that living skeleton tapping on our shoulders or actually gnawing at our flesh, like Death with the Maiden. Sometimes I wonder if some of my hormones, so resolutely channelled in non-sexual directions, weren't actually destroyed when I was a child, atrophied so that only a small percentage remained? After all, if a person has no experience of sex until she is twenty-five years old; if even, at that age, she has to be shown the "seat of pleasure," as they say, and patiently taught that it *is* pleasurable; if, throughout her life, sex continues to have relatively little importance, something must have been killed. A sexual lobotomy, you might say. A psychoanalyst might be interested to know that it can be done without too much damage to the psyche, though it is much more likely to produce an obsessive counter-reaction.

If our family curse is Puritanism, the family virtue is "niceness." We are all nice, even unto the nieces, nephews and grandchildren; whatever violence is in us is masked by good manners, a guileless good will and willingness to help our fellow man. We are gullible, easily taken in by people who pretend to be honest, endlessly taken in by promises; we cannot believe that some people lie as easily as they breathe. We (the generations of my siblings, parents and grandparents) denied and denied (who among us didn't have a sneaking sympathy for St. Peter and the rich young man who cannot give up his whole fortune to follow Jesus?), but never lied; withheld, but never stole. We committed the sin of stinginess of spirit. Was it my grandparents' and parents' fault if the prevailing Puritanism made their fists clench, their eyebrows knit and their faces darken with disapproval, made the words shoot out of their mouths like serpents' tongues? Was it their fault if their inherited prejudices against Jews, Roman Catholics and black people made them commit crimes against their own niceness? My brothers are free from racial and religious prejudice, but are saddened, let us say, by divorce, homosexuality, promiscuity, atheism, etc. Perhaps some of my nieces and nephews are prejudice-free, if such a thing is possible. It is obvious that prejudice diminishes as freedom expands, and that beliefs in general are like vaccines that either take or do not. Religion, which is the source of some of my brothers' prejudices, took for them, but not for me. I become irritated and aggressive when the subject is raised. As for my twin sister, she has overcome our parents' most blatant prejudices, but still believes, like my brothers, in fidelity, family and duty to the community, in all the articles of faith injected into our veins by our parents with excellent results, except in my case.

36

And yet, I have articles of faith—or non-faith. If I didn't, why would I hear myself arguing in a high-pitched voice (just like other arguers in my family) about everything under the sun? Why, if a calm discussion of religion gets under way, does the adrenalin begin seeping into my veins until I actually begin to twitch and sputter? Why this rage? Am I *that* angry with my parents? Is it sexual frustration? I've noticed, though, that inexplicable rage lurks in many, perhaps in all human beings, ready to burst out at the most surprising times; in people who are not in the least sexually frustrated or angry with their parents. It is the infant in each of us, pure ego that cannot endure opposition of any kind. How do you explain otherwise the looks of black hate, the shakings of fists, even by strangers, drivers of automobiles who have been kept waiting for a few seconds, or the murderous fury of friends defending anything one has happened to attack? I still remember with astonishment an acquaintance turning on me when I made a slighting remark about Hemingway, the idea being that an insignificant piece of shit like me didn't have the *right* to talk thus about a great writer. And I am the same, ferocious as a wolf when a friend speaks of Rodin's "rubbery surfaces" and "big feet." "I couldn't see anything except those big feet," a good sculptor friend of mine said. "I'm up to here in waterlilies," he said about Monet. Why did I feel sick with despair? Do I feel that I'm wrong to love Monet if a good sculptor is "up to here in waterlilies?" It must be that. And just as we feel guilty about loving, so we feel guilty about not loving, or about the not-loving of others. "I'd give all of Matisse for one Clyfford Still," said another friend about fifteen years ago, a double blow, pro and con, since I hadn't learned to like Clyfford Still and worshipped Matisse.

Thinking of these threats to the ego, I recall a conversation in the early 1950's with Mark Rothko about Rembrandt, another of my gods. Rothko, who once loved Rembrandt's portraits, now preferred those of Tintoretto. Rembrandt, he said, imposed on his sitters something that did not necessarily belong to them, a deepness, as though he were saying, "Look how profound I am." Tintoretto told the truth about human beings without trespassing on their integrity, and this was the duty of a great portrait painter. This conversation made me unhappy for days. I tried to free myself from it by resisting Rothko's greatness as a painter, as I resisted the greatness of everything I could not understand. I underestimated his painting, seeing it as merely "serene." "I want it to be like the minuet in *Don Giovanni*," Rothko said, pointing out that the serenity I saw was the calm before the storm. Now I understand what he meant — that, in his work, the radiance of the minuet and the tragedy about to break are held in trembling suspension, one over the other or within the other. And his feeling about Rembrandt? Having just seen a big Rothko retrospective, I feel that, particularly in his late work, he is permeated by the spirit of Rembrandt, and that the great formal squares, as dark as death, are, in a sense, self-portraits, abstractions of Rothko's inner torment. The catalogue speaks of "the Rembrandtesque obscurity of the upper portion" of the brown and grey paintings; and of Rothko's reverence for Rembrandt. Was he, as so many men do with women, disagreeing with me for the sake of disagreement? Or did he really believe that Rembrandt was too present in his portraits? Wasn't his own work a long struggle to withdraw himself, his personality and feelings, to reduce his statement to form and colour; wouldn't he have been angry if I had said to him that the late paintings were self-portraits? For I think that the most resolute minimalist is *there* in his work, that Barnett Newman, for instance, or Ad Reinhardt, who went beyond Rothko in removing sensibility as an element of painting, are as present as Rothko; that even if one reproduces photographs of soup cans, those cans of soup proclaim not Campbell, but Warhol. The painter or sculptor enters into fluorescent lights, chunks of wood, electrical gadgets, steel girders, by the fact of his having given them new instructions and a new order.

Rothko was one of many good painters I have known, who, without intending to, had the power to summon up the vulnerable infant in me by reminding me of my nonentity as an artist. Even his kindness made me miserable. He liked a little still life I had done of green pears on a red chair, the paint laid on with a certain freedom which must have appealed to his merciful eye. But the fact that he liked them, instead of pleasing me, revealed their weaknesses, and I wanted to plunge a knife into them and punish their insignificance. In those days, when I was struggling with insufficient means, with no theory or sense of direction to be a painter, I was destroyed by the simple contact with "real" painters: Rothko, Milton Avery, Wallace Putnam, Karl Knaths—all those who were already masters. In me there was a poisonous brew of humility and resentment; and the total inability, because they were so far beyond me, to learn from them—the inability to see what they saw, how they saw, to take even a first step; the infantile frustration spent on rage at the hapless pears on a chair, which seemed like a crystallization of my impotent self.

Sometimes we can come to terms with the infant in ourselves, but we cannot kill it. Aroused, this infant behaves in fascinating ways, awful and uncontrollable. He or she shouts, weeps and raves like a lunatic. There is a lunatic in every one of us, ready to be triggered off by "something," the threat of threats. Lovers breaking up are in a state of derangement, on the edge of madness. I have been that way, possessed by unreason. We are threatened by superior beings, threatened by the fear of being abandoned. The latter can drive human beings and animals mad. Communism. Homosexuality. I know a remarkable woman, accomplished and intelligent, who writes reports, heads commissions, practices psychotherapy, and her madness resides in that part of her that is homosexual, that unadmitted part. To admit it would send her over the edge. Contemptuously, she speaks of women as lesbians and men as faggots; unmarried, she talks of the joys of married life and of heterosexual love. And coward that I am, I never allude to the incident in her life when she was in love with another woman, for this is the trigger and I am afraid to pull it. I begin to tremble at the very thought, just as I tremble at the thought of discussing myself with anybody, afraid to kill or be killed. Isn't the threat, finally, *death* to an essential image of ourselves, to the way we hold our egos together?

I have always had difficulty holding my ego together, for it was battered both by my infinitely slow progress as a painter and by society's generalized threat to homosexuals, which could turn me to craven jelly even while I remained in hiding. Homosexuals live more than others in the shadow of threat. We have committed a crime that has been condemned for thousands of years. Our answer has been to deny it. We lead double lives; we are hated (if recognized) and then judged for hating ourselves. We are judged for reacting bitterly to the unbearable weight of guilt that has been put on us. The most beautiful and loving experiences of our lives have to be kept secret; and the lies we live make us wary and cold. "Cold heart, what do you know about love?" my mother once said to me. At the time she spoke, I was twenty-five and having my first sexual experience with a woman. But it was not my first love.

Three years before, I was in love with a woman and it made me quake with fear and happiness, such flooding happiness that that time of first being in love with a woman still seems like the happiest time of my life. I was twenty-two years old and knew only enough about homosexuality to be afraid of the subject. Long before that, at a debutante party (for we dutifully went through the conventional paces), a young man questioned me, "Have you ever been in love? Do you want to get married?" I said that I hadn't thought about it, but no, I didn't particularly want to get married. He kissed me suddenly. I saw his lips coming closer and pulled away. "Don't you feel anything?" he asked. I said I didn't, not wanting to say that I hated the feeling of this strange mouth pressed against my own. He looked curiously at me and said, "Maybe you're..." and stopped. "Maybe I'm what?" "Nothing," he said. I remember this exchange about thirty years later when what he meant came to me with a blinding flash. A "sort of" or a *real* Lesbian? Had I deliberately hidden myself from myself? How did it happen that I remained so long in a state of total innocence about sex, that I didn't try any of the experiments with my body that other children try? My sister and I were caught one day by our governess lying on the bed with our feet in the air, trying to study ourselves. After her scolding, I never looked at myself again and never wanted to. How well it worked, repression by shame and disgust! The exchange of sexual information that normally goes on between brothers and sisters in a family was taboo in ours and harmless experiments became crimes. With the following exception, our brothers and we never saw each other nude. It was summer; my sister and I were eleven and our brother was sixteen. Our rooms adjoined one another and one night he stole into our room to give us a lesson in comparative anatomy. This ended disastrously, for in the purity of our mean little hearts, we informed. "Why couldn't you have told me that you minded?" said our brother, who had been annihilated by our mother's wrath. Now, almost fifty years later, I know that this brother has been devoured by guilt ever since, martyred like Prometheus, though he did nothing shameful, and that my sister and I are partly responsible. As for me and the fact that I "minded" so much—did it mean that the "sort of" was already latent in me? Or was it our up-bringing that made me continue to be squeamish about men's bodies to this very day, to skirt gracefully around the word "penis," and yet to harbour in me a certain interest in this unruly organ that all men carry about with them?

When my short-term Argentine lover, in the stormy days of our breaking-up, accused me of suffering from "penis envy," I flew into a rage, longing to think of an equivalent accusation for *him*. "You have penis envy yourself," I said, wishing to attack his manhood, for he was sensitive in a general way on this point (he did not know how to drive and it humiliated him to be so capably driven by *me*). But he smiled sardonically. For Freud, penis envy was inherent in every woman, like original sin; for most people now, it is a useful term to throw at women who aspire to self-determination. Or perhaps it is because they are Lesbians? For, if your attitude toward the penis is at all ir-reverent, if you refuse to think of it as the rising sun, the risen Lord, the creation, or whatever, you are immediately suspect. Hasn't Mellors in *Lady Chatterley's Lover* a sixth sense for spot-ting the "Lesbian woman" (*i.e.,* one who pits her sexual will against his)? "When I get with a Lesbian woman, *whether she knows she's one or not* I see red," he says to Connie. Well, Mellors has suffered from women's wills and refusals and frigidity, which (in Lawrence's eyes) adds up to Lesbianism, and since I have a sneaking affection for Mellors, I forgive him. But I don't forgive Lawrence, who might have made an effort to understand Les-bians as profoundly as he understood everybody else. But being an almost "sort of" himself, he was uptight about threats to his manhood. So was my Argentine friend. I understand now why he said during a furious argument we had about Lawrence, in which each tried to claim him as a friend, "Lawrence would have hated you." Yes, I think now, having just read *Lady Chatterley's Lover* after all these years, Lawrence would have perceived the Lesbian in me, the resistance to his maleness — and would have "seen red." At the time of our argument, the sentence, "Lawrence would have hated you," seemed to be groundless, calculated to arouse my fury. Now I think — would he have? Couldn't we perhaps have been friends if there had been no question of our being lovers?

But to return to my sexless childhood, to my grown-up relations, and to the two houses where we spent our vacations. I see now that my choice of Mater's house, The Peak, rather than of Belfield, my maternal grandmother's house, was less an early exercise of taste than an instinct for what made me happy. Belfield had thick stone walls, narrow, almost perpendicular staircases, small rooms full of beautiful old furniture, a basement that smelled of mould, turned butter and souring cream. Everything about Belfield should have made us happy, yet we were less happy than at The Peak. The garden at Belfield was fragrant with lilac and peonies, and you could descend stone steps past a rock garden and take a path that led to the spring, a pool covered with a lacy green plant which heaved and trembled with the perpetual bubbling below. It terrified me to think that if you fell into the spring you could never get out. There were other things to fear at Belfield: a bad tempered cow that chased us and giant Muscovy ducks with their faces entirely covered by red wattles, standing in the mud of the chicken yard, their eyes like brass buttons. But worse than that, there was something almost abstract there, a sense of menace: the huge grey building, a Catholic seminary, that was built on the land beyond the back gate.

My mother's prejudice against Roman Catholics was shared by her sister, Sarah, who fought tooth and nail to keep the land from being acquired and the seminary from being built. Aunt Sarah was acknowledged by everybody to be a great woman. By sheer force of character and intelligence, she became president of a medical school for women, though she had had no medical training, and was given several honourary degrees. She was a feminist at a time when it was hard work to be one. When we were young, she wished even to liberate my sister and me from our subject state. "Do you remember when Aunt Sarah said to mother, 'Suppress, suppress,' meaning that mother suppressed *us*?" my sister asked me not long ago. Aunt Sarah was celebrated for her wit and told long comical stories in which, I began to notice at an early age, she was always the heroine. One was about George Bernard Shaw, who, on a Far Eastern cruise ship, had spotted Aunt Sarah as an interesting woman and had let word drop that he wanted to meet her. Aunt Sarah sent the message that her knees turned to wood if a gentleman wouldn't make the effort to come to see her. And so, in the story, Shaw came to see her. But what I wanted to know was, what did they talk about? Did they match wits? Did they become friends? The point of the anecdote was Aunt Sarah's triumph over male chauvinism, but this seemed to me much less important than her actual meeting with Shaw and I was almost ashamed of her for having put principle before the privilege of meeting a great writer.

But all the happy times were at The Peak, where the sun seemed to shine almost all the time. On rainy days, we would play in a back sitting-room with a fire burning and Balfour (a coincidence that this pugnacious little dog had the same name as our governess) for company; and Percy would bring milk toast for supper on a tray. We were glad to be segregated from the grown-ups, except for the ever-vigilant Miss Balfour, their precept in this case being that children should be neither seen nor heard. In the morning, we had delightful little tasks, for Grandmother employed us to pick rosebugs off the bushes at the walled end of the garden. I can still feel their dry claws on my hand as they clambered out of the can of kerosene and over the edge; I feel the squashiness of their beige-grey backs between my fingers when I pried them loose and forced them back into the can. And I smell the mingled smells of the rosebugs, the kerosene and the roses warmed by the sun with their hundreds of fragrant petals lying on the hot dry earth. Each of us had a little manila envelope tied with a different coloured ribbon, and into this envelope our wages were put, one penny for each five rosebugs. I remember sometimes earning as much as thirty-five cents, paid very solemnly by Grandmother in her morning-room, which was bright with polished silver and blue and white chintz.

There is something of The Peak in every house I have ever chosen for myself, even though there have been no servants, no elaborately served meals, even though the furniture is relatively shabby and the gardens like poor relations. Perhaps it is the perfume of box, lilac, roses and peonies that gets into the pores of every house and is exhaled, or the surrounding peace that I choose by imperious necessity. Now and then, the dreams I have about houses translate my love for The Peak into the image of a kind of terrestrial heaven. I remember one dream in which I found myself in a house, Georgian perhaps, with big square rooms, painted white, and flooded with sunlight that came through French windows. Outside, there was an orchard and the apple trees in it were covered with fruit, like big glowing rubies. My happy dreams have always been visions of sunlit rooms, radiant landscapes and birds.

I wonder now why I felt so depressed always in Mater's city house in Philadelphia, wonder to what extent it formed my tastes and anti-tastes, wonder why some children in the same family absorb and copy the lives of their parents and grandparents and others reject them and determine to do the opposite. Mater's city house was a splendid example of high Victorian rococo, with oriental rugs laid over flowered carpets and every flat surface covered with objects: gilt French clocks, *cloisonné* vases, Dresden figurines, ornate brass candelabra. On a small round table in the downstairs library, covered with a pale satin embroidered Chinese tablecloth (I have photographs and a magnifying glass), there are seven highly polished silver objects and a tall bronze and marble lamp, a wingèd maiden standing on a pedestal and holding a polished marble sphere, half hidden by an embroidered linen shade. Among the silver objects, I recognize with a little rush of joy my plump bird with moveable wings and a head that turns, this bird which I take out of his soft brown bag on great occasions and, with a feeling of ostentation, place on the dinner table. Here and elsewhere, there are objects that found their way by inheritance into our house in Washington: a bronze Buddha on a high bookcase, and next to him, incongruously, a terra cotta mastiff with his nose almost touching the box turtle at his feet. His sharply arched back is turned to the Buddha and behind them is an engraving of one of Raphael's lunettes at the Vatican. On the small wall area between one bookcase and the next, there are ten engravings, miniatures, watercolours and a mirror. The etching of a cathedral interior, the Holbein reproduction, the watercolour of a bluejay, the bronze on the bookcase of the wolf suckling Romulus and Remus (her dangling breasts fascinated me when I was little)—all these moved to my family's house after Mater's death.

One might think that, gazing at the concentration of things (one can't call it a clutter because it has its own highly ordered and intricate and unchangeable composition), I would feel a sense of acute indigestion. On the contrary, having inherited a measure of my grandmother's acquisitiveness, I rove around this elegant antique shop and dwell with real sorrow on the objects I would like to have, that I never noticed until I saw them under the magnifying glass, objects dispersed, sold, gone forever: a bronze bird, its head turned sideways and up; a white china cat with bright brooding eyes; four musical cherubs perched above the open doorway of the solarium; pillows, huge ones, covered with velvet and satin and needlepoint. This leaves the ninety-eight percent that I do not want, the things that were lovingly bought for a lot of money by Mater, clustered together, polished and dusted with a feather duster by generations of Irish maids. And forgotten? Did she look at them? In the hodgepodge of pictures covering the walls were there some that she studied and loved? Did she ever think, where am I going to put these three Majolica cherubs holding bowls aloft? But there was always a place for everything, and in this case, she put them on top of a high cabinet in the dining room, itself filled with crystal beakers and bowls and compote dishes, all sparkling like diamonds. She was like me, I suppose, but her capacity for acquiring things was infinitely multiplied, untinged by the smallest feeling of guilt and shaped by the ideal image of an elegant house. Was my grandmother competing with other rich Philadelphia families? I study the photographs and look for my grandmother's soul, for her real loves and attentions, but I see her soul fragmented; see it most concentrated in the plants that crowd the sunny west window of the dining room. I remember the smell of the sweet olive, a smell that mitigated my city depression; I remember that my grandmother's bathroom was full of plants, and that, at eighty-four, she was found dead there in the bathtub, having fallen peacefully asleep.

The plants spoke of love, whereas the thousands of objects in the house spoke in a loud stage whisper of money. It was not a really welcoming house. There were sofas and chairs covered with velvet on which one decidedly did not fling oneself, but sat precisely. ("Twins, stop fidgeting," Mater often said to my sister and me, but it was not our fault; the chairs were fidget-provoking.) At Christmas, there was only one room in which the joys of subdued romping were allowed, supervised, of course, by Miss Balfour. This was a back study hung with family portraits and miniatures, plus a Rembrandt self-portrait, a Corot landscape, a Rowlandson coach and four in a storm, and a farm scene, highly idealized, in which a donkey gazes at a large pot of milk, a youth stands embracing the head of a cow, and the children and mother are in an unlikely state of cleanliness. Here, we were given a box of toys and allowed to spread them out on the floor and play with them. Carefully, without making too much noise.

One more detail that will perhaps throw light on my grandparents' character. In the dining room, there was a fireplace that was never used for fires, with a carved oak mantle above, the oak inlaid with marble. Particularly striking about this fireplace were the words carved in Gothic letters just under the mantlepiece: "Foster the Guest that comes," it is written, "Further him that maun gang." Between each word is a little rosette; the "gang" turns the corner and is at a right angle to the "maun." This sentence was incomprehensible to me and had to be explained, for a "maun gang" was mixed up in my head with a chain gang. I was prone to confuse words with two meanings, as I had confused the multiplication tables, or to take metaphors literally, as when our governess told me I was "skating on thin ice." Knowing now what the words mean, I try to apply them to my grandmother and her sense of hospitality. She certainly "furthered (perhaps as a family we still do) him that maun gang"; in those days, people were less likely to overstay their welcome, constrained by a sense of fitness and the suggestive silences that hastened their departure. "Foster the guest that comes." Were we fostered? I remember that Grandmother spent a lot of time trying to draw us out and failed; we were miserably shy and she made us shyer. Why? What did she do wrong? What did so many of my relations, including both my parents, do wrong? In this house, there were rules of properness: proper conversation, proper behaviour. Children must be silent when grown-ups talked, mustn't fidget, must cover their mouths when they yawn, must sit up straight at the table with their hands out of sight, mustn't giggle (this was our one safety valve, but was frowned upon). Later, it occurred to me that I was skating on thin ice when I got too near the frontier of properness. I had been "fresh," which meant to want in respect for all things sacred, to answer back. Levity had to be of the right kind. What did Grandmother want to draw out of us? Our opinions? If I had any, they vanished in the drawing-out process. I was backward in many ways, but sensitive to houses that did or didn't "foster" me. Our grandmother fostered my older brother and planted in him family pride and love for his inherited family treasures. His house looks like a simplified version of Grandmother's, with silver displayed on his sideboard and a formal drawing-room that inspires proper thoughts. When I was twenty, I turned against everything Victorian, despised all our family furniture and fell in love with colour, throwing it around in a tasteless and unsubtle way, wearing a green coat, a plaid skirt, a brown hat, a navy-blue sweater. The sensuous use of colour was absent in the houses of my relations, for colour meant a letting-go. My father was angry when I tried to tell him what I saw in Van Gogh. I can almost remember when I began to see colours, having, like my whole family, been blind to them till then. Is it credible that I did not notice the colours of the buildings in Rome? Yet, at seventeen, I hadn't noticed them; indeed, it seems to me that there was almost nothing I *did* notice. I try to make the connection between "fostering" and a sense of colour, but can think of too many drab but welcoming houses. In Grandmother's house, there was above all an absence of carelessness and spontaneity, of sofas sat in and books open, waiting to be read. To my friend, Marie-Claire Blais, all that counts in a person is *coeur*; intelligence, culture, etc. are nothing if you lack *coeur*. My little grandmother, packed with energies and enthusiasm, with her knowledge of English and Italian gardens, with the knowledge that selected each object in her house, did she have *coeur*, the kind that "fosters him that comes," *really* fosters? I would like to think she did, and yet, in my arrogant way, I feel I would have responded, that she would have wakened my sleeping *coeur* (on which, even wakened, I can't always rely). But it was other much humbler people I loved, in the tentative way I loved then, and I remember having the power to distinguish between a real love for children and the humbug kind, which I detested without knowing why. My grandmother imagined that *to will* affection was enough, though I doubt if she spent much time analyzing her attitudes; much more, perhaps, in analyzing our non-responsiveness.

I was mortally afraid of grown-ups, feeling obscurely that they abused their power, but I remember a cousin, one of the eccentrics in my mother's family, who was like a grown-up child, a stout little woman with an oversized head like the Duchess in *Alice in Wonderland*. Her name was Cousin Elsie Keith. Once, when chickenpox prevented me from going to North Carolina for our Easter vacation, and I lay in bed in a state of profound self-pity, Cousin Elsie appeared and gave me a necklace, which I have still, composed of red beads, each of which has a smiling face on either side. Somehow Cousin Elsie had known that I would like this grown-up present better than anything else she could give me; the grotesque little smiling faces made me absurdly happy and I remember a glad feeling of love rushing into my heart when Cousin Elsie put the necklace round my neck.

Cousin Elsie came to see me in our house in Washington, which our parents had bought when we (the twins) were nine years old. It was a five-storey, semi-detached, red brick house, facing a little park, and beyond, the facade of the Roman Catholic cathedral. The house had been quite splendid in its heyday, hallowed by the legend that Alice Roosevelt Longworth, the former owner and the last living daughter of T.R., had stood on her head at the foot of the stairs, in the stairwell where our Christmas trees were to stand so tall that you had to fix the electric star on the summit by leaning over the second storey bannister. Mrs. Longworth was never invited to the house for the simple reason that she was a Republican and my parents were Democrats. The social life of Washingtonians was determined by the party in power; until Franklin Roosevelt was elected, my mother dwelt in the shadows, but from that moment, until a few years before her death, she was free to pursue her social ambitions with an energy that amazed me. There was much leaving of cards at the houses of senators and justices of the Supreme Court, and at the White House; there were special days appointed for this, and days when my mother, too, was "at home." She believed in all these rites and they paid off in the form of invitations which, in turn, generated grand dinner parties given by my mother when the silver service plates would emerge from their red flannel jackets and my mother would get out her Crown Derby dinner plates and Waterford wine glasses and embroidered linen table cloths, and the mahogany table, immensely long with its full complement of inserted leaves, would be decked with all this splendour. Yes, it really happened! My mother lived this way. And during the war, I would go to these dinner parties in my WAVE uniform and engage in sparkling conversation (I thought) with the Attorney General, who, by accident or design, had touched his knee against mine under the heavy tablecloth. It would be dishonest of me to pretend that I never enjoyed myself in these exalted circles or that I wasn't pleased when we (the four children) went to a dance at the White House, and later, to receptions with our parents where we shook hands with President and Mrs. Roosevelt and with General Eisenhower. Who could resist the heady air of great houses and great people? But I didn't fit; I didn't look the part; I was too shy to make conversation with our supposed peers; and above all, I didn't really care. None of us, including my father, cared as our mother did.

She cared, but failed to make lasting friends among the elegant ladies at whose houses she left cards, and whom she never called by their Christian names.

But I must speak of the metamorphoses of the house, changes not so much physical as spiritual. On the back side of the house was a walled yard with two maple trees, an ailanthus growing close to the house that shot up to the third storey, and another strange tree with leaves as big as dinner plates, a garage and a little house my brothers had built and named the Brass Tack Club. Innumerable alleycats prowled along the wall and wailed; bats hung upside down in the wisteria vine that climbed up the back wall of the house, and, on hot summer nights, they sometimes flew into our open windows and brushed our heads with their leathery wings. The earth was hard-trodden, baked by the summer sun, and the grass refused to grow except in the corners. During the war, I tried to dig up worms in the intractable soil of the backyard for the baby robin I'd found in the street and I could only find one worm. A few days later, I had a hard time digging the robin's grave. Nobody loved that backyard; the Brass Tack Club was abandoned and the cats rounded up. It never changed its status and became a garden, despite our periodic efforts to plant flowers, and my mother's surveillance over a somewhat spindly crepe myrtle bush. The growing things that flourished had to seek protection against the house, like the wisteria vine which spread with such prehensile energy that it tore apart the bricks of the house and had to be cut down, almost to the ground.

As for the house—its ghost is full of memories, pleasant and uncomfortable, for it was a witness to all the pains of our growing up—its basement was peopled with the dark shades of our black servants: Sarah, the cook; Amelia, the laundress; Kathleen, Archie, Randolph, Christine—their names changing with the years—except for Sarah, Amelia, and Kathleen, who outlived our mother. Symbolically, rivers of black coal were fed from the street into the bins next to the furnace room, and a horrendous retching was audible even on the third floor, when the furnace was stoked. Every day my mother would descend the steep stairs to the basement and confer with Sarah, the cook, and the others, and it shows something of her true character that they loved her steadfastly and stayed on. As for my sister and me, we scarcely gave them a thought. Sometimes we chatted with Alvernia, the black seamstress, who pedalled away at the old Singer sewing machine in a little room next to our "nursery" on the third floor and who claimed to be able to speak every language, including Egyptian. We stayed upstairs with Miss Balfour and learned nothing from the servants in the basement, when we might have learned much. Most shocking of all, we did not learn what it was, then, to be black. Black people had scarcely begun to rebel; Kathleen, for instance, was unhappy when my older brother asked her to call him by his first name. We were Miss Mary, Miss Hester. My mother held to the belief that you did not entertain black people in your drawing-room or consider them as possible friends. It makes me sick now to think of all this—of the passive state that permitted me to receive ideas and prejudices without questioning them. It surprises me that our black servants, knowing what they knew about us, having endured our sense of superiority, didn't end by hating us. My older brother, so like my mother in many ways, was to become their true friend, to help them in need, to visit them when they were sick and to go to their funerals when they died; I look on his tender propitiation of our sins with awe.

It should have been obvious to me from our lifestyle that we had the means to enjoy it, and yet it never occurred to me that we were "rich." My mother's prejudices embraced not only all those who were "not quite" or "common," but also the "nouveaux riches," who had begun life, she presumed, either as one or the other. To have inherited your money and your possessions was not to be rich, but to inhabit the special and discreet world in which good Philadelphia families lived. Your house could be furnished with Chippendale chairs, Queen Anne tables and oriental rugs, you could be waited on by four or five servants, but it was as though all these visible signs of richness were the legitimate garments of one's class, which, one was given to think, was the only class that had the approval of heaven. To talk about money was vulgar, though you could complain about how much things cost, and "rich" was a dirty word; better to think of one's family

51

as "comfortably off," with a sense of Christian responsibility. My parents were so harried by their consciences, so determined to be good and do good, that they were ashamed of "enjoying" their money. My father had an almost monkish simplicity of soul and the things he loved were reduced to his gold repeating watch (he used to let us listen to its fairy chiming when we were little), a gold pocketknife and a little carnelian owl that sat on an ebony stand. It was our mother, like me, who craved things and who enticed Father on excursions to buy a Ming vase or a Chinese screen; it was she who had a real passion for shopping, but also it was she who drew those nice lines between rightness and luxury, who knew exactly at what point you overstepped the boundary and passed into ostentation. As for us children, I believe we still deceive ourselves with the thought that our attitude toward money and a Puritan rigour of mind prevent us from being "rich" as others are.

I should add that we were so thoroughly insulated from life that we hadn't the faintest idea of what it was like to be poor. We did not have any poor friends or even any whose parents had been poor. Without having our parents' precise notions of the social hierarchy, I had the complacent idea that our status was normal, instead of seeing, as I now do, that we belonged to a very small and snobbish minority. In my present circle of friends, I am the only one with an inherited income, and I listen humbly to the tales they tell of their growing-up in families who fought hard battles with poverty. My childhood, my school and college years were passed among the "privileged," who not only had money, but also were "respectable" in the same sense that we were. It was not until the war threw me with different kinds of people that I discovered that friends sometimes have drunken mothers or ne'er-do-well fathers, that the children of poor parents are often more remarkable than the children of rich parents, that people one knew had abortions and illegitimate children, were divorced, alcoholic, etc., that the professions of law, medicine, the ministry and teaching were not the only honourable ones. My family's sense of hierarchy extended even to shibboleths like the proper pronunciation of "tomato." If you said, "tom*a*to," you revealed that you were "not quite," even if you qualified for "quiteness" in every other way. My mother belonged to a charitable organization which probably still exists called The Girls' Friendly Society, the purpose of which was to go among the needy and minister to them, much as the good ladies in Jane Austen and Charlotte Brontë did. When we were sixteen, my sister and I conducted a class for poor children, the idea being to teach them to sew and to play games such as Going to Jerusalem and Musical Chairs. I remember only my distaste for these strange clamouring little girls whose clothes smelled of stale cooking oil, who could not learn to sew and who hated our games. It was a long time before I learned that we were as handicapped by our wealth as they were by their poverty. They, at least, had an accurate idea of what life was like; ours was restricted by the blinders we wore.

In my mind, I recreate the vanished house and my parents who now inhabit the shadows of death, their complicated lives reduced to my memories of them, faulty and biased, and with so little evidence of their real selves, for I have only a few of their letters, and they did not keep journals. Even in letters, they hid from us and from themselves, and in this, I am utterly unlike them, for in letters I spill out all my joys and sorrows without reticence or remorse. Sometimes, my parents appear to me in dreams, miraculously cured, my father of his tuberculosis; my mother of her stroke, and I recognize them joyfully. Or they are sick, as in a dream about my mother, paralyzed, lying in a bed surrounded by people. She speaks, but no one can understand her; then, I hear words, "Don't worry about light. You'll always have enough to see your way." I took these words spoken in a dream six years after she died as having come directly from her. Now and then during her lifetime she had made me happy by saying something of the same sort, out of a clear sky. "There is something light about you—like the touch of a butterfly wing," she once said to me, who felt, on the contrary, that I must weigh heavily on her. Perhaps it was the memory of this other kind of light that had provoked the dream. It was uncharacteristic of my mother to analyze character or, in fact, to think rationally about anything; she had a "feminine" way of conducting a discussion as something to escape from, instead of as a way of getting at the truth. One could write at length about the tricks that people invent in order to avoid talking about what they don't want to talk about, elaborate and beautiful tricks of evasion, but maddening to a rational adversary. The course of her flight was studded with burrows in the form of entrenched prejudices and refusals. There were things that were too terrible to be talked about at all, such as divorce (my mother did not speak to divorced people if she could help it) or illegitimacy. These prohibitions were expected to apply to everybody in the family; once I was severely scolded when I remarked that a baby which had been adopted by the mother of an unmarried friend looked exactly like the friend. My mother would not even permit the subject to be discussed. At the time, I thought this ridiculous, but I now see how much it reveals of her fierce discretion; she would fly in the face of reason to protect a friend. It is possible that she made herself believe that the baby had really been adopted, knowing as she did that no "nice" young woman would have an illegitimate child. If a person's misbehaviour was outside her circle of friends, my mother was unforgiving, and her not-forgiving was of as pure an ore as her rectitude. By keeping these two qualities shackled together, generations of "good" people were bred and lived to make life miserable for others. Just as Chinese mothers had consented to foot-binding, my mother's mother, and her mother before her, had bound and shrunk their daughters' minds and their will to question the accepted order of things. My parents went to China for their honeymoon, and I remember my mother telling us that she had seen a woman with bound feet, as though it were not a scandal, but a fact of great interest. She had even bought a pair of tiny shoes which I looked at without horror, and it was not until a few years ago, when I saw a bound foot pickled in a jar of formaldehyde at the Musée de l'Homme in Paris, that the crime of foot-binding struck me with its full force.

I ponder now on our mind-habits that enable us to suppress or to torture other human beings or to fill them with guilt; and on my mother, whose habits were set when she was very young. She was not a naturally rigid person (is anyone?), but full of delicacy and gaiety. She *was* "light." I know this not only from memories, but also from studying photographs of her as a young woman, in which her face was often transformed by the most delightful smile. I think of her in our house in Washington and of my parents' room with twin beds made of mahogany, with flowered pink and white wallpaper, with blue chintz slipcovers on the furniture, and a dressing table covered with little china and silver boxes, much like Mater's. In the drawers of the 18th Century highboy, there was a sweet disorder of handkerchiefs and stockings and underthings scented with lavender and rose sachets, for even the messiness of my mother was charming, and on the closet floor, many pairs of long, narrow shoes in a row. I remember the sadness of seeing these elegant shoes and the hats on a top shelf, decorated with fruit and feathers, after my mother's death, testifying to her long sickness when she could no longer wear them. The eloquence of a pair of shoes! Just as my mother refused to wear glasses until she could no longer read the telephone book, even at arm's length, she refused to buy bigger shoes when her ankles were swollen from high blood pressure. She was proud of her hands and feet, proud perhaps of those parts of her which my father had admired; she pretended not to know how to wind a watch because it pleased my father to think that she was helpless about mechanical things. What a strange mixture she was of pride and humility, of grace and rigidity! There was a little corridor between her bedroom and my brother's, with a closet on either side. In one of the closets, my mother had lined the shelves with gold and embossed Japanese wallpaper and had arranged on the shelves a collection of treasures: little tortoise-shell fans and Chinese bottles, cats made of lead glass, ivory and wood carvings, ancient Greek toys and Egyptian scarabs and fragments of statuettes. There, hidden away in the dark behind the painted door, was the fantasy life of my mother, like buried treasure. It reminded me in its surprisingness of the churches of Ravenna, with their plain exteriors and the amazing glimmer of gold inside. Outside the closet, my mother chose and arranged with her unerring eye and light touch, and everything became increasingly formal as you went downstairs. Looking at the Empire of Beauty (a great polished highboy with bright brass drawer handles, with finials and ornamental carving like two breaking waves on the top, about which someone was said to have exclaimed, "It's an empire of beauty!"), the Chippendale chairs and Queen Anne tables, the mahogany table with ten leaves in the dining room, the Ming vase on the mantelpiece and the 18th Century mirror with a carved gilt eagle at the top, you saw that "other" mother, composed of family pride, a less personal love for beautiful objects, for it might have been the living room, the dining room of any conservative American family with inherited wealth and a sense of its own importance. Isabel Archer would have felt immediately at home here.

"Your mother was clairvoyant," said Miss Walker (a real clairvoyant) as she gazed at a portrait I had done of my mother at three ages: young, middle-aged and old. "You didn't have to tell her when something was going to happen; she always knew." Was this really so? I searched and searched my memory and could think of no examples of my mother's clairvoyance. But I knew that Miss Walker could see things that are unknown to me; things that I can hunt for and never find: the magic being shut up in the conventional woman; the paradox of the bird in its cage that refuses to walk out the open door, who does not see that the door is open, and, caught forever in her cage-habits, does not care.

"I see a little cloud no bigger than a man's hand," my elder brother used to say, and we twins would laugh nervously, knowing that he spoke of a storm brewing in our mother, spawned we knew not how. She had what we called her "black look"; it came from something one of us had said or done, something which, in retrospect, often seems ludicrously innocent. I can remember the weight of her stern eyes on me, willing me to meet her gaze, at the dinner table, while I looked at my plate, and of slithering guiltily around the house while the cloud no bigger than a man's hand grew into a towering thunderhead and finally broke when she caught me. "You do *not* say to a young man that you've seen your sister in her pyjamas!" She threw this at me like a lightning bolt when I was more than twenty years old. On this occasion, one of my sister's suitors, who was a house guest, had descended for breakfast and had asked where my sister was. My mother had overheard the fatal words, "The last time I saw her, she was in her pyjamas." This is unimaginable now, as it was even then, but it shows in what a senseless atmosphere of prohibition we grew up. When I went to boarding school, the rules seemed perfectly natural to me, even a welcome relief from home, since, ridiculous though they were, they were, so to speak, visible (don't sit on your bed or don't "communicate" in study hall). At home, there were rules that regulated not only our behaviour and our conversations, but also our thoughts. The mere use of the word, "pyjamas," or worse still, "bed," evidently suggested sex to my mother; or did she fear that these words would suggest sex to *me*? But she needn't have been afraid; our training had been so thorough that nothing suggested sex to me. I would like to know the reason for her real terror of sex, a fear that went beyond convention.

In fiction, the character most like my mother and our governess is the governess in Henry James' *The Turn of the Screw*. One of my recurrent arguments with Edmund Wilson was about his insistence (he had written an essay about it which was accepted as the final word on the subject) that James' governess was a neurotic monster who visited her sexual frustration on the children, Miles and Flora, aged twelve and six, and literally frightened Miles to death. In Edmund's view, the ghosts of Peter Quint and Miss Jessel were creatures of the governess' sex-starved imagination and the children were innocent. To me, this wholly negative view of the governess spoiled the whole story, for wouldn't my mother and my own governess have behaved exactly the same way, more violently, but with less tenderness? I see the story thus: that Peter Quint and Miss Jessel made the children aware of sex by making it quite clear to them that they were lovers, by talking in front of them or by being overheard, and, in Miles' case, perhaps by overt sexual exchanges between him and Peter Quint. That this is not just imagined by the governess is clear from the fact that Miles has been dismissed from school for reasons that no one can even talk about ("I said things," he says to the governess when she asks. "To those I lik-ed," which makes the nature of his crime crystal clear) and that Flora, in a state of delirium, pours forth a stream of "appalling language" about the governess, in the hearing of Mrs. Grose, the housekeeper. It gives you some idea of the moral hysteria of those times that the governess' response to the news of Flora's "appalling language" should be to cry, "Oh, thank God!" and to explain to Mrs. Grose, "It so justifies me!" And the good, solid Mrs. Grose, instead of saying, "Aren't you being rather egocentric?" says, "It does that, Miss!" Mrs. Grose lives in the same world of good and evil as the governess and she perfectly understands her need to be morally in the clear. And it was here that ego, so repressed in other ways (as it was in my mother and governess), worked in women of that time, in the sense of the rightness of their judgements of others. "There had come to me out of my very pity," says the governess, "the appalling alarm of his being perhaps innocent. It was for the instant confounding and bottomless, for if he *were* innocent what then on earth was I?" Edmund's answer to this was that Miles *was* innocent and that the governess was a murderer. But to me, Miles' death, like the young heroes' deaths in two other stories by James, "Owen Wingate" and "The Pupil," was death by terror and guilt. The hearts of the two young men and the boy are not strong enough to bear the image society has of their guilt. Each is suspected of being homosexual, and, in one way or another, James repeatedly killed the homosexual in himself. Note that it is Miles, presumably the stronger of the two children, who dies, for he has made gestures to those he liked, whereas Flora has merely repeated words that she has heard, and in an unconscious state. The thought of this worst of all possible crimes, this unthinkable crime between Miles and Peter Quint, or Miles and his school friends, has induced in the governess an exalted religious fervour, the mawkishness of which makes me feel slightly sick. With her, it took the form of passionate tenderness, a violence of tender willing that was just as hard to take as our mother's blackness. It never occurred to our mother, as it did to the governess, to say to herself, "If he *were* innocent what then on earth was I?" Our parents and governess belonged to a moral school in which guilt was presumed, and it was useless to argue. The wonder of it was that we never "said things," but were scrutinized in the event that we might. Thoughts *might* come into our heads. How else to explain my mother's rush to silence the orchestra playing in our house for our first dance, when they started to play, "It's Sleepy Time Down South"? One would think that this sleepy time would preclude thoughts about sex, but to my mother it suggested them and it would suggest them to us. Our parents' ideas about the crime of sex made their children's lives arid, guilt-ridden or punitive (in my brothers' case) for a long time. Of my brothers' lives, when they were growing up, I know little, but imagine much. During the war, when I was twenty-four years old and lived in the family house in Washington, I was embraced at intervals by a married cousin who spent the night now and then and professed to be "crazy about me." Laughing, I recounted this to my brother, who turned white with rage. "I'm going to tell Mother," he said. I imagined the sequence of events: my cousin disgraced and thrown out of the house; my mother, forever unforgiving. "No, no, no, I can handle it! I promise you I can! I will!..." That moral rage, so familiar to me, fashioned from something as insubstantial as smoke, an idea that hardens the heart and makes people willing to destroy each other in its name. One can almost make an equation: that moral outrage is multiplied by the craziness of the idea held and that the more the idea is untenable, the more drastic the punishment for the person breaking its law. Or is it the more something is tempting, the more it must be punished? Oddly enough, the people who have never been tempted are as ruthless as those who have resisted temptation—and I came to be convinced that my parents belonged to the former class.

But all this moral intransigence and sternness wasn't our real mother, who was an innocent schoolgirl, on whom the doors of life had closed like the doors of the Iron Maiden. She was the brilliant, laughing girl who had won all the prizes for excellence and had been given a carved wooden spoon as the most popular girl in her class. I am convinced that she knew nothing about life except as a schoolgirl might when she married my father, as beautiful as an archangel; he, too, the first in his class. Didn't she say once to my sister, "I cried the whole time of my honeymoon"? So here was a clue, that my father, who was as chaste as my mother when they married, had perhaps frightened her during their first night together, and that this created the horror of sex that she visited on her children. There is a sexual element in all physical tenderness and it was this that was so resolutely suppressed in our family relationships, the absence of which made us so cool and awkward with each other. When we hugged each other, it was without the lovely yielding of real tenderness, and if the latter existed between our parents, they were always careful to hide it from us. My mother created fatal barriers between herself and her children in the name of what was "done," by turning us over to nurses and governesses, by giving us away, in fact, to Miss Balfour, who came when we were six years old and did not leave until we were sixteen. Miss Balfour's moral stuff was sterner than our mother's, and one of our worst crimes was to try to appeal to our mother over Miss Balfour's head. She liked little boys better than little girls. "Little girls are deceitful," she said. Her presence in our family created a lethal triangle, and I see now that this is what poisoned that period of my mother's life: her powerlessness to reach her children, her conviction that Miss Balfour had stolen our love. Miss Balfour had thick, wavy hair, a fresh pink face and beautiful grey eyes; if she had been as kind to us as she was to our brothers, I would have loved her, but she was short-tempered and sometimes downright mean. Sometimes, in order to make some moral point, she slapped us or pinched our arms just above the elbow as we walked down the street on either side of her. We became deceitful to outwit her, and this must have been exasperating, not to mention the awful frustrations of our family life.

After Miss Balfour left us, she took care of a series of little boys, and we would go and visit her. When I saw how tender she was with one of them, how patient, I wept, broke down completely, and Miss Balfour was loving and patient with *me*. By then, she had suffered the torments of *tic douleureux*, had been operated on so that her face was partly paralyzed, and her hair had turned white. I realized how we are formed by the relation we have one to the other, how the words "governess-charges" had made Miss Balfour an overseer; and us, her slaves, how she was ruled by the idea of what she thought we should be, how she thought we should behave, how perhaps she hated having two sneaky and loveless little girls as "charges" and her essential good nature was twisted and deformed. And I remember how happy we were to become friends, to be able to behave as friends. In the same way, our mother was held in the iron frame of the words "mother-governess" and "mother-children." As the years went on and Miss Balfour made herself indispensable, our mother tried more and more frantically to get out of the trap she had made for herself. She suffered torments of jealousy. For a time, until she put an angry stop to it, our older brother used to go and kiss Miss Balfour goodnight as she lay in bed in her schoolgirl nightgown. In any other family, things would have gone further than this, but in ours, the act of kissing your governess goodnight if you were a boy of sixteen was as scandalous as fornication. Yet after this episode, Miss Balfour stayed with us for five more years. Even after she left, her ghost haunted my mother. My father, who had always defended Miss Balfour and considered her a necessary part of the family, arranged for her operation after she had left, and visited her after it in the palatial mansion of her new family to see how she was getting on. This got to the ears of my mother (he had evidently not dared tell her, a fact of some significance, if one is searching in the shadows for truth) and caused another upheaval. Looking back, I remember a period when my mother was continuously in her black state, when she cried day after day. A worldly-wise reader might say that something was certainly going on between my father and Miss Balfour, a reader who did not know my parents or Miss Balfour, one who did not know that the idea of sexual wrong-doing was as terrible as if the act had been committed. It was precisely because there was no accusation my mother could make, because there was no pretext for firing Miss Balfour, that her torment was more acute.

Our poor mother spent the years after Miss Balfour's departure yearning for her lost children and not knowing how to go about getting them back. By then, we were miles away from her, keeping our lives a secret from her, punishing her, it would seem, for having given us away. After my father's death, she lived alone in the big house, trying to carry on her old life, as brave as a soldier, and I can't think of it now without pain. How little we knew of each other; how incapable we were of talking! I remember

61

again the bitter accusation that shot out of her, when, questioning the imminent marriage of a friend and her doubts, I said, "Does she really love him?" "Cold heart," she said, "what do you know about love?" I hated her at this moment—and yet, what evidence did my unloved mother have that I knew anything about love? And if she had any evidence, wouldn't her bitterness have been even greater, as it was on another occasion (I was going to visit a friend I loved, but of the love I could say nothing) when she said, "Another woman?"

Even my sister was unapproachable, embarrassed and cool when our mother suddenly said to her (they were sitting on a park bench and it was after our father's death), "Can't you love me a little?" We all felt—and I knew—that she couldn't possibly understand our lives, that there was no use in trying to talk to her, for hadn't she always been shocked by even the tiniest infraction of her rules? It was much easier to stay on safe ground, to talk about my teaching, about my painting, to go to concerts with her — yes, like schoolgirls — and stay away from dangerous subjects. But why did even these safe subjects create conflicts? Why did it seem to me that there was nothing in the world about which my mother and I agreed when, now, I have the impression that I never bothered really to draw her out? Hadn't she read all the French classics, seen innumerable operas and plays (my mother liked naughty drawing-room comedies and laughed at behaviour that shocked her in real life. "But it's a play," she said when I pointed this out to her); couldn't she recite the names of the kings of England and France? Didn't she love chamber music, and go, year after year, to the concert series at Coolidge Auditorium? But something prevented me from believing that this cultivation of hers was real, for she was unable to discuss why or how she loved books and music. A few years before her death, when she was paralyzed and talked with difficulty, I arranged with a violinist friend to come and play for her in her house and warned him that she might be impatient, or even rude, as she was at times with visitors. He played the Bach partita in B minor, perhaps the most exacting of all Bach to listen to, and my mother, far from being impatient, sat enthralled and afterwards thanked him with all the words she could muster.

Once again, I felt horribly ashamed of my arrogance, of the false idea I had had of my mother's feeling about music. And I realized that even if she found the Bach partita hard to listen to, there was something graciously receptive at the very core of her being, stronger than her sickness, that recognized great music played by a master.

My mother had always been humble — much too humble, I thought. She was impressed by any kind of accomplishment, as long as it was accomplished by an outwardly virtuous person, and this humility appeared in her either as a strength or a weakness. In its strong aspect, it made her capable of listening to the Bach partita, of a silent worship of great art. But her character was fatally shaped by the humility that made her deny her own value and accept the impersonal judgements of society. When she married, because my father was a Democrat, she switched her political allegiance from Republican to Democrat, and from then on, she accepted everything the Democrats did without question. Humility was her primal matter and out of it was fashioned her self-denial, her ferocious loyalties and her snobbishness. She had been humiliated by Mater because she came from a small town and her life in Washington was one long effort to keep a high place on the social ladder. But her friends were often not the great ladies of Washington, but rather relatively simple people of sterling character, who gave me the impression of having stepped from the pages of Dickens, and whom she never called by their first names.

Those friends whom she did call by their first names were all summer friends; with them she laughed and was happy. But even here, there was one whose name brought forth my mother's humility. This was Helen L., who knew Thornton Wilder and other giants, and who founded the Reading Club, of which my mother was a member. As I chase after wisps of memory, think of the high seriousness my mother put into doing homework for the meetings of the club, think of her real awe of Helen L., a genuine intellectual, and think of her awe of another friend, whose mother had been the first editor of Emily Dickinson, I see her in all her touching innocence and see how offensive I was with my mocking sarcasm. Sometimes I would overhear conversations between the friends which touched, not on literature, but on the "servant problem" (a problem which in those days could hardly be said to have existed) or about their husbands' little foibles. I remember noticing uneasily that their indulgent remarks about their husbands always implied their own sense of themselves as *wives*. One and all (including Helen, whose husband was a distinguished scientist, who believed in the superiority of their husbands to themselves), I saw with disgust, and within this rigid framework, like Japanese or Spanish wives, they were quite happy to live and turn any spark of rebellion into a tender joke. These were the terms then of happy marriages — and they were all happily married, for my mother's moral canon excluded unhappily married people. It was the wife's fault, she firmly believed, if a marriage failed.

In the warm summer sunshine, in the gaiety of picnics and parties, in the joy of her garden full of heliotrope and lavender, lemon verbena, rose geranium, all my mother's sweetness seemed to flourish. True, her loyalty to the Episcopal Church provoked a certain grimness, and I see her now of a Sunday morning, wearing her hand-knitted white wool suit, her hat adorned with plastic cherries, and her narrow, pointed shoes, rounding up a cranky flock of children and grandchildren (the latter in starched seersucker and kneesocks, with doleful expressions on their faces) for the eleven o'clock service. That was the trouble: the superego was always at hand telling her how to behave, telling her that she had to go to church every Sunday until she could no longer walk, telling her to badger her children and grandchildren and to be gravely offended if one of them refused her. It was I who refused, and that created another rift between my mother and me, for I refused first to take communion, and then, to go to church at all. There was always in my mother a threshold where laughter stopped, where the rules were invoked and where discussion became impossible. Her summer gaiety was illusory. (Hadn't it been in summer that she scolded me for saying I had seen my sister in her pyjamas?) Alas, none of us ever succeed in turning this intractable morality of hers into a joke, and the sins we committed remained fresh in her mind, like prehistoric animals preserved in a glacier.

The summer mother and the winter mother were the same person, but in winter there was a concentration of loyalties that preoccupied her. In society, she became a redoubtable hostess; in politics, she became president of the Women's National Democratic Club. As a mother, she worked to see that her daughters could ride horseback, dance, speak French and go to the best boarding schools. Our brothers were not polished in the same way and continued to go to our first Quaker school; to be ignorant of the arts of riding and dancing. It was obvious that she was grooming us to be wives, for she drew the line at a college education (we rebelled, however) and put her ambitions and energies into our "coming out," which failed signally to get us husbands. I am grateful to her now for her zeal, and thankful that, among her failures, was the failure to make us carbon copies of herself. None of us believe in the things she believed in with the same fierceness. And how surprising it is that a person so modest could be so fierce! "Your mother is the sweetest, loveliest person!" her friends would say. At her grand dinner parties, she always prevented conversations from becoming heated ("I never talk about politics at the dinner table," she would say), and I can see her beaming face at the end of the long table, her head graciously turning from left to right, or, spotting a guest who hadn't spoken, launching a question that would draw him out. She was much loved for these qualities by the courtly gentlemen of Washington.

It amazes me that she could put so much moral energy into the most insubstantial beliefs. I remember the summer mother, the light-hearted one, and her fury, when, one Sunday, the curly-haired, black-eyed minister of our church began intoning the Creed. She and her friends assembled and inveighed against the dangers of becoming "high church," seeing the minister, with his love for music, for sculpture and flowers, as an emissary of the Pope himself. To him, it was natural to inject a little art into the Episcopal service; to my mother, it was a crime. She won, of course, and eventually the minister, the only one of his kind I ever felt close to, changed to a church that was "higher," where he could let himself go, and an uninteresting and non-artistic man took his place.

Just as there was a right and wrong about the smallest details of the church service, just as these details engaged my mother's full moral attention, so too there was a rigid sticking to society's rules, as exigent as the laws of the land. I have said that my mother played the social game, but it seems to me that her psyche was geared to success or failure, that she was vindicated in a deep personal sense if she was invited to the White House and humiliated if she was *not* invited to something she considered a test of her social standing. During the war, a garden party was held at the British Embassy to honour the King and Queen and it became the kind of event that provokes intrigues, family quarrels, the kindling of furious social ambitions. Despite her efforts, my mother had not been invited, but worse still, her niece, who was married to the third son of a duke, had been, and the fortunate couple was staying in our house. The day of the garden party, it rained so persistently that the ladies' big hats collapsed and the collars of the gentlemen's morning coats turned green. Our bedraggled cousins appeared at the dinner table and as they told about the disaster of the party, we all began to laugh, helpless releasing laughter, and I remember my mother laughing until tears rolled from her eyes. It was over, this terrible test, and perhaps, at that moment of relief, she saw how little it mattered.

I have staked out in my mind an area where my mother felt unthreatened, for I see now that every day had its threats, that, if we seemed to be walking across a minefield, it was because our mother had this feeling herself. I see her now in the innocence and isolation of her safety spots, opening her tea basket in the compartment of a European train, heating water over a can of Sterno, handing us enamel cups of weak tea and Klim, the powdered milk of that time whose mirror name delighted me, and Petits Beurres. I see her outdistancing us all with her loping tourist gait, like a Tennessee walking horse, and, white-faced, sitting on a broken column at Hadrian's Villa, overcome by the Italian sun. I can feel her confiding arm in mine on the last trip we took together, during which I puzzled her by behaving like a sulky child; and the softness of her hand which so irritated me by gently stroking mine. In her mind, it seems to me, I had been changed into my father, with his depressions and his endless arguments, but with his power to protect her. In *my* mind, I was the unmarried daughter whose duty it was to take care of her mother, and the fact that I was compelled to fill this unwelcome role infuriated me. But by then, when she was in her seventies, my mother was an angel of patience and whatever differences we had were invariably my fault. These came from my feeling that we belonged to different species and that I was yoked to my so-different mother by an obligation which I could not accept.

Could we, I wonder, by some kind of consciousness-raising, have reduced all those threats that my mother felt? I am still convinced that I could not have told her any of my secrets (my sister, to whom I have told them, disagrees. "Mother knew more about you than you think," she says, but has no evidence to prove it), that she could never have understood my love for women, that, just as she had refused to speak to her oldest sister for twenty years because her sense of justice was outraged in a quarrel over their mother's will, so she would have refused to speak to me, and would have read me out of the family circle as well. Hadn't she had her first stroke at her club, watching McCarthy on television, the man who was abominable to her not only because he was a demagogue, but also because it was rumoured that there was a homosexual relation between him and Roy Cohn? To me, the convulsions that my mother had then were the outward sign of her loathing; and I was glad I'd kept my secret tightly locked away. And yet, there are Miss Walker's words, "Your mother was clairvoyant," and my sister's insistence that I could have talked to our mother, that she would have understood. Even now, my heart begins to thump with the old fear and sickness that came over me at the very thought of talking, that made it impossible to talk to my twin sister until recently—the old fear provoked by my mother's grimness, by an alarming sideways twitch of her set mouth that made us all tremble. I think of Lesbian friends with mothers who are still alive, who live near their mothers at their own risk, who spend themselves in a futile effort to placate them, consenting to hypocritical silence and coming to believe in the necessity, imposed by their mothers, of lying low and pretending to be invisible. I know mothers who have sent their daughters to psychiatrists, mothers who denounce their daughters behind their backs, mothers who take the fact of having a Lesbian daughter as an excuse to feel martyred. Which one of these stereotypes would my mother have chosen, she who cared with her whole soul about society's rules?

Too often, it is the mother who makes the rules and the daughter who cares about her who compromises and in so doing, permits her mother to become a tyrant. A veritable snakepit of taboos prevents the mother of a Lesbian daughter from loving her with any constancy. One might expect the fact that mothers naturally love their daughters the way women love each other (*i.e.*, with passionate tenderness) would help them to understand love between women. On the contrary, every woman is seen as a threat to this love, which, since it is "virtuous," is prevented by a taboo from ever becoming incestuous. The mother of a Lesbian stands between her daughter and her daughter's lovers like a dragon; it is as though she were snarling, "Keep away from my property!"—for she, the mother, is the only woman a daughter may legitimately love. Unfortunately, Freud was too busy with the Oedipus complex and too baffled by the psychology of women, who, for some strange reason, kept rebelling against their conventional role, to go into this other complex, to which no one has yet given a name. No doubt, Sappho had a mother who was anxious about Sappho's women lovers, and if her name had survived, the complex could have been named for her. No doubt, this anonymous mother was glad that Sappho had men lovers, too, just as a contemporary mother of a married Lesbian daughter swallows her aversion to the idea of women lovers as long as her daughter is "faithful" to her husband. Since she has been fashioned by the patriarchal society we live in, her first reaction to her daughter's marriage is delight (she need no longer be ashamed of her); if her daughter continues to have Lesbian attachments which aren't too visible, the mother prefers to think of them as adventures in which love plays no part. How strange it is that the purest element of a relationship between women is seen as the most threatening, the love that binds them together; and yet, it isn't strange, for it is this love which excludes the mother. The nameless complex which makes mothers love and hate their Lesbian daughters simultaneously, can never, like the

Oedipus and Jocasta complexes, be said to be resolved, for society never sanctions Lesbian love as it does heterosexual love. When a son or daughter marries, the mother's bond with her son or daughter is dissolved in the ceremony of marriage and this official sanction helps her to bear the pain. Since she had been taught to accept the idea that a husband or wife takes priority over a mother, she must at least make an effort to play second fiddle. But a daughter's love for another woman is condemned by society, and a mother simply cannot believe that her daughter loves another woman more than she loves her own mother. One sees the mothers of Lesbians making frantic efforts to win back their daughters: bribing them, making them feel guilty, placing themselves bodily between the lovers in an act of non-violent resistance by living in the same house with them, this last, the worst punishment that a Lesbian couple has to endure. I have observed this and have seen the hate it spawned between the mother and the daughter's friend; I have seen the daughter wrap herself in a protective silence that made communication and honesty impossible. I've suffered from the mealy-mouthed atmosphere of respectability in which it is not permitted to show any signs of affection, to hold hands, to touch the person one loves in front of the dragon-mother, who pretends that she is fond of the daughter's friend, the mother always there as a super-spy, who gives you the impression, even in the night, of keeping her ears cocked for telltale sounds. It is drama quietly playing itself out below the surface of politeness and compromise and it leads me to this uncompromising conclusion: that Lesbian daughters should keep a safe distance between themselves and their mothers and should not harbour the illusion that they can share their lives, even if they seem to love each other. And I will continue to doubt that I could have talked with my mother or that any good would have come of it. My sister, married, with four children, her life a reflection in some ways of our mother's, of course could talk to her, could feel that anything she said would be understood. But I am thankful that I lived those last years of her life in a dishonest shadowland and am convinced that its air was the only air she could breathe. It was not only to protect myself, but also to protect her from the killing force of the word

69

or words: homosexuality, Lesbian, that could not be said or attached to a person without triggering a sort of moral madness.

There is a beautiful episode in *Through the Looking Glass*, a little parable about the power of words to change love into fear. Alice finds herself in the wood, "where things have no names," and meets a fawn, who shows no fright, for he cannot remember what he is. "So they walked together through the wood, Alice with her arms clasped lovingly round the soft neck of the Fawn, till they came out into another open field, and here the Fawn gave a sudden bound into the air, and shook itself free from Alice's arm. 'I'm a Fawn!' it cried out in a voice of delight. 'And, dear me! You're a human child!' A sudden look of alarm came into its beautiful brown eyes, and in another moment it had darted away at full speed." People of my mother's generation were armed in their minds at the sound of certain words, and the triggers cocked to go off. How could she possibly have endured the naming of her daughter with a word she could not say herself? Like Alice and the Fawn, we could only be friends in a wood "where things have no names."

Reading over the few letters from my mother that I still have, I study her large, firm handwriting with the same distance between every word, the same distance between the lines, the same pressure on every letter—her handwriting that scarcely changed from the time she was sixteen until she was seventy—look at the self that is enclosed in the closed "o"s and "a"s, at the discipline that even stiffened words expressing tenderness. I find a letter she wrote in answer to one of mine, written a year after my father died, and I see her suddenly, defenceless and loving, as her real self was. "You have hit upon the memory that troubles me most," she says, "the sins of omission, all the little things I might have done for your Father and didn't do. You are all very good, quite the best and most considerate children in the world. What I can't understand is that a year has gone by.... Well, yesterday has passed and I wonder at people's kindness. Downstairs are lovely pink lilies that Mrs. Warren sent me and Miss Edith Bache sent me roses, and Mrs. Crouse a sachet, and best of all, you wrote me." Signed "your loving Mother," the only time, for it was always, "Love from Mother."

70

I have another letter from my mother, written to my father in 1919. The handwriting is like that in the 1941 letter, but it leans more exuberantly to the right. She has a trick of looping letters back to cross her "t"s, and extending the arms of the "t"s so that they form airy horizontals: "Mrs. Roberts to tea"—the "s" of Roberts soars back, encloses the vertical loop of the "b" and darts forward to form a long line with the "t"s of "to" and "tea." She has been reading. "I'm so deeply immersed in *The Old Wives' Tale* that I can hardly tear myself away, also *Le Consultat et l'Empire* is becoming rather sad and I know I am going to suffer fearfully over Napoleon's downfall, much as you may rejoice in it." Then the roster of tea guests, a habit my mother stuck to all her life, and the electrifying words about my brother, "I don't care to have him playing too much with girls." And about me: "Her latest trick is to throw herself on the floor joyously when she comes into the room to speak to any ladies." (I was two years old.) I read these letters and am struck by a sense of our mutual crime, my mother's and mine, of not having reached out to each other more diligently, more patiently. But how? For there before me is her handwriting: so set, so regular, like chicken wire. The wit, the sweetness, the cleverness come through, but if you can reach out to touch it with open hands, you strike the wire and are hurt. "Quite the best and most considerate children in the world." "Is it true? Is that really how it seemed to you?" I want to ask her. If it was true, perhaps I managed to hide my devils from her better than I thought. Perhaps she only remembered the moments when we were loving with her and forgot the other moments; forgot her own black states as well. Many people's memories allow them to do this convenient erasing job. I sometimes wish my own did, that it did not tend to filter out the good times I had with my mother, leaving the things of which I am ashamed.

Chapter Three

The taboo on any discussion of love by Lesbians has been quite recently lifted by a general breaking out of the silence imposed on us, and at last I feel free to speak about the place of love in my own life. To begin with, I should say that love has always taken a secondary position in my life, secondary, that is, to my work as an artist, and that this disqualifies me as a great lover or one who can talk confidently about love. As I look back, I see myself constantly seeking an orderly life with a friend, rather than with a lover; a life with an artist who would have a working schedule and tastes much like my own. I sometimes wonder if I was looking for a twin, if I am, in other words, a true narcissist, though I already had a twin. Could it be that my own fraternal twin (who chose a path the opposite of mine) and I were incompatible even in the womb, that I spent the rest of my life looking for an identical twin? If so, I never found her. My falling in love had nothing to do with the ideal state I aspired to, and the differences between me and my lovers became more and more pronounced as time went on. At the beginning, I would be carried away by a genuine and selfless passion which I believed would be eternal. I made imprudent use of the word "forever," and was surprised by my frequently abrupt transformation from a tender and adorable friend to an irritable person, who would refuse to make love, who would insist on getting up early in the morning, or sleeping the entire night (on resuming my normal life, in short). What had happened? Why? I couldn't explain. I just felt in my whole being that it was over, that I was no longer in love. My love and I had fallen into familiar roles and we would play them out to the end. The more she loved and needed me, the more cranky and sullen I became — and this acted on her in a poisonous way. Barbara Deming and I, superficially so alike, so fitted to be true lovers, became temporary enemies through this process of need and refusal. For I would refuse not only love, finally, but also the whole idea of the couple, with its exigencies and its absence of freedom. In talking about love, I want to explore these fatal changes: from something so joyfully given and received, to something bloated with guilt and resentment, with self-justification and judgement of the other. The cycle was sometimes interrupted; and sometimes, my love would get tired of *me* and I would suffer the torments that I visited on others, but I cannot think of any love of mine that did not have its dark and suffering side, its turning inside-out which would last for longer or shorter periods, and then, go through another mutation into friendship of the most harmonious kind. Could we have been such loving friends without the initiation and the pain, the possessiveness and the shedding of possessiveness? I doubt it. The tender vestiges of sensuality lie at the bottom of our friendships and remain at a level I can absorb, and we no longer ask more of each other than we can give.

I said at the beginning of this book that I was introduced to sex at an age when most adults have years of sexual experiments behind them. At twenty-four, I had no idea that there were parts of my body that could be "aroused," either by myself or by someone else. I had never touched or explored my body or, by accident, discovered the pleasure of masturbation. I literally had to be taught where, how and what feeling I was supposed to have: I remember now the relative feebleness of my first sexual response and how it was a long time before this mysterious little flicker of response turned into a genuine orgasm. But I was already capable of falling into that joyful swooning state that is synonymous with falling in love, of suffering from nervous indigestion at the thought of the loved one; I knew well the tremor that travels the length of one's body with no exact location, and the drunken waves on which one is gently rocked. All this had been happening to me since I went to boarding school at fifteen. Here "crushes" were permitted, even smiled upon, as long as they didn't "go too far." At that time, I had no clear idea of what "going too far" meant. Most of the girls at my school were in love with boys, and they huddled around portable phonographs that played "Night and Day" and "Paper Moon," talking about their boyfriends and their love lives. Even though I was excluded from these huddles, for I couldn't even pretend to have a boyfriend, I gathered that they stopped short of "going the limit." The meaning of this awful phrase I could only vaguely imagine, but it was plain that the girls on top of the hierarchy of love had *almost* gone the limit. Today, when going the limit is as natural as brushing your teeth in the morning, this must be surprising. Forty-five years ago, it was still thought of as a frontier, and once you had crossed it, you could no longer be thought of as a "nice" girl.

But in the matter of crushes, the limit was so unthinkable that I never heard it discussed. It is strange that precise memories relating to something that I knew nothing about come back to me at all, and come back with the suggestion that, even then, I had an inkling that there was a forbidden element in a crush: the danger that it could get out of hand. I see our house-mistress, Miss McNeil, at the end of a long table, surrounded by laughing girls; we are joking about crushes, about who has a crush on whom. Suddenly, Miss McNeil strikes her fist on the table and cries, "You will *not* talk about crushes!" Since we detest poor Miss McNeil, one of many authentic spinsters at the school, we imitate her afterwards with explosive giggles, and crushes continue to be a subject of burning interest. The girls who had almost "gone the limit" and who were often people of importance, the captains of teams or the heads of self-government, were the chief objects of worship. I see before me now the captain of my basketball team, with her black hair and severe face, like Sir Lancelot, dressed in a green tunic and green stockings, and the retinue of younger girls who loved her from afar. I, too,

75

loved her, but my serious "crush" was a jolly, plump girl who had a habit of squinching up her grey eyes and smiling at me in a way that made me weak with joy. Not long after she left school, she got married and I was one of her bridesmaids. I saw her years afterwards, the mother of many handsome boys, as kind and smiling as ever. The percentage of non-marrying girls in that school was amazingly low; I and a girl, who, in our callous way, we called a "drip," were the only ones in my class who did not get married.

Of the memories faintly tinged with "evil," I have two. In one memory, we are "walking the lane" in twos and threes. The lane was a straight, tree-bordered avenue that stretched from the big wooden school building to the gate at the far reaches of the property. Beyond the gate was a street which had a streetcar line; this was the world and it was as remote from us as Mars. We walked the lane, arm-in-arm, every single day, rain or shine, down to the stone pillars of the gate and back to the grassy ellipse in front of the schoolhouse. I remember during one of these walks, I heard a girl describe a crush she had and her physical feelings were so precise that those of us who were listening knew that she had "gone too far." My other memory is of being in the math teacher's room. Miss H. was small, with an intelligent hawkish face; she wore tweed suits and walked with a long stride, her hands in her pockets. Though we were merciless about the other spinster teachers, we loved and respected Miss H. She was sitting on her bed leaning against the wall, and, at the foot of the bed, a girl named Alice was stretched out like a languorous cat. Alice was as beautiful as a Botticelli angel, with golden hair falling on her shoulders, finely chiselled features, transparent pale skin and clear blue eyes, and when I looked at them, something in Alice's attitude and the way that she looked at Miss H. — and the tenderness that I saw in Miss H.'s look — told me that they loved each other. Alice married, of course, and Miss H. — what ever happened to her? What happened to all the "sort of's" — or the real or severely repressed Lesbians — for in those days, there wasn't one married teacher in the school? Of their lives, I knew nothing; and I felt no curiosity, since it took me a long time to learn to care about the nature of people's lives.

But at least I looked at people hard enough to remember the pent-up suffering in their faces. In those days, it was a curse to be single, and many of these women—plain, badly-dressed, having never been loved by a man, having perhaps repressed their love for other women, having thought of it as a deadly sin—were sombre and lonely and accursed.

Presiding over us all was a woman who was too much a goddess to be called a spinster—Miss Louisa Fowler, whom I feared as goddesses should be feared. Morning and evening as we sat in study hall, she would call the long roll of our names and we would confess our lapses from the rules. "I sat on my bed, Miss Fowler." "I communicated, Miss Fowler." It was forbidden during study hours to acknowledge the presence of another girl by a smile, much less to speak to her. In the corridors between classes, we filed, expressionless and silent as nuns. But this didn't prevent certain girls who sat in the front rows of study hall from turning around and looking with soulful eyes at their crushes. It was the duty of the self-government board to report these lapses to Miss Fowler, if the girl herself failed to report them. I think now about Miss Fowler's power to strike terror into timid souls like mine, to convince eighty-five girls that there was some sense in the preposterous rules that smothered us. I think of the way we worshipped her—our stately, severe goddess, with her frosty blue eyes and creamy Virginia accent. She looked with a tolerant eye on crushes and seemed particularly radiant at the big costume dances where we all danced together. It was one of the peculiarities of the time that you could foster love between girls and yet be horrified if it became serious.

What to make of that oddest of school rules—that if you got a letter from a boy, not only did you have to report it to Miss Fowler, but also your answer had to be mailed out by her? This rite was solemnly adhered to, I now think, because girls who got several letters a week and who reported them developed a particularly close relationship with Miss Fowler and could see her much more often than those of us whose only reason for going to her office was to be reprimanded. I would see girls come out of her office and hear her mellow laugh through the open door. I would be filled with envy. Miss Fowler loved these "normal" girls and was thrilled, later, when they got married, as they invariably did. I should add that as a scholar, she liked intelligence and that I rose in her estimation when I did well in college. What she disliked in me (for I was never one of her favourites when I was in school) must have been the sneakiness of the slave, my paralyzed shyness with her, and my childishness. For my age, I was exceptionally unaware, both physically and mentally, and I look back on that dormant person with surprise—surprise that some part of me functioned at all and was able to write papers on Shelley and Shakespeare and win various awards. But my mind did not wake to a sense of its own working until I was in college; and my body, later still. As a schoolgirl, I was silly and superficial, full of imprecise emotions and undigested knowledge which fooled people into thinking that I was deeper and brighter than I was. I remember putting on a show of sorrow when Mater died and wearing an expression which became known as my "whipped dog look." It consisted of gazing pensively and mournfully into space. Miss Fowler must have seen through me, deep into my immature heart; I felt watched by her and unloved by her, and my worship was tinged with resentment that was sometimes close to hate. I felt unappreciated, even if I felt that there was not much to appreciate.

My school must have been the last stronghold of innocence in the United States. Miss Fowler's mission was to turn out pure, honourable and responsible girls; she was King Arthur and we were the knights of her Round Table (before they were beset by their various troubles). We were steeped in Christianity and spent most of Sunday going to church, singing hymns and saying prayers. The members of the self-government board were imbued with Miss Fowler's sense of mission, and the ambition of every girl was, at month's end, to get a Golden Report, which meant not only excellent marks, but also not breaking a single one of the innumerable and unnecessary rules. I never got a Golden Report. If the conduct of any girl threatened this beautiful moral order, she was expelled or called up before the self-government board. In my time, several girls who were a class ahead of me, who had been caught smoking, were punished by not being allowed to graduate with the others. I believe that

Miss Fowler was an example of a truly virtuous woman, one of the last of the great head-mistresses who loved her work and her girls, in whom even a practised eye could perceive no signs of frustration or repression or guilt. With her, you felt that her sternness was part of her magnanimity and that her definition of good and evil had been handed down from heaven. Fortunately, I was never tempted to rebel, except in insignificant ways, and my crushes stayed within the limits she considered a normal part of growing up. It got back to her, however, that a certain girl had described the feeling of being in love with another girl and this girl was asked to leave. Seven years after I graduated, in the training school for the WAVES in Northhampton, Massachusetts, I became aware of what was so conspicuously missing at my school, and I was able to recognize the excitement of smothered fires and looks exchanged, appraising and desiring. The students at my boarding school had almost all been "normal" girls who would eventually marry; the WAVE trainees were single women, mostly ex-school teachers, "sort of," or "almost," or "fully-fledged" Lesbians (fifty percent in these categories, I would say, to make a modest estimate). I was still on the fringes, a "sort of," unknown to myself, yet I was somehow wary. I guarded the secret of my first love within me, the first step in my sexual awakening which had taken place so late.

My first love was the innocent kind of which Miss Fowler might have approved, if, instead of being women in our twenties, we had still been schoolgirls. But she would quickly have recognized the moment at which we crossed the forbidden frontier and were "in love with each other." I was teaching English at college and my friend was doing graduate work. Our love is the story of all first loves, except that it was never, as they say, consummated. The odd thing about it was that our happiness, instead of provoking dour looks of disapproval, seemed, with one exception, to be contagious, and our friends and relations were infected by it and became happy themselves. This, of course, added to our feeling of innocence. The one exception to the general acceptance of my first love was an unmarried middle-aged cousin, in whose house I lived, a professor who was loved by everybody, but was so shy that she scarcely dared raise her eyes to look at her students. I began to notice her agitation when my friend telephoned, as she did almost every day. I remember being sick and lying in my upstairs room. Laura came up to see me, sat by the bed and took my hand, and this, the first overt expression of our love, made me tremble with joy. When, I wonder, were the iron rules that now prevent women from even holding hands without disapproval, clamped on us? Or men, for that matter? In the nineteenth century, women held hands, embraced each other passionately, and even slept in the same bed, and this was accepted without suspicion (but woe unto you if you "go too far," as does a fellow teacher of Lucy Stone's in Charlotte Brontë's *The Professor.* In this, to me, unmistakable passage, Charlotte shows her loathing for Lesbian attachments, she who has written with such tenderness in *Jane Eyre* of the love between Jane and Helen, who dies in Jane's arms; and in *Shirley,* of the love between Shirley and Caroline.) We know too much now about the forms of love-making and it is assumed that a great friendship between two women includes love-making. Somehow my cousin had learned the dark secret that women really *do* fall in love with each other. I would like to know how she learned it; had she been taught by experience? The difference between Miss Fowler and her cheerful acceptance of crushes and my cousin's dark forebodings lay in the difference in age of their students. My cousin knew that when two grown women show signs of loving each other, it is "dangerous and unnatural." She knew that my friend's visit upstairs lasted too long and she mounted the stairs and appeared in the doorway. Frightened, I withdrew my hand from Laura's. I knew that while I might enjoy holding her hand without having feelings of guilt when we were alone, the appearance of anyone at all would make my heart beat with terror. From that day on, I would be overcome by alarm and disgust with myself if I thought that I had been discovered and exposed. My cousin and I were too shy to talk to each other; she continued to be agitated and I continued to be swept along on the glad tide of love. I was so naïve then that I made no attempt to conceal my happiness. I liked to look at Laura across the distance of a room that was full of people until she felt my eyes on her and met my gaze. Her eyes were dark and warm and her melodious voice spilled out warmth, like a warm spring. We played the banal old game of catching each other's eyes and holding them, while my soul fainted with joy and my body quivered. Yes, this kind of love without sex used to exist and would build like an airy pleasure dome for weeks and months, without the intensity and obligation of sex; there were no let-downs, only a sustained state of bliss.

It is a kind of love that can still exist between women, but is almost impossible between a man and a woman. Laura and I continued to hold hands and hug each other until the summer holidays began. Then, we spent a night at a girls' school, the headmistress of which was a friend of Laura's. In retrospect, I see what wasn't clear to me then; the headmistress, unlike Miss Fowler, accepted the idea of love between women, and with kindly complicity, she put Laura and me together in a room with a big double bed. I lay there rigidly, sick with nervous tension, not touching Laura. After a while, she reached toward me and took me in her arms and I remember my ambiguous feelings even now — of fear and relief. It was the beginning of something new, on the borderline of wrong-doing; we both felt so without saying anything. Yet everything about that first night was what is called innocent: our embraces, our chaste kisses, my pyjamas and Laura's nightgown. As I look back, I find it amazing that we were able to make up rules as we went along, that it was such a long time before we kissed, that the little bit of exploration we eventually tried frightened us so much that we stopped. We could spent entire nights without sleep, simply kissing and embracing each other, and the next day, we would stagger about in a state of delicious exhaustion. Far from feeling frustrated (perhaps I was without knowing it), I was in a state of radiant happiness, such as I've never known since. This happiness lasted till the war separated us; I joined the Navy and Laura joined the Army. I was initiated into sex by a fellow WAVE; and Laura fell in love with an officer and married him. During the last night that we ever spent together in the canopied double bed in my mother's house, I told her about the WAVE and tried to show her what I had learned. It was something I will always regret, this shattering of something between us that was childishly pure. She reacted violently and did not forgive me for a long time— perhaps she never has—though we see each other sometimes and embrace with the same old warmth. But we never talk about our old love for each other.

Chapter Four

Lately, I have had the feeling that my mind has slowed down, that it is like a box of wet matches or is full of wet sawdust, that it cannot take fire, smothers sparks, that it is slow and heavy. In conversations, my thoughts have scarcely been able to emerge as words, and sometimes, I forget the beginning of a sentence before I get to the end. Because of this, I've felt sorrowful, mourning the time when my thoughts danced and my responses were as quick as light, mourning my loss of feeling. Along with this sombre indifference, I feel plaintive self-pity or the destructive wish to pick people to pieces, to scatter the pieces like chaff, to be rid once and for all of everything that troubles and diminishes my ego. And then comes guilt, that useful corrective, which has always been an essential ingredient in my character. It starts working and it says, "You're being mean-spirited and ungenerous," and all the rest, but the bile and spleen remain and have to work themselves out in some other way. I am not in a state of grace. I am unworthy of even receiving what Martin Buber called the "tiny grace of every day."

But, trudging up the hill this day in my spleen-state to get the mail, I saw two bluebirds and was puzzled, seeing first their white and rusty breasts, the meditative set of their heads and their bills like black thorns. Then, as one of them fluttered off, I saw his blue back, the unmistakably vivid blue of a bluebird. I had looked at just the right moment, a quite arbitrary moment, yet this happens to me surprisingly often, this vision of birds suddenly there, as in a dream. And I am back in Wellfleet again, in the chilly springtime, looking out the kitchen window at eight or ten bluebirds, some young and grey-blue, restlessly moving down to the ground, from tree to tree, and singing their sweet uncertain little song. Birds, that was one of the things we had in common, Barbara and I, for I began thinking of Barbara Deming and our life together.... Barbara, with her great patience. She kept so still one day in the woods that a baby woodpecker landed on her head. That reverence of hers on walks, touching her finger to her lips, barely breathing, whispering "shh"—a reverence that sometimes made me want to trample on the dead leaves and shout, at least after my first delight had worn off. It is fascinating to think about the little things that get between two people and finally crack them apart, despite the things that bind them together. We loved the same books, music, paintings; the same rather austere life. We were both artists (painter and writer); we even looked alike, tall and flat-chested, like awkward boys. Sometimes people mistook one of us for the other; I once argued with a stranger who angrily insisted that he had seen me on TV (this was after Barbara had become famous for her radical political action). But we soon ceased to run along parallel lines, for each of us had her own evolutionary route to follow. Barbara moved outward, toward engagement and the forging of her own courage, while I, though I was carried along for a time by her example, stuck doggedly to my private and tiny graces.

I had fallen in love with a story that Barbara had published in *The New Yorker*. This story, so delicately written—about an adventure a young woman has in Italy, about the presumption on the part of an Italian who wants to make love with her and her resistance to him, humourous and firm, a resistance that has an underlying desperate will to it—was so close to my own experience that I immediately felt as if the writer were an old friend. (Fifteen years later, I again fell in love with a book, literally struck with the lightning of it, and again, met the writer and loved her, which shows, at least, that art is as real to me as life.) It turned out that Barbara was the life-long friend of my friends, the Poors, and that, one day, when I was visiting them, she came over. She was almost six feet tall, with long arms, a swinging gait and a deep voice, like a man's. Her gestures seemed self-conscious and slightly theatrical. She had a way of suddenly straightening up, clicking her heels together and saluting. I discovered later that she was not at all self-conscious and this has enabled her to do things which would have been impossible for me to do — I, who have an exaggerated sense of how other people see me. Barbara does not care what people think of her appearance, how she dresses, or the gestures she makes. If she likes a coat, she will wear it until it falls to pieces; she has a saint's indifference to fashion, the exigence of which torments me. I see her now in my mind's eye — in a shapeless loden coat and baggy pants, her head swathed in one of those hoods that covers your nose and chin. I see her as a hieratical figure, like a sage in a Chinese painting. When I first met her at the Poors, I saw her serious face with her kind, mournful eyes, framed by straight dark hair and bangs, and her long hands in continual motion, shaping her thoughts. There were immediate arguments between her and the Poors, and her deep voice sounded like a big ship in the night, steady and relentless. Even then, I was conscious of her dogged will and her absolute conviction of being right; of an earnest moral weight. But also, I was aware of a searching and sensitive attention that immediately included me in her life.

How quickly it all happened! How quickly one falls in love and decides — I want to spend my life with this person whom I scarcely know! Barbara and I spent our first night together in her aunt's house quite soon after we met; she, alarmed by my ardour (she confessed later); I, troubled by her strangeness. She talked to me at great length about her loves; about the women she had loved and still loved and would always love. It is characteristic of her never really to fall out of love. This is another difference between us. Loving, needing love, her body's need for love, helpless as a baby with longing — all these weighed me down. Little by little, through longing and refusal, we changed each other and my ironically too great ardour diminished and resisted and became sulky after its first joyous fling. Ours was the story of two bodies out of tune with each other, each making life difficult for the other. And our earnest conversations, or rather, Barbara's discourses on giving and taking (I was supposed to do a little more giving) did little to bring us back together, for the power of reason will not resolve the mysteries of body chemistry, despite what Barbara thought.

How can I presume to think that I know Barbara, even now that our troubles are over and we are dear friends again? How can we know anyone, except in relation to ourselves? According to this relation, we judge and analyze, going so far as to think we know more about another person than the other person knows about herself. With this presumption of knowing Barbara, I would say that she has often been blinded by her will and that this will has two aspects: one aspect, identical to faith, is deeply religious; the other is closer to wishful thinking—or to the unconscious exercise of power. In a remarkable essay about *Hamlet*, Barbara explored the aspect of will as wishful thinking; it is the action of the play, she says, driving each character to wish things to be other than they are. The question is: when is will an act of faith and when is it an act of aggression? By her faith, Barbara is able to make people change in good ways. Something in her, says Jane Gapen, who lives with her now, "tugs at one's devil / Unmistakably, one's devil wants to fly out / and throw itself at her feet." And these people, whose devils fly out and humble themselves before her, say that she is a saint. Living with her for fifteen years, I saw both faith and will; and her earnest rationalizations of will. My devils, far from throwing themselves at her feet, snarled and snapped and resentfully lay in wait. Looking back, I see Barbara as life-directed by conscience (but not necessarily my conscience), whereas what finally broke us apart was the coming of Marie-Claire, who *is* life, pure and simple. We argued interminably about conscience—it being, for Barbara, something inherent, like a soul, that could be discovered in oneself and cultivated; and for me, something akin to the superego, planted in us by family and society, nourished by guilt. These arguments and those we had about religion stimulated my devils. I have already said that discussions about the existence of God often made me angry (this anger is quite common, I was glad to see when I read Isherwood's *Christopher and His Friends*), but there was something particularly infuriating about Barbara's patient portrayal of God the Father, insisting that I was not to imagine Him as a person with a big white beard, but as pure spirit. To me, pure spirit was still masquerading under the name of God and Barbara and everyone else who believed in Him had access to a secret that was denied me for some reason, and thus, they felt superior. Barbara denied that she felt superior, but the maddening calm that emanated from her when she talked about Him (always Him — a fact that was later to strike her with the full force of its patriarchal sexism) was in itself a sign of superiority over my unseemly rage. Why were there so many people who didn't have consciences and who didn't believe in God, I wanted to know? Familiar questions, to which true believers have ready answers. In my case, she said, I believed in God without knowing it; otherwise, why my passion for nature? This would provoke my angry reply that many painters have had a passion for nature, Henry Poor among them, without believing in God, but there was no way of convincing Barbara that it was possible *not* to believe in God.

Now, years later, no longer under pressure, I can talk more calmly about religion and can state my beliefs. I believe in the miracle of creation, however it came about, in the oneness of time, and in destiny, as opposed to chance, somehow allowing for a tiny exercise of free will (but I will never know if this is really so). I sit here peacefully writing and thinking while people are being blown up, burnt, decapitated, drowned, raped, tortured, starved — and with this knowledge, I do nothing but tend my little garden. . . . And Barbara, where is she? She, whose conscience still pursues me, who still has the power to make me feel guilty. She is on the Florida key she has chosen with her refined unconcern for everything, except for what is essential to the work of herself. It is hot there and dampness seeps up, through the porous coral soil and flowers, to become mould on her precious books. She has chosen, with her friend, Jane, a painter and poet with her own finely-honed conscience, to lead the life of a recluse. Her joys consist of small revelations: a mango on the newly-planted tree, a vision of sea horses or a baby octopus in the place where she and Jane swim, or a frigate-bird hovering far away over the gulf. The flat landscape, with its straight roads and canals, bordered by the naked roots of mangroves and their impenetrable growth above, seems to symbolize the serious and inexorable nature of her quest. Intensely, she and Jane meditate on the scandals of life—and they act: to suppress a film in which one sees a live woman tortured and mutilated; to defend an Indian woman who has killed a man who has molested her daughter and was attempting to rape her; to convince men that they, too, can share the joys of motherhood by suckling their babies. Somehow, somewhere, she has been delighted to find that certain men can secrete milk, and to her, this could be a solution to the problem of their jealousy. This concern of hers rouses my indignation that always lies just below the surface. "They want everything," I cry, "even to have babies! As if they haven't enough already! Let them be jealous!" But Barbara thinks that this particular form of jealousy (the mirror-image of penis envy?) is at the bottom of the clash between the sexes. She thinks that fathers should mother and mothers should father, in short, that androgynous beings will save the human race. And, as usual, a shadow like that of the "monstrous crow" in *Alice* falls on me, and with it, comes gloom and the old sense of difference between Barbara and me. I want to ask her what she is going to do about the nine-tenths of the world where macho ideas still reign supreme, about the emergence of ever-stronger strains of women who like being women, like insects who thrive on insecticides? But like all real revolutionaries, Barbara is not disheartened by the weight of evidence. She has her own evidence burning in her, her personal victories and the changes she has wrought in flinty hearts. She acts on the world and, at the same time, is writing a beautiful novel about her love for another woman. I begin to accuse myself for the nth time of another form of envy: envy of Barbara's faith that keeps her doing good and believing in herself. I would like to be able to think that the artist in her is the more important being, that her novel is more important than her radical ideas. But I have witnessed the long training that prepared Barbara for the double role of artist and radical activist, each necessary to the other. These two sides of her nature come together in the harmony of herself—gentle, stubborn, profoundly searching beyond the barriers of reason. She has in her both artist and saint, and I, forever uneasy with the idea of sainthood, resist and humbly salute her! How hard it is not to judge ourselves by comparison with others and not to concoct reasons for resentment from these comparisons!

Barbara has always had the power to provoke in me the old anxiety that identified me with Martha in the New Testament when I wanted, like Mary, to be praised by Jesus. How did it happen that the two great friends of my life were both Mary's in the purity of their concentration on the "one thing"? Martha is "troubled about many things," said Jesus, "but one thing is needful and Mary hath chosen that good part." I remember a sermon we heard at boarding school on the theme of Mary's choice. "Mary's *choice*," intoned the minister, drawing out the sacred name of Mary and rolling the "r," then seeming to savour the word "choice," as though it were a succulent piece of roast meat. It was clear that this minister had no sympathy for Martha, who had prepared the dinner and was probably washing the dishes while Mary sat at Jesus' feet. I sympathized with Martha, reflecting that Jesus was not unlike other men who expected women both to sit at their feet and to tidy up; but I envied Mary. When I lived with Barbara, my Martha-anxiety would build and build, until the inevitable explosion. Sometimes at dinnertime, while I busied myself with many things, Barbara would sit in front of the fire in the blue velvet-covered chair with her long arms hanging over the sides of the chair and her legs, in their green slacks, bent at a firm right angle, lost in thought. The fact that this attitude reminded me so strongly of her father, that it seemed to be saying, "I'm waiting patiently for my dinner," made me still more furious, for the role of Martha that was imposed on me was reinforced by the role of wife. When my explosion came, it seemed to Barbara like gratuitous aggression and she would brood for so long about the injustice of it that I would begin to feel guilty. She hated to be taken by surprise: to find such a distance between the way she felt and the way her perfectly innocent behaviour was construed. She would earnestly set about cleaning the house or cooking, but after a week or so, she settled back into her Mary-state. But her avoidance of housework, which she did very efficiently, was nothing to Marie-Claire's. Perhaps Mary in the Bible also maddened her sister by doing everything wrong, until Martha finally said, "You listen to Jesus, I'll get the dinner ready," and this state of affairs continued until Jesus got the impression that Martha *preferred* to be busy.

There are people in the New Testament who seem to have been invented to make people with uneasy consciences feel guilty. My father was haunted by the story of the rich young man who gave generously to the poor, but refused to give up everything, for it was his own story. We would all like to be able to pass through the eye of a needle (this ability seemed very remarkable to me when I was a child) by remaining the way we are. My conscience, too, has always been nagged by the rich young man, by Peter and Thomas, and finally, by Mary, whose choice Jesus preferred. The only parable that cheered me up was the one about the man who buried his one talent, for that, at least, I hadn't done. Both Barbara and Marie-Claire, without meaning to, remind me that I am less entire than they are, that I can deny like Peter, doubt like Thomas, disperse myself in the quotidian like Martha, and balk at the eye of the needle like the rich young man. Both of them have, in a sense, already gone through the eye, have lost themselves and saved themselves, while I seem, in the tradition of my family, to protect myself, consider the pros and cons, to be driven by the Martha in me, while longing for the beautiful entirety of Mary.

But suddenly (a happy thought), I see Martha and Mary as one. My Martha-self has busied herself for the two Marys in my life, and for *me*, harbouring within myself the twin poles of spirit and domesticity. Is it possible that the Martha-me, with all her fusspot order and irritability, has been a kind of wife to the Mary-me, has tended the little flame of spirit, such as it is, taken out the ashes and blown life into the somnolent embers? I think of a tiny painting by Rembrandt in the Louvre, of a philosopher seated in shadow at his open window, through which one sees the golden light of late afternoon. In the right hand corner of the room, there is a hearth with a little flame burning and an old woman poking at the flame with tongs. In the centre of the philosopher's study is a stone spiral staircase, winding into darkness, forming a black vortex, like the centre of a snail shell. I was dumbfounded by the beauty of this picture, with its compression of symbols and their dense meaning. The hunched old housekeeper who keeps the little fire burning is like an aged Martha and reminds us that a certain simplicity and earthiness are necessary to nourish thought. The centre of the spiral staircase contains the lightless mystery of the philosopher's voyage into thought, while he sits motionless, himself a centre, a mind which seems to have dreamed the subject-matter of the painting. The painting is about the singleness and stillness of real attention; the staircase is like the vortex of an ear which can hear silence, just as the story of Mary's choice is that of a person who knows how to listen. I have always been plagued by the sense of the shortness of my attention-span and my ability to be distracted and I have invented exercises for this: to let words, music and paintings enter my senses, without being trammelled by a single irrelevant thought — but, invariably, thoughts intrude, buzzing away like winter flies on a sunny window. With all my attempts at rationalization, I cannot love the Martha-me, who actually cares about what the house looks like almost as much as she cares about listening to the Word. The strength of the Marys of this world lies in their real indifference to messiness and dust, to what they eat and wear, in short, to all the concerns of Martha. My Mary-me chooses one hundred percent Marys as friends and the Martha-me is impatient and nagging, feeling the familiar envy and impatience with *myself*. To be entire! To pass in one's concentrated entirety through the eye of the needle!

I have been reading over my letters to Barbara from 1953 on, those hundreds of letters kept by her, brimming with my life, which the present me remembers so inadequately or inaccurately. I read them to re-discover the person who was in love with Barbara, who longed for her when we were separated, who wrote daily letters and consumed hers with that voracious impatience

91

that only lovers know. My truest thoughts, feelings, vision of people and of nature are in those letters, so why am I awash now in wave upon wave of guilt and a sense of my cowardice; this, along with the secret pleasure I take in reading my own letters, as if they had been written by someone else? At the bottom of it, I think, is the pain of knowing that we cannot know one another, no matter how close we think we are; that words are useless, that they compound misunderstanding; that when we have hurt each other, words strike like sabres or fall like heavy stones; that our most private and delicate feelings cannot be conveyed or guessed at. Reading some of Barbara's letters to me at the end of our life together, I ache to think of the turmoil in her, her anguish at discovering the image that Marie-Claire and I had of her, so far from her image of herself. Who knows, perhaps these self-images are the true ones and the ones that people form of us, based on the inadequate evidence of their senses, are less true? In the course of my fifteen years with Barbara, my image of her seemed to clash repeatedly with her self-image. She, with all her delicate perceptions and conscience, will never know how much weight her passion, her longing or her sense of moral rightness put on others. A blind spot? No, a part of her so vulnerable that I never dared to touch it, the literally sacred self-image, which, when it comes tumbling down around our ears, throws us into panic and despair. "But I should have been able to sense it, too, and that I didn't is a horror to me and makes me doubt myself in a new way I never have before," says Barbara, at the end, when I gathered strength to speak honestly (but to speak honestly is to inflict pain). And which of us knows, notices, second by second, our effect on others, feels the wrongs we have done, the weight of carelessness, too much vehemence or not enough love?

It sometimes seems to me, reading these hundreds of letters, that I have lived more fully in letters than in life; that the self that writes is more capable of loving than the self that lives in propinquity with someone, feels threatened and defends her precious territory, growling like a dog. In our letters, Barbara and I exchanged our lives, our souls and senses; the joy, pain and comedy of every day that we were separated, as we were unable to do when we were together. There is a gossamer lightness in the letters we wrote during our first separation, when I went off to study at the art school run by our friends, Henry and Anne Poor. I was older than any of the other students and I suffered because of this. I suffered from being a student; from painting badly; from being in a new kind of relation to my friends, Henry and Anne, now my teachers, with their awe-inspiring authority. In my state of depression, I wrote Barbara, "How thankful I'll be to get away from everybody here—the students, I mean. So nice, but each of us whacks against the other, a maddening whacking of individual wills and visions. I suppose that's the point of being a student...." Later, at the same school, I go through the kind of change that is like a turning inside-out, that can be either a misery or a joy. "As for people—how very queer it is now that the sickness of soul is gone. I love them; they love me. How easy they are to talk to! How gay and gentle they are! And in all of us the same thing has happened. We are captured by the innocence, the seriousness, as though HVP's spirit had entered into us.... Oh, I wish you'd write about it—how people are transformed!" As I think about Barbara, about the selves of our letters and about our physical selves in our daily lives, each "whacking" against the other; as I look for the differences that put a distance between us, I see something inherently unstable that sleeps in me, a capricious alter ego nourished by the petty circumstances of every day. "Ah! Ne puis-je savoir si j'aime ou si je hais," says Racine's Andromaque. Racine's characters are in a perpetual state of readiness to turn inside-out, but the mechanism is simple. They love when they are loved; they hate when they no longer feel loved. The women, at least. With me, the poles are not as far apart as love and hate; they are, rather, positive and negative. The positive pole is love. In this state, everything is easy: to pay a certain kind of loving attention, to look intensely at another person without the perfidious need to criticize, to listen, to smile, to live in a kind of psychic sunshine—it is all so easy that one cannot believe that the lurking alter ego isn't dead once and for all. Just as revolutions have their period of euphoria and loving fellowship, followed by bickering and ruthlessness and even civil war, so I have always had small scale revolutions in myself,

93

sometimes several in a single day—euphoria and backlash, one following the other so predictably that it should no longer surprise me. In the period of backlash, I no longer know what my true feelings are, even toward those I love. My heart is deader than a stone. But Barbara does not suffer from these oscillations and I am sure that once she has decided that she loves someone, there is always a substratum, a solid core of feeling, that she can depend on and recognize, that will take the shocks of daily "whackings." One might say that she is physically unable to turn "inside-out," that some fortunate mechanism in her prevents her from ever being spiteful, stops her from repeating gossip or believing the mean things that people say about each other, prevents her, if she likes a book, a painting, a person or a cause, from being influenced against it, him or her. This steadiness of love is a saint's virtue, for every saint that ever lived must have loved like Barbara (and not lurched like me), but it prevents her from seeing the changes in people or causes that she loves. Secure in her own love, she can be heedless of the warning signals.

"So many things seem filled with the intent / to be lost," says Elizabeth Bishop in "Poem." Losing, for Elizabeth Bishop, is a form of art, and, like every art, it can be practiced and perfected and thus accepted. Elizabeth Bishop believes in the permanence of loss, while I believe in a process something like transmigration: each loss is a death, with a soul that reappears in a new and different life. Every love seems to contain its "intent to be lost"—and to be, in some cases, re-discovered; and, in other cases, replaced. I sit here at the window, looking out, and I feel my identity with Lily Briscoe, the painter in *To the Lighthouse,* who is the artist in me and who knew, too, the loss—of the power of seeing—who suffered cycles of sight and blindness. I look out at the desolate beauty of winter, the white-dappled spruces, like a million cloaked magi, with clouds of snowsmoke rising among them, stirred up by the thumping and whistling wind. The snow is lying over the fields in great sheets and lumpy eiderdowns and blurring the rusty-iron leafless trees that border the fields. The sky is a warmish grey, the beautiful palpable grey that the painter Lemieux loves—a grey which I cannot arrive at in a painting, no matter how hard I try, in which there is light, like reflections in pewter, but no shadow. I look at the ragged fringes of icicles on an eave I can see from the window and pray that my vision of winter and its beauty will quench my fear of it—my insistent identification of the Canadian winter with death. In spite of my artist's elation, I feel my insides begin to churn with winter-anxiety, but I have discovered something important in this dialogue between the aspects of myself—a clue, perhaps, to my turning "inside-out." When I am in love, I am like Lily Briscoe, making of love a work of art, giving it that totality of attention one gives to painting a picture or writing a poem. There is a pre-love state when one wavers, slipping in and out of love in a most surprising way, with the illusion that one can control the situation, and then suddenly, it is too late; the situation is uncontrollable. One is now in a state of obsessive attention to the other person, wholly positive, as art is, a magical jump into the unreality of continuous joy; or, in the absence of the other person, the joyful despair of longing. All artists use love as the material of their art, but writers are able to burn it, so to speak, like fuel. Marie-Claire, I see now, transforms love into art and this acts as a reactor, replenishing her life. Perhaps Barbara, too, keeps love burning through this perpetual exchange between art and life. Or perhaps each of these friends burns physically more steadily than I do. For me, just as a painting can be called finished and a frame put on it, so every passion contains its end (its "intent to be lost") because my everyday self with its flagging attention and its irritability pushes away my artist-self. In painting, too, I suffer from the yawing movement (attention-indifference) and I can turn violently on a painting that I have liked or tear a drawing into little pieces. Something, nevertheless, has kept me struggling to be an artist: a persistence that gets me over the wastelands with the momentum generated by the times when love and attention burn. It is an alternating current, however, so different from the fierce solar energy of the masters who, in one day, could produce more than I can produce in a lifetime. Did they ever know times when the brain was inert, when the eyes refused to see and the spirit was petty? Was Keats talking about this when he cried (to Shakespeare), "Bright star, Would I were steadfast as thou art!" Does every artist sometimes

95

have the sense of flickering and failing?

Yet I think that the negative times are necessary, that, in some strange way, they give life to the times of attention. But how much of my life as an artist have I lost, muddling along until I am once more in a state of grace? I had this in common with Barbara, that we both needed a fixed schedule and time—oceans of time—out of which to distill a bit of good work. And we both still have the feeling that life is short; we get panicky if our schedules are disrupted and we are ferocious about interruptions. But Marie-Claire's energy burns so intensely that she does not have to worry about time. Barbara and I have become artists the hard way, through a long exercise of will and discipline, and Marie-Claire was born an artist, with all the prodigious energy of a bright star.

As artists, Barbara and I are alike and plod along at the same determined pace. She is probably as rebellious as I am, as we confront the idea of growing older and older, losing energy, losing brain cells, perhaps even forgetting what we are so anxious to accomplish. We are close to each other now, for the reasons that we are alike, this anxiety about time being one of them. But we are unlike in crucial ways that I try to analyze. "It is almost as fascinating as depressing, how difficult it is to learn from experience." Barbara wrote this to me when we were in the process of separating. "I think back now to the times when I went off to the South or to Saigon or North Vietnam and, feeling scared, tried to draw closer to you, each time in the process, driving you further off. I do finally recognize that the mere fact that I felt impelled to take these actions made me, as you put it the other day, strange to you, so how *could* you turn toward me?"

It happened so gradually, our separation. It began with the light tapping of the wedge that was going to drive us apart: her conversion to pacifism through the reading of Ghandi and the beginning of her involvement with the Committee for Non-Violent Action. My first mocking impulse changed to respect, to awe of these people, who lived their beliefs, who were willing to die for them. I became a pacifist myself and joined the NECNVA. I limped along after the brave ones, handed out leaflets against nuclear testing in the atmosphere and joined demonstrations. I bailed the NECNVA out of their financial difficulties, and, with Barbara, sat through endless meetings. In a letter to Anne Poor, written on September 30, 1963, I describe one of our weekends at the farm that I bought for the NECNVA. "Bobbie and I spent the weekend at the Voluntown Farm and got back close to midnight last night, absolutely done in after at least twenty hours of sitting on hard chairs TALKING. I never say a word and shrink into the smallest compass of my large ego; but Bobbie says a lot and says it better than anybody. I feel like Mary and Martha [I am forever obsessed by their story] and find it really restful to go into the kitchen and scrub one hundred potatoes.... Marj [Marj Swann, who with her husband, Bob, ran the NECNVA and were among the most heroic and committed of its members] begrudges every minute not spent doing the horrible tasks of leafletting, vigilling, walking, ringing doorbells, in short—non-violent direct action. How anybody can really *like these things,* I simply can't understand. They are always talking about how people become more 'committed' in the process of doing them, whereas I become so much less committed that I think I'd rather be blown up than ever have to hand out another leaflet or stand soberly in front of another war-making establishment. But perhaps it's just those silent hours on the hard chair that make me feel this way."

And so it was, that I was there in their midst for years, driven by my conscience to help, to give the appearance of belonging to them, and in reality, ever aware of the dead weight of myself and of the resistance that was finally to puzzle them so much when I shed my pacifist ties. I had begun almost immediately to doubt in the depths of my being what these wonderful people told me: that the more one acts, protests, the braver one becomes. I was becoming less brave; I had a mortal fear of going to jail. Barbara went to jail again and again; she spent a hellish month in a cage with eight friends in Albany, Georgia. (Out of this experience was to come her beautiful book, *Prison Notes.*) They were protesting a city ordinance forbidding black and white people from marching together down a main street. While she was in this cage, I wrote, "I'm there all day long, but I'm not there and can't be there—and there is the perpetual contradiction between

97

this quietness, between where *you* are, as you let your thoughts fly over Wellfleet, and the real horror that you're all living.... What to tell you? All the little quail kicking vigorously close to the herb bed, dislodging seed from the snowy ground. The mourning doves. And the soft russety feathers of their shoulders glowing pink in the marvellous light." I took refuge in birds, tried to believe they were as important as the life of sacrifice. But I was a victim of my relentless conscience. I became exceedingly moral. "I've just written Governor Sanders and President Johnson, reminding the latter that he has professed a belief in the right of dissent." I fired letters and telegrams off in every direction, this being a relatively easy form of moral protest. But my conscience kept torturing me. I added a postscript to the letter about writing President Johnson: "I'm so *ashamed of myself,* so ashamed of this shameful resistance and refusal and inexpressible pettiness of soul." I was ashamed of not having joined the march that landed Barbara and the others in jail, but not ashamed enough to risk my own neck. Meantime, Barbara was risking her neck more and more—and almost getting killed in the process. She became braver; she seemed to be refining every vestige of ego from her nature. She had temporarily given up her artist's life while I still clung desperately to mine. She went with a small pacifist group to Saigon to demonstrate against the war in Vietnam and they were set upon by students who had been bribed to make trouble, and bundled out of the country. She came back to Wellfleet a heroine; journalists came to the house, more or less hostile, and meetings were arranged so that people could listen to her story. Marie-Claire and I, proud to be friends of Barbara, nevertheless quivered with secret fears—that the house would be bombed or set on fire—but we wrote indignant letters to the local papers, protesting their treatment of Barbara's mission. Our letters were published along with an insulting answer to one of Marie-Claire's letters. As an alien, she was afraid of being thrown out of the country for associating with radicals and we were both convinced that the house and the telephone had been bugged. "What if they are?" said Barbara. "We haven't any secrets."

A large question worried at our souls in those days of moral testing. What are you willing to die for? A friend, expressing admiration for Barbara's radical actions, said to me, "I'd rather die than go to jail." Thinking it over, I decided that, just as I would rather be red than dead (this, too, a choice that kept being posed, almost as an accusation, in every political discussion), I would rather go to jail than die. But Barbara was willing to go to jail *and* die. Thus, at the time of the Cuban missile crisis in 1962, she went off to New York to protest with her pacifist comrades, while I elected to stay home. "You don't want us to be together?" meaning to *die together*, she asked. And she was hurt when I said no. In fact, I didn't want to die anywhere. I was angry with Khrushchev, Kennedy and Castro for holding us all hostage; angry with those friends I met in the village who seemed so cheerful and resigned. "If it happens, it happens," said Paul C. "I'm ready to go." It was almost as if they were glad to have the problem of their deaths settled in such a spectacularly simple way.

As usual, I was split between my two selves, worrying on the one hand about how much my choice mattered, was it cowardly, was this the moment at which you were supposed to know right from wrong; and thinking furiously about Kennedy and Khrushchev and the risks they were taking in the name of power, reducing the fate of the world to a game of "chicken" that was played by only two of the world's billion inhabitants. To me, my immediate world had never seemed so beautiful; I felt like a hen swelling to twice her normal size, spreading her wings to protect the chicks gathered under her. In the crystalline light of the end of the world, I smelled the sweet damp October air, saw a towhee scuffling diligently in the fallen leaves, sounding like a mouse in a wastepaper basket, heard his whistle, "Your tea!" and saw sun and shadow pass over the blue-grey reticulated trunks of the locust trees which I had tried to paint or draw so often. I went for a walk, as nostalgic as if it were already a memory, in Paradise Valley, where one could find abandoned cellars and the bones of buried blackfish, where in spring, clumps of double narcissus were just visible in the lush grass and lilacs still bloomed close to the ruins of old homesteads. That same day, I took a last look at the bay and the calm ocean, which seemed to say, "Don't worry, we'll be here after you're gone." At the ocean's shore, two sandpipers were running in their shadows over the glassy sand. My kingdom of heaven was here on earth, with the defenceless non-human lives that would be destroyed so wantonly by remote decisions to bomb, just as later, during the war in Vietnam, I suffered for the great forests and their defoliated trees and saw the forest floor littered with dead animals and the small, bright-feathered bodies of poisoned birds. These were the victims who could not fight back, beginning with the prodigal earth, turned to hardened clay, dust and potholes full of fetid water, to the marvellous leaves, turned brown, to the rice fields with their young jade-green plants obliterated, moving up through the chain of life, to the swollen bodies of dead pigs and water buffaloes, to chickens and cows, to dead babies and little children. All those who have not been asked, "Are you willing to die?" Who, even if they had voices to cry, "No, no, no!" would be victims of the impersonal game-players. Somewhere in me, along with a measure of cowardice, was a decision, not moral like Barbara's, for she knew what she believed in and would stick to it no matter what, that my life lay in this caring about the life around me. The meetings, telegrams, letters to the President, all those things were done in obedience to the superego (in this case, Barbara's conscience, which served to point the moral way to so many of us), while I tried to remain attentive to my own rhythms, to the messages that I received when I kept very still.

It was easier to feel this way when Barbara was off "fighting for us," as the friend who would rather die than go to jail put it. When Barbara was home, the issues became huge, occupying the whole house, it seemed, and squeezing me into a defenceless corner. It was useless to try and take a moderate position with Barbara, there was only one "correct" position to take—the radical one—and a radical position exacted radical action. Even if you were incapable of acting radically (by some alchemy of faith, she excused me from this), you had to believe with your whole heart that change was possible—and anyone who wasn't with her was against her. My dilemma was often to be neither for nor against —and this was impermissible. I have never known a more persuasive arguer than Barbara. Like an octopus, that much maligned egghead of the deep, with its great domed forehead and intelligent eyes, she would clasp you in her many arms and suck out the counter-arguments until you were bone-dry. She used to hang on to Edmund himself, who could demolish me with two testy words, "No, no," and force him into a rational discussion. She was not dismayed by people whose faces were distorted by hate, who shouted at us as we stood in picket lines, "Filthy puke!" etc., words that made me want to turn and run for home. Even people like this could be persuaded, as she persuaded her jailor, the big brutal police chief in Albany, Georgia, and made an almost-friend of him. Somehow, it was harder to persuade her brother, her sister-in-law, the ones nearest her. And it was hard to *keep* me persuaded, for I backslid again and again, as I fell under the influence of this person or that. About Cuba, for instance. Was what happened all the fault of the United States? Had Castro been a Communist all along? Or if Cuba became Communist, wasn't it the result of the self-fulfilling prophecy (this an ingenious piece of radical sleight-of-hand, for it had to be proved that the radical position was never wrong)? How much easier it had been during World War II, when it was perfectly clear that the Allies were right and the Nazis were wrong, when it never occurred to me, or to anyone I knew, to be a pacifist, when, even though I fulfilled my tasks in the Navy in an uninspired way, I suffered no pangs of conscience.

Contact with radical pacifism in the persons of Barbara and the NECNVA convinced me that all my comfortable beliefs were wrong, that the United States was governed by liars and hypocrites, or well-intentioned weaklings like Adlai Stevenson and Hubert Humphrey, who could be made to lick the boots of whatever power they served. And wasn't it true that all our "liberal" heroes compromised, that Stevenson and Humphrey had to defend Johnson's Vietnam policies against their real convictions? Didn't I read that when, at his ranch, Johnson ordered Humphrey (his choice for Vice-President) to kill a deer, Humphrey, "who abhorred hunting," shot a deer, and that Johnson, to test his loyalty, then ordered him to shoot another? The relentless exposure by Barbara of the infamy of everybody in government, the fall from grace, even in the peace movement, of wayward brethren who had compromised with the "liberal" enemy— all this made me less and less sure of my power to decide anything. I remember a moment, a kind of fatal conversion to Barbara's view of Cuba during the heady time just after the revolution and before the missile crisis, when she had actually succeeded in talking to Castro and urging him to take a less aggressive position toward the United States. She had been listened to courteously, but with sceptical firmness, for it was just after a ship had been blown up, presumably by the United States, in Havana harbour. It had been easy to believe in the Cuban Revolution at the beginning, easy to look on the doubters in the light of one's superior and more radical ideology, but more difficult as time went on. My conversion to Barbara's viewpoint made everything simple again; I needed only to believe those reports that were favourable to Castro and to disbelieve the others. The thousands of refugees who swarmed out of the country were all reactionaries who didn't have the guts or the altruism to stay; the American friends and relations who cast doubts on the Cuban paradise were middle-class liberals who clung to their own privileges and were afraid of losing them (like me, I thought guiltily). I argued passionately with these friends, just as, later, I was to argue that the war in Vietnam was a monstrous crime committed by the United States (about this, I have not changed my mind). If the seed of doubt was sown in me by a brother or an anti-Communist friend, I had only to read one of myriad pro-Castro articles to restore my uni-vision.

Now, many years later, I am silent and subdued. Didn't Castro throw all of Cuba's homosexuals in jail? Don't the refugees in Miami tell sombre stories about the life of dissenters, the conditions in Cuban jails? The homosexuals have been released, and it seems, re-educated, whatever that means. What exactly *is* their position now, I would like to know? But the material for indignation and despair is so copious: hundreds of great crimes and thousands of smaller ones, down to the slow seepage of poisonous chemicals through a billion bloodstreams. The chain of life is threatened and so is the atmosphere we breathe. There are Davids and St. Georges all over the world, standing up to Goliath, slaying the dragon, or pumping him full of tranquillizing darts. Barbara is one of them; she never loses faith. And I am back again cultivating my garden.

Chapter Five

I think now that there are two beings in me: one, who has been free to make choices and shape my life; the other, bumbling along, trying this and that. My free self, as my mother said in my dream, somehow has always had light to see her way. I see an image of armour, suits of armour, fitted on human beings, particularly on women, that inhibit their natural growth; I see helmeted heads, or those in boxes or behind bars, that appear so often in contemporary sculpture and painting, impersonal portraits of beings fixed forever in their rigid lives. Every human being, says the American Declaration of Independence, has the right to "life, liberty and the pursuit of happiness." The pursuit of happiness. Those audacious words ring with 18th Century optimism, but by the time my parents were born, happiness had become synonymous with duty and virtue, thus becoming a by-product, if you were lucky, of a properly lived life. I remember a conversation with my mother in which, when I said that it was important to be happy, she became grim and thoughtful and said, "There are other more important things." "What?" I asked. "There is such a thing as duty," she said. I seem to see her peering out from the depths of her helmet, having convinced herself that, since she was *not* happy, doing her duty created a satisfaction that was better than happiness. She thought that the pursuit of happiness was selfish, and she wanted indirectly to say to me that *I* was selfish. Looking back now, I regret the kind of selfishness in me that she was thinking about (my airy unawareness of other people), but not the kind that enabled me to wriggle out of all those suits of armour, just before the nuts and bolts had been tightened for all time. The suits of armour in my life (imposed by the sense of duty beloved by my mother and by the guilty conscience that drew me to saints) took the form of a stint, after college, working in the Works Progress Administration; my three years in the Navy; and my uneasy role as part-Maecenas, part-active member of the NECNVA—and served to teach me what I wasn't and what I couldn't do well. Many people conscientiously assume the roles that their choice of "duties" has imposed on them and cease to ask themselves, "Why am I doing this?" Roles, self-imposed or otherwise, are like love-states that we accept without question while we are in them. They make us what we are, even the bad roles, for every choice is both a kind of mask, to which we conform, and something inner, that alters us from the inside-out.

The history of women has been that of beings without the power of choice, whose very lives have been imposed, and whose liberty has been bounded by the confines of their imposed lives. We like to think that, in the Western World, we are free to choose our lives (this to me is what is meant by the "pursuit of happiness"), but don't these free choices lead women into the same old traps? Barbara wrote an essay, *We Cannot Live Without Our Lives*, pleading, with all her eloquence, for the right of each woman to her own life; for each woman's right to refuse the ancient woman's role of living everybody's life except her own. My mother accepted the idea of self-denial and the clashes between us were between her denial and my assertion. I slithered repeatedly out of traps I had voluntarily entered when they began to threaten the indestructible sense I have always had of my "self." Sometimes these traps took the form of love, or other people's possessiveness of me ("Ils veulent me mettre le grappin dessus," as Cézanne, who hated even to be touched, put it); sometimes they were other people's ideas of what I should be, or how I should behave. I remember once when an aunt cornered me at a

Christmas party and said, "Why don't you get married? You're just an ordinary American girl." The ideas people have of us are saturated with a kind of burning poison, like the shirt of Nessus, and they stick to the skin of our "selves," for although there is an affirmative voice that cries, "Can't you see that this is my real self?" another self-doubting voice is slyly whispering, "Could it be true?" And isn't this babble of interior voices—protesting, defending, resisting—the tissue of every human relationship, except the translucent state of being in love, which, according to Donne, mixes two souls together and makes them one? "We then, who are this new soul know / Of what we are composed and made," he says, celebrating the marvellous illusion of love. (But did any poet turn against his loves with more violent disgust at the moment of disillusion?) The first danger signal flashes when the mutual knowledge of good things, of which "we are composed and made," turns to knowledge of the weaknesses that go with them; when the sharp eyes of love begin the process of finding fault and correcting. Then, lovers claim that their vision of love has given them the right to demand radical changes; and the self, so gladly given, begins its withdrawal into solitude.

I ask Marie-Claire, "Do you think the wish to change the beloved is a sign that love is waning?" She answers uneasily, "So you think I love Hélène less," for Hélène was the friend that she was then trying to rescue from a state of *accidie* and inertia. Marie-Claire, the exception to every rule, arrives like a hurricane in people's lives, bringing to every love the gift of life, with its concomitant demand, "Live!" We cannot live without our lives! And if it isn't apparent what your life is, she has the uncanny ability to find it for you, unlike those who think they know "what is best for you" or those who "mettent le grappin dessus." Every love, for her, becomes a work of soul-freeing; and she always seems surprised when the beloved resists, with the stubborn conviction that she knows herself better than Marie-Claire knows her, or when she resists with growing rage, because Marie-Claire, once engaged on her work of regeneration, batters away like a piledriver. Fortunately, we recognize in each other our autonomous and unchangeable "me"s, like two knights who lower their visors before a friendly joust. She pushes and I resist, furiously sometimes, but her pushing is always in directions that I want to take: toward more air to breathe, a greater indifference to what people think, toward liberty and "the pursuit of happiness." Certain of her loves close in on the integrity of their selves, like Hélène, who was wrestling, like Jacob in the embrace of the angel. We hate it when someone points in the direction that we intend to take and says, "Hurry! Hurry!" We prefer to have the sense of having made our own decisions.

I was thinking not long ago about Marie-Claire and her clairvoyant intuition, about her beneficent pressure that gets people's backs up, but which pushes them in positive directions. I had waked up with a terrible headache, intensified by the sharp yelping sound of old Gillou, our dog, who is black, stone-deaf and sausage-shaped, who was outdoors, making a circumlocution of the house at 5:30 a.m., wishing to get into the house, to climb the stairs and throw herself down on the brown sheepskin rug in my room with a loud thump and a sigh. I had pretended to be asleep—and deaf like Gillou—to the plaints of Marie-Claire, who, as she went downstairs to let Gillou in, walked on her heels with the determination that very small people often put into the act of walking, and I, who took satisfaction in stepping silently as an Indian on the balls of my feet, thought, for the thousandth time, with a certain irritation, how can she make so much noise? The whole house shook. And how, every time she unbolted the bathroom door (and why did she have to lock it?), could she make it sound like the crack of a pistol? These little things, part of the unconsciousness of Marie-Claire's immediate physical life, later set me to wondering if perhaps now was the time to tackle the most difficult subject of my life—namely, Marie-Claire, my love for her, our love for each other, our life together. It was an ideal day for such a difficult project—a summer day, sparkling and cloudless. Looking out at the sunny fields, at a male bobolink with still imperfect markings, who was sitting on a fence, at the swallows that dipped below the edge of the hill and soared into view again, I saw a long slender bird land awkwardly in the little spruce tree, saw his bill open to say, "Chik!" while his tail wagged sideways, as though a string were attached to it.

It was a young brown thrasher with the look brown thrashers have of having outgrown themselves like adolescent boys. "Chick-wag, chick-wag," the bird cried, an alarm call, it seemed, though there was nothing to be alarmed about. Walking in the garden after that, watching the almost visible growth of the zucchini, looking at the lettuce luxuriating between the stems of marigolds (I had read that vegetables and flowers, like city people, like propinquity), I tried to keep in my mind the brown thrasher, the sun sparkling on the upturned faces of the marigolds, and, at the same time, the mystery of Marie-Claire, who more than anyone I have ever known, was and is unknowable, guarding the secret of her "I am." She is mysterious, even to herself perhaps, for how can anyone explain the ceaseless activity of a trillion brain cells with their trillion messages and recollections, packed into the so-recognizable head with its high forehead hidden by thick hair, black eyebrows (other members of the family wear these eyebrows too—a brother, two cousins, an aunt—and it is always a surprise to me to recognize their dark authority above different features) and eyes that turn from brown to gold—this delicately beautiful face that I have tried to paint or draw hundreds of times: the fine bone structure of the nose around its bridge, the narrow jaw and chiselled lips that suddenly stretch upward in a "v"—a tender smile, unlike anyone else's—or parting, become a merry, but somehow discreet (because of the aforesaid narrowness) grin. Her eyes—a subject in themselves—the right eye without much visible eyelid, very tidy, like a Chinese or Eskimo eye; and the left eye, opening wide, anxious and tragic, with a wide eyelid. This eye, which seems to concentrate and throw out beams of gold light, is almost hidden under her hair which, as time goes on, encloses her face more and more, until she begins to give the impression of a person resolutely hiding and watchful. (There is a wayward sister of hers at the National Gallery in Ottawa, a little portrait by Whistler called, "Lily-in-our-Alley," a girl with thick red-brown hair hiding her face—which is the face of Marie-Claire without genius—with a trace of vulgarity in her mouth, and all her energies concentrated in her seductive charm.) In my paintings of Marie-Claire, I often use raw umber for the right eye and yellow ochre for the light-filled left eye, and finish my work in a state of despair, for it is almost as difficult to arrive at the inner truth of someone as it is to arrive at the truth of a face. Marie-Claire's face, when I first met her, still had childish elements (Marie-Claire was then twenty-three) and I found it infinitely moving when the wind blew her hair back from her forehead and I could see the graceful dome of curving bone just under the hairline and the bluish tint of her skin, fine-drawn over the temple. The colour of her skin—like Byron's perhaps, which someone said was like an alabaster lamp lit from within—has always had a luminous pallor, refusing even to be browned by the sun. To suggest her in a painting, I mix a little raw sienna with much white and it isn't right, as it isn't right for her delicate, chalky-pale child's hands, with their slender fingers and long thumbs and surprisingly strong grip (like the strong tread of her feet). Looked at from certain angles, Marie-Claire's face is quite round—her eyes set in a width of Mongol cheekbone—and her nose seems to turn up. I used to paint her as a wise, merry owl—but then, I would see that her cheeks were hollow and that the hollows were created by the length and determination of her jaw. As she turned her head, her face would become narrower and the bone structure more visible. In every painting or drawing, I would catch some fleeting truth about her face; something that people would immediately accept as a likeness, but not *the* truth, which is, in fact, that a painted face is not alive. But what about those painted faces that *are* alive, I thought? What about Rembrandt and Goya? What about the little Vermeer in Washington, a woman whose face is shaded by a hat and in the shadow cast by its brim, you see the light in her eye and the moist gleam of her lips? What about that *look* in Rembrandt portraits, which Rothko had come to dislike, as fathomlessly deep as the universe? Well, I would think morosely, Marie-Claire should be painted by Rembrandt and not by me —Rembrandt rather than Goya or any of the other great por-traitists—for who better than he could suggest the unknowable world behind eyes that may perhaps be looking, not directly out of the picture, but into infinite space? Yes, the secret is in the eyes (what would the Mona Lisa's smile be without her inscrutable eyes to emphasize its ambiguity?) and Marie-Claire's eyes, so direct, so steady-gazing, have a special power of seeing behind walls, across rooms, of penetrating people's souls and throwing them into states of feeling bewitched—and angry at feeling thus. Didn't Barbara's brother refuse to let Marie-Claire read his daughter's hand (she has an extraordinary gift for this), evidently afraid of what she might see? Didn't Edmund call me into his study, as if I were an errant schoolgirl, and dress me down because she had written in a book, still in manuscript, about the death in a skiing accident of Paul, a young man whom our French friend, Odette Walling, had taken to be her son? "Now, look here," he growled, "Odette called me to say that Christopher has gone on a skiing expedition and that Marie-Claire has killed him off in her book." Edmund had not read the manuscript, but Odette had and she insisted that Marie-Claire, who had written about Paul's death months before, had Christopher in mind. It was useless to argue with Edmund, who could be as irrational as a maddened water buffalo trampling everything in its path. I, too, was on trial for sheltering and defending a witch. Edmund's fury was symptomatic of the fear, harboured by the good people of Wellfleet, that even if Marie-Claire hadn't yet put them in her books, she might, but coming from him, it was strange indeed, for hadn't he the ruthless eyes of a writer and hadn't he, when he wrote his two novels, prepared his own friends for a ritual feast and served them up in recognizable form?

"She sees everything," people said nervously, holding against Marie-Claire that strange power which, even in her state of mute shyness (for her English was scanty when she first came to Wellfleet), she could not hide. So they punished her (as seers are always punished) with every means at their disposal: by ignoring her, by spreading lies about her (some almost comical, such as the one that she had persuaded a friend of hers, a distinguished Roman Catholic abbé, to visit us in order to convert me), by turning Edmund (who was responsible for our meeting) not only against her character, but also against her work, which he had discovered with amazement—and Marie-Claire did not fight back (how could she?), but sat silently among these people who felt so threatened by her, her eyes absorbing and emitting energy, while her fine-sculptured ears, under their cape of hair, recorded every word they said and stored it away for future use.

Thinking about Marie-Claire's face, hidden more and more completely by the thick helmet of her hair; about her body, swaddled even in hot weather by layers of shirts, scarves, vests, jackets, jeans and boots, I speculate. Why does she go to such lengths to hide herself? For it's all of a piece, the reduction of her body to a pair of eyes, to a pair of nervous fine-boned hands (and feet to go with them, but these are mostly invisible); and the hoarding of her inner life, her pain, until it can spill out in a book? At first I blamed the nuns, who had, I thought, made Marie-Claire ashamed of her body. When we first met (Edmund had arranged for the three of us to have lunch in Cambridge), Marie-Claire was dressed like a convent girl, wearing a blouse with a Peter Pan collar, a black jumper that fell well below her knees, a raincoat that was much too big for her, and sharply-pointed black shoes with high spike heels. She had bought the raincoat, the collar of which she always pulled up around her ears, without trying it on, this being one of the eccentricities that I discovered about her, little by little. She would wrap it around her small self, pulling in the belt, but not tightly enough to call attention to her bosom, which she kept tightly bound and about which she had an obsession — the opposite of that which makes women with small breasts wish them to be bigger. She would buy blouses several sizes too big, to conceal her bosom and would leave her jackets unbuttoned so that they could not accentuate its curves. Later, I mocked her when, at the village supermarket, she would furtively slip a packaged bra, the dimensions of which might or might not be correct, among the produce in the shopping basket. For just as she refused to try on shirts, pants or coats, she refused to try on bras — and nothing horrified her more than when a saleslady swept close with the intent of putting one on her over her clothes in full view of the people in a shop. Hence, the supermarket solution, if one could call it that, for half the time the bras she had snatched up were the wrong size or shape and they had to be thrown away.

Marie-Claire carries her phobia about being seen trying

something on so far that, if she is given a present of a blouse or a jacket, she carries it off and buries it, like a dog with a precious bone, and at some time of her own choosing, appears, self-consciously wearing whatever it is, with the perceptible hope that no one will embarrass her by mentioning it. She refuses to wear either sleeveless blouses or those with short sleeves, and to cover her neck, she invariably ties a scarf around it, though it is the normally beautiful neck of a young person. As for bathing suits, she has a horror of them and appears in one, wriggling with embarrassment, nervously pulling it down over her shapely legs, or up, lest someone catch a glimpse of her breasts. I believe that she ceased to swim, not only because of her terror of drowning (she paddles about in shallow water much as my mother used to, for my mother had once sunk to the bottom and stayed there long enough to be frightened for life), but also because of her preternatural modesty. But if I accuse Marie-Claire of being a victim of the nuns and their false sense of decency, she denies it, not wanting to admit that she is unfree in any respect; whereas I take pleasure in blaming my own exaggerated modesty on my governess and my mother.

At this moment in time, I am looking at a postcard—a photograph of a little bronze seated goddess. "Estatuita de Astarte," it says on the back—and it is to be seen in the Archaeological Museum in the city of Mérida, in Spain, where Marie-Claire and I passed several gloomy and quarrel-filled days. Astarte has the proportions of Marie-Claire; her hair is cut in bangs and is combed behind her ears, à la Egyptienne, the ends resting on her full, high, rather childish breasts. She is short-waisted, like Marie-Claire, with a little round belly, legs held tight together and feet that are planted on a cube. She is smiling a remote smile and she has lowered eyelids. Marie-Claire looks like Astarte, but her legs taper down to delicate ankles and narrow, perfect feet, much more graceful than Astarte's. Sometimes, in these days of her relative liberation, Marie-Claire goes barefoot and wears shorts cut off with scissors, but often on a hot day, one sees her in the same ragged shorts with multi-coloured kneesocks and heavy shoes, with a long-sleeved shirt and the invariable scarf to conceal (one might suppose) the immodesty of her neck. And oddly enough, this passion for concealment, for burrowing—or whatever it is—extends to the night, when Marie-Claire wraps herself in the cocoon of five or six blankets, no matter what the temperature, and pulls a wool shawl around her head and over her face, so that one sees nothing but an indecisive mound of wool.

Habits. What do they mean? How much light do they cast on a person's character? I have the idea that even the humblest objects should be treated with respect. A toothpaste tube, for instance, should be rolled from the bottom. Marie-Claire tortures toothpaste tubes beyond recognition and I look upon their poor twisted bodies with sympathy. I wish sometimes I could cultivate the carelessness that seems to go with greatness of spirit. Haven't I seen the mangled paint tubes of great painters many times, and their palettes which, more often than not, are mountainous accretions of little dabs of dry paint, with not a square inch of the surface visible? My palette, orderly like everything I touch, is a half-circle of logical colours, enclosing an oiled area of smooth brown wood, which I clean after every day's work. When I read about the lives of great painters, I am relieved to learn that certain ones were tidy and I identify with them, even if they aren't my favourites.

In the house, I play a game with Marie-Claire, of which she is totally unconscious, which concerns the putting away of household objects: cutlery, pots and pans, glasses and plates. Brooding on her seemingly trivial habit of changing the places of these objects as soon as they *have* a place, and, if I accept the changes, of going back to the old places, in short, of keeping me in a perpetual state of guessing, it comes to me that she is all of a piece; that she is always in a state of flight, refusing to be pinned down. Just as she will move a plate from cupboard to cupboard, she will never give a direct answer to a direct question, answering with something quite irrelevant, until I have repeated the question several times in a voice of mounting irritation. Her sense of privacy is threatened in a million ways each day and in my mind's eye, I now see her scurrying psychically in every direction—to prevent herself from being caught. And now, the meaning of one of her strangest habits becomes clear, this being her refusal to pay for anything with small change. The result of this habit is the accumulation of mountains of pennies, nickels and dimes (she sometimes uses quarters), which one finds in plastic bags, or in jars, a jumble of change from every country in which she has lived. I appropriate the mountains of change and am hard put to get rid of them; I can be seen in shops labouriously counting out pennies, while the salespeople eye me coldly. In this case, I decide, Marie-Claire is simply carrying a step further her idea that orderly habits denote a smallness of mind. The use and counting of change imprison her soul and keep her generous spirit from taking wing, whereas bills of all denominations give her a sense of freedom. She keeps thick wads of these bills stuffed in her pocketbook and disperses them, like autumn leaves, in the form of tips, which pains my penurious soul. After many years of living close to her, I finally begin to understand that the sin of *mesquinerie* (which is worse than murder in her eyes) extends its arms, like an octopus, and includes every kind of consistent order, except cleanliness, which for some odd reason, she places higher on the scale of virtue than I do. But perhaps even here there is a connection, for just as I am careful in small ways about money, I wear the same shirt for days on end, and just as Marie-Claire disperses dollar bills, she changes her shirts and multi-coloured socks several times a day, leaving piles of discarded clothes in corners, like the piles of discarded coins.

We two, Marie-Claire and I, are like the old grey mare and a fiery little pony yoked together — or would be, if the yoke hadn't become so flexible with the passage of time that each can now go at her own pace. Marie-Claire, so timid and yielding when I first knew her, is no longer timid — and yields to no one. I remember with wonder the person who nestled under my protective wing so sweetly, who, in those first months of our love for one another, would throw her arms around my neck fifty times a day, like a child, or wake me up out of a sound sleep with the anxious query, "Tu dors?" One would have thought that her will, which flashes now like Excalibur, existed then only to conform to mine and Barbara's and that her occasional storms of tears were those of a sensitive child with a boundless need to be loved, instead of the fierce welling-up of real grievances. But in Marie-Claire, there were symptoms of restlessness, to which I paid insufficient attention. She would put in disappearances—as other people put in appearances—vanishing with magical totality from a shop or a street, as though she had put on an invisible garment. Her disappearances would cause my heart to beat with fear and then with exasperation—and my blood still drains from my heart when I remember a time in Truro, Massachusetts, on a beach, one side of which sloped steeply down to the rushing Pamet River. Lying in the sun, with closed eyes, next to Marie-Claire, I had a sudden sense of her absence, stood up, and, with a fainting heart, looked in every direction with the conviction that she had fallen into the river and drowned. I remember then the miracle of her head rising above the edge of the slope, her shy smile, her pale shoulders and arms, the somewhat top-heavy effect of the upper half of her body, with her full breasts bound tightly by her bathing suit, diminishing to childish hips and graceful legs, and her narrow feet, like Egyptian feet found in tombs, stepping over the warm sand.

"L'amour vit dans ses propre régions inhumaines, sous un règne de terreur qui n'est que le sien," says Marie-Claire in *Les Nuits de l'Underground,* which speaks so profoundly about love between women. The disappearance on the beach symbolizes for me a series of deaths and resurrections that I lived with her, each with its apprehensive terror. The first and worst was at the beginning of our life together, when, as we were out walking, Marie-Claire hard on my heels, a thorny branch snapped back and struck her left eye. A little cloud of blood appeared at the edge of the iris, and she, believing she had been blinded, was like a stricken bird that sinks down and prepares to die. For weeks, though her sight came back, she was troubled by fog and spots that flew crazily across her field of vision, and the light of day was a torture to her. The terror that she silently lived through was expressed by her state of physical weakness; she was exhausted by the slightest effort and had to be helped to climb the hill to the house. It was as if the light of her genius had been threatened with extinction, and indeed, for a time it was, for she could not see to type and stopped writing entirely. Meantime, I was sick with the sense of my own responsibility. Why had I proposed the fatal walk? Why had I not told Marie-Claire to keep a safe distance behind me? And I raged against the insensitivity of all those, including eye surgeons, who implied that Marie-Claire exaggerated her pain and helplessness, and who went so far as to suggest that it was possible for her to get along very well with only one eye.

Marie-Claire had come to the United States like Daniel entering the lion's den—a small, vulnerable, yet courageous Daniel, who could keep the lions at bay, but could not prevent them from baring their teeth and snarling. At that time, most Americans (including me) knew nothing about Canada, and even less about Québec. Canada was a place that sent its unwanted cold fronts southward and could be blamed for the rigours of winter in the United States; or it was a place where you went fishing, hunting and skiing—and in Québec, people "quaintly" (as one of my brothers said) spoke French. That Québec actually had writers and a literature of its own, was inconceivable; all the Québécois, in American eyes, were poor and more or less illiterate and earned their living cutting wood or scratching a bare livelihood from a rundown farm. "I see something dark in them, an impoverished spirit," said a friend in Wellfleet. It was a surprise when Edmund Wilson put Québec on the literary map with his book, *O Canada*, in which there was a chapter about the work of Marie-Claire and other Québécois writers. Marie-Claire came to the United States with the reputation of having been "discovered" by Edmund; nevertheless, she was referred to by Wellfleetians as the "Canuck," which, as everybody knows, has the same derisive content as "Wop" or "Frog." It irritated people that she could barely speak English and that Québécois friends, who spoke even less, would come to visit. "Why can't they learn English?" asked Henry Poor. One still has the feeling, now that Québec has asserted its identity, that Americans think it is getting far too big for its britches and it will get what it deserves if it "goes too far." Americans are pained by French road signs when they cross the border and by the incomprehensible language of the Québécois. And the Celtic and Latin Québécois are physically as different from Americans as the so-called "gooks" in Vietnam, with their lovely small-boned bodies, were from the big American soldiers who despised them.

My friends in Wellfleet suddenly all seemed big and careless, and even those I loved became strangers to me in their relation to Marie-Claire. Alone with them, everything was the same, but if I spoke of Marie-Claire, particularly if I spoke enthusiastically, a silence fell—and I felt that she had been locked in a cell and was beating on the walls. One of the worst American sins is suspicion —and enthusiasm is always suspect. Edmund had said that Marie-Claire had genius, so it had to be proved that he had been carried away; that the books she had already written weren't *that* remarkable, that she was beginning to peter out as a writer. The second novel she wrote in Wellfleet, *Les Manuscrits de Pauline Archange* (a masterpiece, I thought) was pronounced to be a bore and Edmund bluntly said to me, "Marie-Claire writes too much. She's incapable of judging her own work." Edmund liked to accuse her indirectly this way and he became, then, in person, the prison wall on which *I* ineffectually (for he never listened to me) beat. I was unable to remind him that he wrote books year after year and that the shelves of my bookcase were weighed down by them. And what about the great writers of the past: Dickens, Balzac, Henry James, who endlessly *wrote* without giving a thought as to whether or not they were writing "too much"? But no, there were different rules for a woman who was still in her early twenties and who was somehow supposed to practice book-control as one practices birth-control. Edmund, like so many others in Wellfleet, became a rhinoceros (as in Ionesco's play) and began charging blindly around, trampling the fragile things in his path. It was only after Marie-Claire had left Wellfleet that he returned to his old admiring sense of her; it was as though she had died and the Wellfleetians were released from the spell that had struck them blind and savage.

I had begun my relationship with Marie-Claire with the hope that everything I found touching and beautiful in her would be visible to my friends and my heart almost broke at times when, at parties, she was treated with indifference, when I would see her sitting silently while everybody laughed and talked around her, her eyes painfully burning in her white face. My friends showed no curiosity about Canada or tried to draw Marie-Claire out and had already sized her up, judged and condemned her, so that she was like a forgotten prisoner in the dock. When her eye was threatened, when even this almost fatal accident failed to move them, I judged my friends by their sadism in disposing of the eye and by their impatience with Marie-Claire's psychic breakdown, as if this was necessary (like the blinding of Oedipus or the blinding of Rochester in *Jane Eyre*) to humble her invisible but suspected pride. The accident happened while Barbara was suffering in her prison cage in Albany, Georgia — and because of it, I no longer needed to feel guilty about my joy at being alone with Marie-Claire. But it was as though Marie-Claire had to be punished for my joy and for my having forgotten to live vicariously every moment of Barbara's hell. Why couldn't I have borne the full weight of the punishment instead of having myself inflicted the worst of it on Marie-Claire?

When Barbara emerged from prison, emaciated as if she had been in a concentration camp, she and Marie-Claire and I went to Markoe Island in Florida, where we joined the three members of the Poor family for a holiday in the sun. Marie-Claire, still suffering from the light, was subjected to the blinding glare of the white sand and to the hostile and equally painful glare of our friends. What was she doing there? Why had she attached herself to me? Why had she come, just at this moment, when Barbara needed to be alone with me? These unspoken questions seemed to shout in the heavy silences between us. The Poors, our dearest, most respected friends: Henry and Anne, the two painters; and Bessie, the writer — each so powerful alone — joined together to form an impregnable pyramid which could not be stormed or even approached, which, in fact, had no entrance. They did not speak to Marie-Claire — for how could they speak to a person who did not exist? Marie-Claire sat miserably in the sun-dappled shade of the stunted bushes at the top of the beach, her wounded eyes hidden behind dark glasses, while the rest of us swam and spent long hours sunning ourselves. And I was caught in the middle, loving our friends and hating them for hating Marie-Claire, not knowing that in the course of time, they would come around; that the ferocious Bessie, so like a little carnivorous owl when she was angry, would suffer a sea-change, becoming so gentle, so generous and humble, that one wondered if Florida and Wellfleet had been the kind of bad dream that seems to go on forever. (But that was when she began her slow journey toward death — when she had cancer of the throat — and her vocal cords were removed.) As for Anne and Henry, the two titans who reigned along with Edmund in my life (Anne still reigns), who had something of the arbitrary cruelty of all gods (and all human beings?), they were influenced, as Edmund had been influenced, by a kind of dazzling fiction, shot with thunder and lightning, that required its villain (Marie-Claire) and was more tempting for them to believe than the truth. Bessie, like all writers, erected her "palace of thought" (as the narrator does in James' *The Sacred Fount*, that marvellous book about a writer's manipulation of life and his sense of omniscience) out of her own bitterness and disappointments as a writer.

On one occasion, having succeeded in detaching Anne from her parents, I aided in building a "palace of thought" by being cowardly. Instead of saying that Marie-Claire and I loved each other (I was unable to share this secret with anybody, for I had observed how even the slightest indication of my love made my friends jealous and I shrank from delivering the *coup de grâce*), I told the story of the injured eye and gave that as a reason for protecting Marie-Claire and bringing her to Florida. My virtue in not wanting to hurt people was balanced by my fear of what people would think of me, a flaw which even the submissive Marie-Claire of those days was quick to discern. Yes, I cared what people thought, I hated to be judged by my friends and I was mortally afraid of being judged by my family. I executed a remarkable series of dance steps, like a solitary waltz — forward, sideways, back — steps of defiance, prudence, cowardice, not wanting to hurt anyone, nor to endanger my reputation as a "wonderful person." Back in Wellfleet, Bessie lectured me about the problem that our friends had with this new triangle. Could they invite Barbara and me together as before, or did they have to invite Marie-Claire, too? I said I didn't give a damn whether or not any of us were invited and that if they were real friends, that wouldn't be a problem—and went home in a fury, though I now see that the ever-meddling Bessie at least had a social point. Bessie, like others, used as an argument for the expulsion of Marie-Claire that she was a writer who needed to be close to life, unaware that even Wellfleet contained enough material for several novels. Another friend told the three of us that we were "locked in"—that Marie-Claire was locked into her life with Barbara and me, and that she was even more fatally locked into her choice to love and live with a woman. These analyses were dangerous because they contained a germ of truth—and I resisted them with the blind instinct of self-preservation. It was true, though (I did not know at the time how true), that Marie-Claire was being forced to live a life that was unnatural to her; that her wings had been clipped, but she adapted herself so lovingly to my life and concealed her rebellion so well! Part of my prudent sideways dance steps were done to convince myself that all was well and that Marie-Claire would be happy with Barbara and me. I knew that Marie-Claire suffered from the general hostility. I knew that she was being ground between the two millstones of Barbara and myself, but it never occurred to me that this life, which seemed so perfect for the three of us as artists, was as hard for Marie-Claire as living in a convent. She wanted to live the delirium of a city life, with its marvellous encounters, its bars, its joyous blending of night and day. The Puritan discipline of Wellfleet was gradually eroding her love for me, even if she wrote like an angel there. Barbara's departure to live with her new friend set us free, but not, as I supposed, free to love each other at last. Marie-Claire had begun to beat her wings violently and turn in her cage, like a bird that feels the compelling urge to migrate. It was the end of her innocent and generous pretense to be what she wasn't, but I did not understand this yet and had to be given a series of hard lessons. For a time, we seemed to belong to two different species; we went to Spain where I endeavoured to be a conscientious tourist, while Marie-Claire went to bars, defying the Spanish rule that women must be accompanied, where she stared down men who made rude remarks and women who looked at her with contempt. She was far from me, living in her own future, in the reality of a photograph we had both seen

121

in a bookstore in Barcelona. It was of a writer Marie-Claire had met in Paris when they both won literary prizes there. This writer — her face, with its prominent nose, like a sheep's, her pale melancholy eyes, and mouth that was both sensitive and sensual, her silver hair cut short, like Joan of Arc's — looked out from its place, among her books, and entered into Marie-Claire, as if a spell had been laid on her. From then on, I suffered from my new identity as someone who interrupted her thoughts, who demanded attention and answers, with my nagging schedules and my apparent conviction that our life would go on in the same old way. I, too, was under a spell, that of a self whom I hated, who would become increasingly jealous and self-pitying, while Marie-Claire moved in her own direction.

This sombre self, bent under her own weight, was a different person from the one, transported by turbulent joy, who grew out of our first meeting — at lunch with Edmund — when Marie-Claire poked at an omelette without eating it, when she and I walked distractedly through the Fogg Museum, she firing questions (what do you think of Virginia Woolf, Kafka, Katherine Mansfield?), when, in the rearview mirror, as I drove off with Edmund, I saw her little figure in her belted raincoat, waving, a joyful smile on her face. I was forty-five and she was twenty-three; I was too old for her. I explained a week or so later when we were alone in my studio and she had come out with the disarming question, "Could we love each other?" I really felt too old; I resisted. Then I felt the years dropping off and wings seeming to grow from my heels and shoulders. "She's a force of nature," Barbara said about Marie-Claire. She began to take me by storm — with letters twenty pages long that required hours to decipher and books she was anxious for me to read: Simone Weil, Mauriac, Breton, Kafka — until I began to feel persecuted and begged her to stop. "Mais c'est tout ce que j'ai à te donner," she said, and I felt like a brute. I was convinced that I could resist the "force of nature," about which Barbara and I smiled. And I was surprised when my feet seemed to be swept out from under me and I found myself floating on a flood-tide, without even reflecting that I *should* resist. Every falling in love is a repetition, and yet, it is different every time. My love for Barbara had been like a spring sunrise, like the adagio movement of Schubert's "Trout" quintet. Because we were the same age and the same shape, because we were both white, Anglo-Saxon Protestants, well-bred, with prosperous families, with similar habits of sobriety and high seriousness, our love became sedate and respectable — and we were accepted in Wellfleet (after a preliminary soul-searching by the wives of Edmund, Henry Poor and others) as an authentic couple, who seemed to have walked to the strains of the wedding march from Tannhaüser. Marie-Claire and I chose for our music, *Rosenkavalier*, with its lovely ambiguity; I identified myself with the Marschallin and Octavian, and Marie-Claire (who, like Octavian, was in love with an older woman) played both Octavian and Sophie. We would sit clasped in each other's arms listening to Lotte Lehmann, Rise Stevens and Eleanor Steber, while I told Marie-Claire how, once, at the old Metropolitan Opera House, I had sat in a box over the stage with a friend, breathlessly waiting for the moment the friend had described, when, at the end of the opera, Octavian wraps his long black cape around Sophie, bends his-her head and kisses Sophie on the lips, a long and passionate kiss, as the two walk slowly offstage, for in real life, the friend said, they were in love with each other. Even after years had gone by, Marie-Claire would still ask me to tell her about the love between those opera stars — and the trio from *Rosenkavalier* would still fire us both with tender nostalgia.

Borne along on the current of love, I would drive to Cambridge to see my little friend in her basement apartment with its grimy windows, through which one saw the legs and feet of passers-by. Marie-Claire kept a bicycle chained in the lobby of the apartment house, and before all its vital parts were stolen, she would ride into Cambridge on her quest for life. After the demise of the bicycle, she would walk into town or take the subway in whatever direction it happened to be going, and would sit in bars for hours, trying out her English on deadpan or arrogant Americans. Our friend in Wellfleet, Odette Walling, concocted the idea that Marie-Claire was engaged in continual love affairs and expiated her sins by regular confession at the Roman Catholic church down the street. If Marie-Claire went to Mass before she met me, it was because she was under the spell of Simone Weil and could think best about Weil's purity and mysticism in the atmosphere of a church. One of her few friends in Cambridge was a woman professor, remarkable for her virtue and the goodness of heart that so often goes with immutable views about right and wrong. She tried to convince Marie-Claire that Simone Weil's ideas were dangerous for true Catholics. She was also one of several good friends who were inexorably opposed (as Catholics are) to love between women and who did their best to steer Marie-Claire away from what they thought of as her fatal choice. With her Octavian-like weakness for older women, she felt impelled to pour out her heart and confess her leanings to every older woman she met; I was the first to make no attempt to save her from herself.

Marie-Claire lived with the intensity of someone who is alone most of the time. She nourished herself on the kind of little roast chickens that turn on spits in supermarkets, on minute rice and yogourt, worked on her novel, read night and day and roamed Cambridge and Boston. With my Martha-instincts always alive, I scrubbed the sooty floor of the bathroom of her apartment, tidied up the kitchen and brought her things to cheer the place up, which provoked one of her surprising bursts of tears, for she was proud of her underground lair. On November 22, 1963, I set out for Cambridge from Wellfleet (Barbara had gone off on a long protest march against the U.S. policy toward Cuba), turned on the radio and heard the news of Kennedy's assassination. Instead of turning back, I went on—toward Marie-Claire—and I think of this terrible time, which I could have chosen to share with my American friends, as a turning point in my life. I chose instead to affirm my love for Marie-Claire, who, isolated by the terror and panic of the whole country, needed me. So I drove, weak with fear, in pouring rain, in a colossal traffic jam, while the radio voices went on and on, repeating, filling in, launching hypotheses. Oswald, the presumed assassin, had already been caught. He was a member of the Fair Play for Cuba Committee, it was said; he had passed out their leaflets. Barbara and I were members of the Committee, and at that very moment, Barbara was somewhere in Georgia, marching with her friends to protest

124

the government's policy toward Cuba. They would all be rounded up and thrown into jail and so would I, I thought. When I finally got to Marie-Claire's apartment, I sat on the bed, with my head in my hands, and said, "It's the beginning of the end." I remember that Marie-Claire's face, lit up by the pleasure of seeing me, became anxious, and fear, like heat lightning, flickered in her eyes. There was a faint irritation in her voice, a pleading that seemed to say, "Stop thinking just for now about the terrible event that has spoiled this time together." She was there in her immediacy, giving life to me, like a blood transfusion—the merging of our lives under the sign of terror—and I felt the warmth of love flooding me and restoring me. I drove back to Wellfleet at midnight and I was there the next morning to fend off my friends' questions ("Where *were* you?") and to share their fears. Word came that Barbara and her friends were safe, that they were going to continue their march—and the country had already begun one of its miraculous recoveries. From then on, I had two selves: one, the wingèd secret being who loved Marie-Claire; the other, a person who quaked in the shadow of outside terrors that simply seemed to change form, until they coalesced in the continuous terror and revolt caused by the war in Vietnam.

My secret-self shed years of life and my soul danced in spite of the outer weight: the guilt of hurting Barbara; the pain of Marie-Claire's ostracism. Marie-Claire and I worked in separate rooms in my studio, and letters, poems and drawings poured from us in a steady stream. Marie-Claire wrote to me under the pseudonym of Christian Deslarmes; I replied in the person of a misanthropic version of myself. She posed for me, sitting quietly while ideas for novels raced through her head, and my portraits of her were a constant and painful reminder to Barbara (and to jealous friends in Wellfleet) of my love for Marie-Claire, a kind of physical and irrefutable extension of it. I began to do illustrations for one of Marie-Claire's books, at first to amuse myself, but then, with the knowledge that an unknown part of myself was being tried and used. The reaction to these illustrations from my friends was almost uniformly hostile; they were so different from my lyrical landscapes and ink drawings of flowers and marshes that they were judged to come not from me, but from some false spirit which possessed me. I could read their thoughts, "This isn't really you," but in doing the illustrations, I found that I could see what I had never seen and know Marie-Claire's world, in spite of my own inexperience. I would have liked to call on my inner eye as Redon had in his illustrations for Baudelaire and Poe; or Demuth in his illustrations for *The Turn of the Screw*. I worshipped these masters, absorbed something from the comic violence of George Grosz and studied Chagall's Bible and La Fontaine's illustrations with awed delight. My opinion of my own work made its usual dizzy leaps, up and down, according to my painter friends' reactions to it, but I never quite lost faith in my illustrations, even when people said, "Oh, how amusing," or, "They're *fun!*" or reacted as squeamish Americans are apt to do, with an embarrassed silence.

Marie-Claire's response to my work was invariably to say, "C'est beau. C'est merveilleux," either because she was trying to say what I wanted to hear, or because she was intuitively aware of my intentions, even when they weren't realized. Her attitude caused me to exclaim that I wished she would say what she thought and stop trying to flatter me, and for me to accuse her of being unable to see when something was really bad. And Marie-Claire, knowing that I did not want to hear that something was bad, kept on insisting, "Je l'aime!" She herself began to show an astonishing aptitude for painting and was exploring every kind of medium and trying experiments that I, with my one-track mind, never tried. In a couple of days, she could turn out a notebook full of enchanting little abstractions or fill a whole drawing pad with her improvisations, inspired by Matisse, Chagall, Nolde, Picasso — by all the painters that she knew — but she always kept her own identity. I felt a little jealous of the rapid progress she made, reflecting that she could just as easily have been a painter as a writer. One can think of many great writers who have also painted (Victor Hugo, e.e. cummings, Henry Miller, to name three), though one can say of each of these that their painting is deficient in the seriousness and density of their writing. But Marie-Claire is, I think, better than any of them.

In general, I did not feel jealousy of her, but awe for the

126

miracle of a mind like hers, in which there seemed to be no compartments or passages leading to dead ends, no walls to dismantle, no spaces full of inert matter, but an electric free-flowing of impulses, memories, intuitions, emotions, fears—a universe, in short, in violent motion. That our so-different minds could understand and nourish each other was another miracle, wrought by love. I have noticed in the course of my life that certain people could enlarge my powers by the generous giving of their own, and other people could diminish them. Sometimes, under the spell of a good tennis player, I played well, or I talked brilliantly, it seemed, in conversations with brilliant friends, or, when Gardner Jencks, the benign Svengali who gave me piano lessons, was at my elbow, I played better than I ever could play by myself. This flowing of higher into lower worked like a kind of chemistry, though the levels had to be exactly right, like the adjustment of locks, so that a ship can pass from one to the next. It works best between lovers—in the stage when they feel the communion of body, mind and spirit—passing each into each. Later, that part of Marie-Claire that rebelled against her imposed life almost made us strangers, just as Barbara and I became strangers for a time. I found it impossible to recognize my defiant little friend with her new enthusiasms and her rages at anyone who refused to share them. There was a gloomy and painful period when we seemed to become irreconcilable, when I was, like a large bird, moulting and temporarily flightless, and Marie-Claire was out of sight or coming back to dart about me in mocking circles.

We both sometimes wonder how it would have been if we had fled together from Wellfleet, instead of living our triangular life with Barbara, though I know that if I had to do it over again, I would still be paralyzed by the same scruples. In short, I have changed less radically than Marie-Claire, for whom it would be unthinkable, who can scarcely believe that she was capable of what now seems like generous folly and masochism in the name of love. The triangle that Barbara and Marie-Claire and I formed for six years was earnest and well-intentioned—even loving—but unworkable, as I, who have held every possible position in triangles, believe that they are all unworkable. In the

127

course of my life, I have played the role of A, the injured spouse
(to speak in conventional terms), B, the injurer, and C, the person who intrudes on A and B with her love for B. For those
with tender consciences, each position is untenable. One may
think that A is the one who suffers most, isolated by the love
between B and C, but A's suffering and jealousy are powerful
weapons that can frighten B and C into giving up their love, and
then, the three suffer equally. Or A, by falling in love with C, in
her turn, will attempt to create a more nearly equilateral triangle,
an inexorable piece of human geometry that prevents any two of
the three from being close to each other. For such is the strength
of the equalizing instinct that C then falls in love with A, thus
leading to a suffering B. So it was with Barbara, Marie-Claire
and me, who tried so hard to make our triangle work in the context of the equation: I love Marie-Claire, Marie-Claire loves me,
Barbara loves me; thus, Barbara and Marie-Claire construct a
fragile love which threatens that between Marie-Claire and me.
Consider the problem of trying to discuss schedules — when and
for how long (it comes down to this) can any two members of
the triangle be alone together; the torture of discussing this, for
not one of the participants wishes to say outright that she wants
to be alone with another. And since it is particularly painful for
Barbara (who feels insufficiently loved by both me and Marie-
Claire) to propose leaving us alone, she suffers even more if we
imply that we would like to be alone. When the three are
together, the atmosphere — charged with pain, with frustrated
desire, with the impossibility of being openly tender without
causing more pain or of showing a preference, the unspoken
wish by Marie-Claire and me that Barbara will cease to care so
much and become indifferent to both of us — becomes rigid and
artificial. Barbara, suffering, puts on a mask to conceal the
heaviness of her heart, a kind of clownishness that irritates me
and scares Marie-Claire; Barbara weighs heavily on us and on
herself. Any A will react in this way, with uncertain control of
feelings that are surging sickly within, and will stop (or not, as
the case may be) just short of exploding into open jealousy and
violence.

Inevitably, during all those years, the three of us had our good

Consuelo Kanaga

Marie-Claire Blais, Wellfleet, Massachusetts, 1965.

Jill Krementz

Edmund Wilson.

Mrs. John Wister, my maternal grandmother, with her family. My father, Edward Browning Meigs, upper right; my mother, Margaret Wister Meigs, lower left, with my brother, Julian; Hester and Mary, the twins, on my grandmother's lap; brother Charles, lower right.

My mother, Margaret Wister Meigs, with twins Hester (left) and Mary (right).

Margaret Wister Meigs with her children. Clockwise from left: Mary, Charles, Julian and Hester.

My father, Edward Browning Meigs, age 18, Philadelphia, Pennsylvania, 1898.

My mother, Margaret Wister, age 20, before her marriage, Philadelphia, Pennsylvania, 1903.

Consuelo Kanaga

Barbara Deming, Wellfleet, Massachusetts, 1955.

Henry Varnum Poor, New City,
New York, 1968.

Consuelo Kanaga

"Life-Portrait of My Mother," oil, 50" x 60", 1958.

135

Illustration for Marie-Claire Blais' *The Manuscripts of Pauline Archange* from *Illustrations for Two Novels by Marie-Claire Blais*, Exile Editions, 1977.

Illustration for Marie-Claire Blais' *St. Lawrence Blues* from *Illustrations for Two Novels by Marie-Claire Blais*, Exile Editions, 1977.

times together. In our little summer house in Maine, surrounded by huge fields and an apple orchard, we read aloud every evening after dinner: Chekhov, Pirandello, and all of Ibsen—and the sombre greatness of Ibsen's plays, shared with my two friends, remains with me as a marvellous binding memory. And before these evening readings, when the great fields turned an unearthly green under the flaming sky, we would go out and play ball, while the dogs ran in crazy circles, round and round us, until it was too dark to see the ball. But lurking in every good time was the night's menace and the hard realities of the triangle: Marie-Claire alone in her little room; Barbara and I together, but separated by our separate roles. The chivalry practiced by me (to diminish the suffering of Barbara) prevented Marie-Claire and me from ever spending a night together when Barbara was in the house; and it was Barbara (whose footfall stirred such complicated feelings in Marie-Claire) who would leave me and slip into Marie-Claire's room to say goodnight. And this was a benign form of triangle, which we wanted to make work with all the strength of our hearts!

After six years, Barbara found another love—and Marie-Claire and I were left together, but by this time she was exhausted by the struggle, having tried to live a wholly unnatural life, the victim of a hate campaign initiated by the virtuous married women of the community, frightened by having had to share in Barbara's political life, irritated by my cowardice—for wasn't it a form of cowardice to have allowed our love almost to bleed to death? She longed to live more freely. She had adjusted to her caged life with such heroism that I believed that it was bearable, but once free, with the energy of all freed slaves, she turned violently against it. After her listless attempt to live my life for another year, she fell in love with the French writer, whose photograph we had seen in Barcelona, and another triangle was formed, this one, a deadly variety, on the points of which A, B and C are all impaled. In this case, Andrée (the French woman) had her eye on me all along (she was drawn to monied Anglo-Saxons) and Marie-Claire, in the generosity of her heart, encouraged us. Why she invariably throws her friends together in this way requires a deeper study in the mechanics of the triangle and in the workings of her

137

masochism and guilt feelings. With this impulse of hers, joined to my equalizing instinct (which has elements of destructiveness and punishment in it), the seeds of disaster were planted and sprouted almost immediately. I believed myself to be in love with the dazzling Andrée — who sang French songs and laughed like a joyful and innocent child, who loved life ("J'aime la vie!" she kept exclaiming), who quoted Apollinaire and knew Racine by heart — for the month that it took to change my entire life. I found myself, as in a dream, arranging to sell my beloved house in Wellfleet, packing up all my belongings, buying a house in Brittany that Marie-Claire and Andrée had found, and flying to France with the two dogs. By the time the furniture arrived, Andrée had revealed her Protean personality, with its furies and avidity, and cuckoo-like, she had begun to push Marie-Claire out of the nest. A terrible year followed, too charged with melodrama to be believable. From the very beginning, by throwing jealous scenes, Andrée had prevented Marie-Claire and me from speaking to each other alone. Having isolated us, she then attempted to make us hate each other by mutual mind-poisoning — and in this, she almost succeeded. It is inconceivable to both of us now that we let ourselves be so manipulated. And yet, I have only to remember what we called Andrée's Medusa face, when her eyes seemed to start from her head, when her girlish skin would turn bright pink, when a volley of stinging words, like machine-gun fire, would rattle out of her mouth, or remember the crushing weight of her sulkiness, her refusals to eat, her withdrawals to her room and the clamourous sobs that echoed through the night, to understand that irresolute self who could not escape from the trap that I had so diligently constructed and walked into. For Andrée practiced the art of terrorism with consummate skill, alternating it with tearful repentance and insinuating charm, accompanied perhaps by a volume of poetry or a scarf from Yves St. Laurent. One was so thankful when this other being reappeared that one was only too willing to propitiate the monster. Many times, with mixed feelings of admiration and disgust, I watched Andrée cozen Marie-Claire, just after having launched her poison darts, or turn her back on her for several days. It was an amazing demonstration of seduction and honeyed pleading ("un tout petit sourire, mon chéri") and before my eyes, Marie-Claire would turn from a person with defiantly flashing eyes to a grateful and helpless child. Andrée needed Marie-Claire and her technique was to keep her paralyzed but alive, so that she could eat her at her leisure.

Andrée could in another life have been one of le père Goriot's daughters. She adored luxury and like many French women, she could tell at a glance where you bought your clothes and what your income was. She would traverse Paris to buy the best cheese or pâté, and if anything less exalted was offered her, she would dismiss it with the words, "C'est infecte." She and her husband (for she had a husband, a charming man whose avocation was to invent ingenious excuses based on Freud for the outrageous behaviour of his wife) would look about in a restaurant and pronounce judgement on the other diners — "des têtes immondes" — and I remember that one of Andrée's fearful outbursts was provoked by "un français moyen, vulgaire" who had the temerity to wear a handmade Irish sweater. Andrée thought of me as an inexhaustible well, but I had an inherited sense of self-preservation and was prudent about money, and it was, ironically, Marie-Claire who gave her last penny and I who gave less and less to feed the insatiable Andrée. I believe that our relationship ended, not because my love for Andrée dried up, but because my money did; and because, despite all Andrée's efforts, she was unable to break the bond between Marie-Claire and me. It was for this practical reason that she announced to me one day that she was leaving, hoping perhaps, in vain, that I would make some objection. She had played all her theatrical roles and had even attempted a mad scene, falling in a heap on the bathroom floor, breaking a plate, talking in a high, childish voice, sitting with her mouth open and her alarming eyes glazed and unfocused. I was taken in as usual and convinced that I would have this deranged creature on my hands for the rest of my life, but Marie-Claire, toughened by her suffering at Andrée's hands, was furious. "Elle n'est pas folle!" she cried, while I bent over Andrée, and Andrée shot Marie-Claire an unmistakable look of hate. Marie-Claire had been gathering her forces to act. The mad scene had been precipitated by a lunch that she insisted on having alone with me, a lunch at which we compared notes about Andrée and laughed hysterically. The day that Andrée announced that she was leaving, I drove her to the station so that she could catch the evening train to Paris, both of us pretending to a sadness that neither of us felt, and when I returned to the house to tell the incredulous Marie-Claire, we danced with joy for the first time in over a year. It was another reduction to the two of us together, but it did not last. Marie-Claire took off, beating her delirious wings, and I packed up everything again and crossed the ocean to Canada, with the same two dogs and a Breton cat. And so it was—in a nutshell—though you cannot squeeze lives into a nutshell. Perhaps, by being tried for fourteen years, Marie-Claire and I have proved that the bond between us is both elastic and indestructible and that it rests, with all our differences, on some strange communion of spirit rather than of flesh. We are both free now, not to leave each other, but to live our lives in the context of this odd fidelity.

Part Two
Dolly Lamb and Lily Briscoe

She could see it all so clearly, so commandingly, when she looked; it was when she took her brush in hand that the whole thing changed. It was in that moment's flight between the picture and her canvas that the demons set on her who often brought her to the verge of tears and made this passage from conception to work as dreadful as any down a dark passage for a child. Such she often felt herself — struggling against terrific odds to maintain her courage; to say: "But this is what I see," and so to clasp some miserable remnant of her vision to her breast, which a thousand forces did their best to pluck from her.

Virginia Woolf,
To the Lighthouse

Chapter Six

When I was thirty-five years old, before Barbara came to live with me in Wellfleet, my neighbours were Mary McCarthy and her husband, Bowden Broadwater, who had chosen to live in the same village as Mary's ex-husband, Edmund Wilson—a choice which would have profoundly shocked my mother, but which merely provoked endless gossip among the Wellfleetians. Had they made this choice because a beautiful old house was for sale there? Or was Mary looking for the subject matter for a new novel? In any case, she acquired both.

I met Mary McCarthy in Newport, where she and Bowden had spent several summers—and where I was under the wings of Leonid, the painter, and his wife, Sylvia Marlowe, the harpsichordist—in a big wooden house designed by Sullivan, overlooking antedeluvian grey rocks and the blue sea. Mary terrified me, for it was a time when her tongue was preternaturally sharp and her green eyes glinted dangerously, when the swift flicker of her smile would make you wonder whether or not she were friendly or ferocious. But we became friends, nevertheless, though I felt more like a timid household pet, and she and Bowden did their best to introduce me to their Newport friends, some of whom lived in palaces—"cottages," they were called— and with whom I felt as Lucy Stone does in the presence of

Ernesta Fanshawe in Charlotte Brontë's *Villette*. With these people, I felt that here lay the gulf between my family's discreet denials of money and their conspicuous pride in their money. The Newportians behaved like rich people, a fact which seemed to fascinate Mary and Bowden, not displease them as it displeased me. For Mary and Bowden, the Newportians were not threatening, but rather, subjects of literary interest and analysis. Just as during the awful period of my coming out in Philadelphia, I had been unable to disguise myself as a typical debutante; just as I listened with distaste to the chatter of the other girls in the ladies' room, as they powdered their noses and patted their hair in place and carefully smeared lipstick on their mouths, so too, I was disgusted by the superficial chitchat of the Newportians and was unable to answer the kind of questions they put to me. I even had the feeling that, had it not been for the protective presences of Mary and Bowden, these people would have torn my awkward and serious self to pieces.

I had had no intention of buying a house, but one day, I drove to Cape Cod with Bowden and Mary to see two houses that were close to each other and for sale. It was 1953—a time before Cape Cod began to sink under the weight of its summer population, when beautiful old houses could still be bought for a song. The two houses that we looked at were red and yellow and are still there surrounded by locusts, oaks and pines: the red house, higher up the hill, with a big box bush crowding the front door, and, at the kitchen door, a quince, whose red-orange flowers flaming in the sun proclaimed that spring had come, even before the shadbush in the woods sent up its white smoke signals; the yellow house, some two hundred feet away, halfway down the hill, screened from its more elegant and older neighbour by wild roses and blackberries. We fell in love with the two houses at first sight, and indeed, they were both irresistible, perfumed by the smell of box and the slightly mouldy cold air inside unheated houses which have spent a lonely winter. The yellow house was furnished. In fact, the beds were still made and elegant fawn-coloured flannel trousers and other clothes still hung in a closet. Mary and Bowden decided to buy the red house and I decided to buy the smaller yellow house, so we made haste to arrange the sale with Miss Freeman, the little limping real estate agent with a stentorian voice, who, as a high school teacher, was said (Bowden divulged this) to have slept with every boy student in her class. The red house immediately became known as "Mary McCarthy's house," just as later, when Mary sold it to me, it became known, after a decent interval, as "Mary Meigs' house." Mary and Bowden painted the panelling white, like fresh cake icing, and the walls, pale pink and the ghost of lemon yellow. They filled the rooms with graceful and formal antique furniture and fresh flowers—exotic flowers like ronunculas and anemones and freesia, which came from heaven knows where. The yellow house became a kind of temple for the objects I loved, while the red house, befitting its age (it was said to have been built in 1790), with its wide brick fireplace at a slight angle to the rest of the long living room, the uneven horizontals of its twenty-four inch floorboards and verticals of the corner timbers, which threw bookshelves completely out of kilter, became a dwelling worthy of Mary and Bowden, who made a work of art of their life, with *fêtes champêtres* and dinner parties which they spent days creating, and over which they presided brilliantly, often dressed in matching black and white. Their formality was like that of Colonial Britishers who dress for dinner in the jungle, and after their summers in Newport, Mary and Bowden aspired to a standard of perfection like that of the characters in Henry James' *Ivory Tower*, which was somewhat incongruous in Wellfleet, since it was peopled with bohemians.

Meantime, I lived in the yellow house with the worn furniture that had been there when I bought it, and gradually, augmented by antiques that I picked up on foraging expeditions — solitary orgies of snooping and discovery—or which I found on the village dump: such as a mahogany armchair and an old sea chest for which I made a cover. I spent hours scavenging on the beach and clung, like a miser, to my collection of sand dollars, fish vertebrae, the skulls of dead birds, and stones. My relation with Mary and Bowden continued to be friendly and apprehensive. I doubted Mary's affection, just as I was to later doubt Edmund's, after seeing her spent sleepless nights going over conversations and re-editing my part in them according to what I would

147

like to have said. I was haunted by the fear that she felt an obligation to invite me to the red house and I imagined discussions between her and Bowden about the extent of their responsibility toward me. As an exercise of pride, I invented excuses for not accepting their invitations and the fact that they were endlessly kind and helpful tortured my scrupulous and paranoid conscience. I was less afraid of Bowden than I was of Mary, and Bowden and I became comrades of a sort, but even this made me uneasy, for he spent hours spinning out the gossip of the entire community with a strange half-smile, his dinosaur eyes (Mary said he looked like a pterodactyl) magnified by thick lenses, watching me, it seemed, to see how I would react.

Bowden and I were bound together by a common secret which both of us took great pains to conceal. It was obvious to me that he was a homosexual, and obvious, no doubt, to Bowden that I was a Lesbian who was still in the closet — even though there was nothing to prove it. Homosexuals, as we know from Proust, have extrasensory means of recognizing each other. But Bowden, in the triumph of his marriage to Mary, extolled the wonders of heterosexual life while I listened, silently rebellious. He had the look of wanting to extract all the details of my life; of perhaps knowing them already. He was like a pelican digesting its fish and making a savoury mess of it, which it then regurgitates for the infant bird — in this case, Mary. Bowden acted as an extra pair of eyes and ears for Mary, I thought. While she sat writing in the little front room where itinerant clergymen used to sleep, with the circular bookcase turning on its stem like a Lazy Susan, with the arcane matter of her work, Bowden, when he wasn't painting or puttering away at the house, would be out gathering information for her and subjecting it to the digestive processes of his agile mind. When Bowden talked to me, I would feel myself slowly, very slowly, being swallowed and reconstituted.

While Bowden, with his eyes on me, talked lazily about heterosexual love, I found myself sliding toward one of my ritual tests, for he proposed himself as a mentor one night when Mary was away and we were having dinner together at my house. I prepared myself for the ordeal with two dry martinis and we went to bed. For me, it was over in seconds and I proved, at least to myself, that I wasn't frigid. But like so many things in life, like the radical action that I failed later to develop, the first proof meant nothing if it was followed by failure. I fell into a sleep induced by satisfied desire and alcohol, leaving Bowden to his own devices. I did not wake up until dawn, when I saw him stealing toward my bed. I had a headache and a sense of disgust with myself. I said urgently, "No, no, no!" as alarmed as if he had come to rape me, and I was grateful to him for going back to his own room and for his subsequent delicacy and forbearance. I had given him rich material for an enlarged portrait of me as a non-woman, afraid of sex; perhaps this was fed discreetly to Mary (without going into detail) and was useful to her when she made me into Dolly Lamb in *A Charmed Life*, her book about Wellfleet. Oddly enough, I had no feeling of having betrayed my friend. My experience with Bowden, I thought, could only have made Mary laugh the laugh that I liked and feared, that was somehow a medium of speech, or vice-versa, for she talked with a kind of fixed laugh, while her green eyes narrowed between black lashes until one could only see their malicious glimmer.

The two houses were linked by a single well with an ancient pump which was in the round cellar of the red house. This pump, with its indiscreet hawking and belching, disclosed to Mary and Bowden when I took a bath or flushed the toilet in the yellow house and it was ultimately the cause of tactful hints dispatched by them in my direction to the effect that I should sever the umbilical cord by having my own well dug and my own pump installed. To me, the pump was an odious robot bearing false witness against me (I, who was so careful about water), for how could they be sure that its testimony corresponded to my bath-taking and toilet-flushing? I was only too glad to shut it up by getting my own well, but I worried about the details that the pump had contributed to the portrait of me that I knew Mary and Bowden were constructing. I was sure they held anguished conferences over the problem of the pump and how to bring up the subject without hurting my feelings and invading my privacy. They were like that, worrying about my feelings, my solitude (which I enjoyed), and how to mitigate it; indeed, about every detail of my life. Their kindness to me had a double edge: it was a concern for my welfare, but it contained within it the plain suggestion that my welfare consisted in following their advice.

I had the feeling not only that they thought that I was infinitely malleable, but also, that I *wanted* to be transformed by them; it was as if they were fitting a ghostly skin over me that I could not shake off. A conversation comes back to me. They were discussing my choice of a smoke-grey sleeveless dress of pleated chiffon. "You've decided to become the kind of person who wears that kind of dress," said Bowden. "You've chosen your type." Everything in me surged up in protest; it was all wrong, this analysis. He had put the cart before the horse. I had chosen the dress, I explained, not in order to define myself, but because I liked it. "Exactly!" cried Bowden triumphantly, and my insides began to churn with a familiar turmoil. I couldn't bear it when people squeezed me into corners, reduced me to clichés. I had enough trouble supporting the severity of my own self-analysis and didn't need any outside help. Because I was mild and polite like everybody in my family, people thought I was waiting to be told you are this, you are that. My mildness was a smokescreen, like the smoke-grey dress which seemed so suitable, yet both Mary and Bowden seemed to have decided it was the whole truth. "If there was anybody else inside her," Mary says about Dolly Lamb, "it was a creature still more daunted and mild and primly scrupulous than the one the world saw."

A writer's witchcraft is at work in this long passage in the book where Mary, as though she had constructed a doll-fetish that was able to stick pins in itself, makes Dolly (me) conform to her real life view of me, the one I had sensed before she wrote the book. Dolly, a painter, has made friends with Sandy Gray, a free spirit, thrice-divorced, against whom she has been warned by Martha and John, the characters who correspond in the book to Mary and Bowden. (Mary McCarthy, too, assumed the identities of both Mary and Martha by choosing Martha as her pseudonym, adding, for good measure, the surname SINNOTT, for Martha in the book is obsessed by moral niceties, just as was the real

Mary.) Sandy drops in on Dolly, fluttering her timid soul, looks at her paintings and pronounces judgement. "Her work was sick, he told her—cramped with preciosity and mannerisms. Underneath he discerned talent, but it was crippled, like some poor tree tortured out of shape by a formal gardener. She needed to be bolder and freer." Then follows the crucial passage, in which Dolly analyzes herself, her efforts to "let herself go," and her repeated failures with a succession of teachers. "The leap forward, the breakthrough—never was accomplished. She parted from each master sadly, with the knowledge that she had disappointed him." At the end, Dolly blames her "teachers and well-wishers; *they* had promised miracles and then let her down." And she cries out to Sandy, "But I am precious. . .I'm inhibited. I'm afraid of life. I'm decadent. That is *me*. Why can't I paint that if I want to?"

"That is *me*." Before the book was written, I had already felt this terrible judgement without appeal settling over me—a judgement composed of circumstantial evidence. Mary and Bowden worked as a team from the outside in, piling up the observable details of people's lives and drawing their own conclusions. I remember another conversation about souls. Some people had souls and others hadn't, Bowden said, looking at me with his ambiguous smile. I knew he was thinking that he and Mary were among the few people with souls and had recognized this in themselves, just as the elect used to recognize themselves in the days of Cotton Mather. I felt with all the power of my being that I, too, had a soul, that all living creatures have a soul, but the fact that Mary and Bowden did not say so made me uneasy, and pride prevented me from asking. What if they said that my soul was still embryonic; what if they proposed themselves as midwives for the soul that they would have brought to birth by their benign influence, as a mother creates musical taste in an unborn baby by playing records of the great composers or by taking it to concerts?

How to prove, against the weight of evidence, that you are the person you feel yourself to be? And to what extent are you that ideal person forever racing ahead of the other touchy self who is ready to feel so puny and infinitely small, to turn so furiously on the arrogant self and reduce it to size? It seems to me that my life has been one long effort to induce these warring selves to live in harmony with each other; to become one, like lovers, and yet these selves still split apart without warning. When I first read Mary's book, it was as though I were nibbling imprudently at a mushroom, like Alice, and shrinking so suddenly that my chin knocked against my feet. For Mary mocked not only the outward Dolly: her preference for instant coffee (she had presented me with a coffee pot to correct this, for there were miniscule lapses in sensibility that bothered her sense of "correctness," as much as the pea under her mattress bothered the sleeping princess), her collection of shells and bones ("Stop hoarding!" Sandy Gray says to Dolly about these, "It's your own shit you're assembling there, in neat constipated little packages." And, as it turns out, Dolly is "given to constipation."). I minded less these little brushstrokes, even when they were false. I had never been constipated, for instance, but I saw how essential to Mary's sense of comedy it was to make Dolly Lamb all of a piece. If she hoarded shells, if her work was "cramped" and "crippled," it followed that she *must* be constipated. Freud himself had discovered the link between constipation and artists' blocks and Mary could not resist the temptation to elaborate on the anal theme when she said later of Dolly that she was "industrious, even in her pleasures, like a sober little girl making mud pies." I did not suffer either from the physical appearance of Dolly: "her neat dish face," her body "curiously flattened out, like a cloth doll that has been dressed and redressed by many imperious mistresses." None of this mattered as much as it mattered that Mary seemed to want to quench my faith in myself, that she activated the dormant seeds of doubt that made me so ready to hate myself and my work. And the turn of the screw was that it is not Mary McCarthy-Martha who judges Dolly's work, but her spokesman, Sandy Gray, who has the virtue of honesty. "After the first day, he never glanced at her paintings; as soon as he got to know her, his abrupt honest mind had simply dropped the idea that she could ever do anything serious." And at the trial where Dolly testifies in favour of Sandy, she says, "He hates any kind of dishonesty or compromise; that's why he doesn't like my painting," thus sticking a few more pins into the doll-fetish.

By the time Mary's book came out, she and Bowden had left Wellfleet after having spent a triumphant year in the old house, which took on some of the atmosphere of Parnassus. The gods of literature and learning had wandered freely there. Once, Mary brought Robert Lowell to the yellow house and insisted that I show him a landscape, with which I was struggling, in the little shed where I worked. I refused to get the painting, with the conviction that it was unworthy to be seen, and Mary, like a mother with a timid child, set out resolutely in the direction of the shed, with me in her wake, protesting. It was a strange fact that when someone I respected looked at my work, I suffered a shame similar to that of a person who has been stripped naked and set on a block to be sold as a slave. Robert Lowell looked at my landscape and murmured something which seemed to have come from his perception of my suffering and I suffered more than ever. I was like Lily Briscoe, "who's braced herself to stand the awful trial of someone looking at her picture."

Later, I thought of this incident in the light of Mary's book and the contempt for my work that she expressed through Sandy Gray. The feelings that I felt and my reaction to the incident spread in me like poison. It was as though all of Mary's victims in Wellfleet had been struck down with a wasting disease. I saw them, pale and shaken, unsure of themselves, unsure of everybody else (for this awful image of themselves might now be accepted as the true one), and I dragged myself about in a state of doubt and self-loathing for a long time. It meant nothing to me that Dolly Lamb was the nicest person in the book (with the exception of Martha-Mary) and that Martha says to her, "I love you, Dolly." This "I love you, Dolly" was propitiatory, like Mary's smiles—either that or it was supposed to give her the right to be cruel. Her choice of alter egos for me seemed to be part of her exercise of transforming power, for hadn't she said to me that I reminded her of Emmeline in Elizabeth Bowen's *To the North*—Emmeline, who wasn't even an artist like Dolly Lamb, but floundered through life in a charming, near-sighted way and worked in a tourist agency? Was Mary like my Aunt Bessie, saying to me, "You're just an ordinary American girl"? "You're a

153

good little child in your pinafore," says Sandy Gray to Dolly Lamb. "You love Mummy and Daddy and Nanny and little brother and sister and your teddy bear. Some day you may grow up to be a woman." He has guessed from the prudish way in which Dolly lives that she has never been in love with a man. Ha! So *that* was it! Re-reading the book, I pounced triumphantly on the hoary old idea, so cheerfully sexist, implicit in Sandy's discovery. The love of a man—this panacea for all women artists' hang-ups—was as loudly and constantly advertised as Dr. Scholl's corn plasters or Burma Shave, though I could think of many a woman artist who had loved men without the promised results. It was sad to find that Mary-Sandy, like Bowden with his hymns to heterosexual love, believed in the liberating power of the penis, just as though the Brontë sisters, Emily Dickinson, Jane Austen or Rosa Bonheur had never existed. What a wonderful surprise it would have been if Dolly had said to Sandy, "No, but I've loved women!" Sandy would doubtless have answered that loving women was just a prelude to loving men, or a poor substitute, since this idea is one of the beliefs of every "normal" man.

The truth about Dolly Lamb was that she did not know whether or not she was a virgin. She had had an inconclusive experience with a man, interrupted by a sailor, "on a boat... behind a stack of steamer chairs.... The older she got, the more men hesitated to tamper with her, because they thought she was a virgin, and she could not correct this impression, because she was not sure." This muddle in Dolly's head makes me laugh, for it seems like the ultimate refinement, the final brushstroke (after Dolly's state of constipation) in Mary's picture of a person who was almost totally repressed. This information about Dolly Lamb must have come from my recounting to Bowden (faithfully transmitted to Mary) a tale from my life in Washington, during the war, when as a WAVE, I lived in my mother's house. My WAVE friend who had introduced me to sex simultaneously encouraged me to complete my education by making love with a sailor named Jerry, a gentle young man who had become our friend. One evening, Jerry came to the house and we climbed the stairs to the "nursery" on the third floor, lighted a fire in the fireplace and began to embrace each other on a worn old buffalo skin. We were interrupted by a knock on the door. It was my older brother, the self-appointed guardian of my virginity, who said that he thought he smelled smoke. We were still fully dressed in our respective uniforms, but we moved guiltily away from each other. After my brother left, we resumed our embraces half-heartedly and he reappeared, still smelling smoke. Hot-faced and cranky, I was unable to say, "For God's sake, will you leave us alone!" for at the time, I was taken in by the earnestness of my brother's concern and I decided that fate was against the loss of my virginity, at least with Jerry. It was six years before I gathered my courage again and had a genuine love affair with another gentle but tormented young man. This time, I might, if I had been a young bride in the primitive Italian village where the affair took place, have hung up the sheet the next morning for all to see. Instead, I stole with it to the kitchen, where there was nothing but a stone sink and a bucket of water that had been brought from the piazza, and scrubbed with might and main, as fruitlessly as Lady Macbeth, for the next day I saw Pepinella, my ferocious little cook, with her near-sighted black eyes, bending close to the bed and scrutinizing the sheet, which was still damp.

The experience of actually losing my virginity, which took place a year or so before Mary's reign in the red house, evidently had not turned me into a "woman" in Sandy Gray's sense of the term, because this would have been visible to Mary. As for the moment when Edmund horrified me with his question, "Aren't you really a sort of Lesbian?" that was yet to come and I was still resolutely hiding my head in the sand like an ostrich. Though Mary and Bowden had many ways of knowing through overlapping friends that I was a "sort-of," they never gave any proof of knowing and I decided that Dolly Lamb's sexual ambiguity was a reflection of Mary's unsureness. Or was it her discretion? In this one instance had she decided to withhold her power to kill? I think so now, remembering the time when, with her drawling chuckle, she had said of two friends of mine, a woman of fifty and her younger friend, "I saw them sitting on the beach and they looked like a couple of old lovers." I flared out at her in response, "Why do you have to watch people like a cat and pounce on them?" and cried bitterly afterwards when I was alone. I had guarded my own secret, but had given it away by so fiercely defending my friends, even when, in her candour, Mary had spoken the truth. This was the year before Barbara came to live with me, an event which was a kind of public proclamation, but in spite of which, I continued to believe that no one used the word "Lesbian" about either of us. I had once been called "Schizzy Mary" by a homosexual friend in New York, and it was years before I understood that what he was talking about was my tendency to think "I am not *really* what I am." To have been a Lesbian in Mary's book would have been much worse than not knowing whether or not I had lost my virginity, and in my craven way, I was grateful to her for staying her hand.

Andrée, too, made me a character in one of her books, a book of vengeance, which both Marie-Claire and I refused to read. Certain friends read it though, and we were able to judge its deadliness by their reactions. "There are always two sides to every question," said one friend, but we would not read the book, even in order to defend ourselves, and no doubt, in our friends' minds, the ghostly fictional selves are still attached to us and always will be. Mary McCarthy composed Dolly Lamb of truths and falsehoods—even generous falsehoods. In a passage of the book which makes my head reel with its contradictions and tantalizing flattery, the one which begins, "I love you, Dolly," Martha continues, "'You're so loyal...Forgive us for bullying you.' 'All my friends bully me,' said Dolly cheerfully. 'Anyway, Martha *I* admire you...But you do make me feel inferior. You always have. When you're here I burn the muffins.'" And Martha replies, "Honestly, I'd much rather you didn't burn them. I love perfection in my friends. I don't grudge you the seashells or having a better character than I have. It makes me happy." Am I, reading the book, supposed to believe that Mary McCarthy, in person, is speaking through Martha, who has said to Dolly, "I like your shells" or through Sandy when he says that they are her own shit which she's assembling? I love Martha and hate Sandy, but since I am always prone to disbelieve those whom I love when they praise me; I tend to accept the harsh judgement of Sandy, whom I suspect of being the judge in Mary. At no time, be it noted, does Martha give an opinion of Dolly Lamb's paintings. She leaves that hatchet job to Sandy!

But did Mary expect to be taken so seriously, to have to cope with friends who pulled on their fictional alter egos like body stockings and were then unable to wriggle out of them, who, with their guilt feelings and pained reactions, made her think she had been correct in her analyses? Did she know that I wasn't mild inside, wasn't always loyal, had, at times, a terrible character, and that, above all, I resented being bullied? Did she really think that I had a better character than she? Was she saying, "Please be loyal, no matter how I treat you," or was there a Dolly Lamb in her mind who had nothing to do with me, who developed as a comic exercise that led where it listed?

The reader is probably thinking at this point that I was an idiot to have been haunted by Dolly Lamb, to have been tortured by the question, "To what extent did Mary mean her to be me?" But it was as if my self-esteem were hung as a kind of forfeit around Mary's neck. Having my self-esteem gave her the power to shatter me or to preserve my life— and I seemed, then, to have the ability only to see myself through her eyes. Dolly Lamb was like a confirmation of my worst fears, the personification of the hateful seen self, and, for a time, she silenced the proud, even arrogant person inside me, whose stubborn certainties kept me going.

Chapter Seven

Mary, with her unerring accuracy, had hit everything that was vulnerable in me: the indecisiveness of my life, the tightness of my work, my prudish habits. She had even let fly an arrow in the direction of Dolly's money and stirred up the old guilt in me. "Perhaps it was her money, Martha had lightly observed; perhaps she [Dolly] was like the rich young man in the Bible who could not accomplish his breakthrough unless he sold all he had and gave to the poor." I search my memory; had I ever said to Mary that my father was haunted by the story of the rich young man and that I, too, had allowed the story to trouble my conscience? It seems to me that we never discussed it, or the fact that, in the Bible, Jesus elaborates on the attitude of the rich young man toward his money. "How hard it is for them that trust in riches to enter into the Kingdom of God!" The key words are "trust in riches," which, I think, means to take them for granted, like the rich young man who was virtuous in every way, but who clung to his "great possessions." My attitude toward money is a mixture of thankfulness and uneasiness; of possessiveness and a wish to purify myself by giving it away. To me, money only belongs to you if you have earned it and there is something shameful about unearned income, reflected in the inevitable question, "Do you make a living from your work?" Even in my good years, I have never made a living from my work, but I hate to confess this. I am glad to be able to say that I have had a teaching job at Bryn Mawr College and was in the Navy, but I can still be accused of never having *had* to earn a living, and consequently, of having a less professional attitude toward my work, of not pushing myself, etc. I have friends with inherited incomes, artists who are sure of themselves in some way that I am not sure of myself, for I have been constantly buffeted by guilt of one kind or another and I have always been tortured by the idea that people thought (as Martha thinks about Dolly Lamb) that my money prevented me, that it would always prevent me, from being a serious artist. I endeavour to think about Georges Sand, Byron, Toulouse-Lautrec, Berthe Morisot, Degas, Henry James, and a great many others who never had to worry about money. They all succeeded in becoming great artists in spite of their easeful lives. I knew one thing: that if you had money, you had to tie yourself to the mast, like Ulysses, and shut out the voices—not of sirens, but of your own friends. I have had to cast off, little by little, not my "trust in riches," but my mistrust of myself. I started painting seriously too late to acquire the confidence that people who have started very young have, the kind of confidence that Marie-Claire, for example, has as a writer. Just as I was, for a long time, a "sort of" Lesbian, I was a "sort of" artist, working steadily, but with a quaking and touchy heart.

I remember times when painter friends would come to my studio to look at my work, often on one of those summer days, golden and blue like a day in Italy, when the sun would beat down on the scorched grass, still green in the shade of the locust trees, and turn the front of the studio a flaming rose-red, a day which I would begin in high spirits, until the session in the studio when I would feel creeping up in me the sickness of apprehension. The paintings I liked in the morning would change in the afternoon light, and as my painter friend would look silently at them, I would begin to see through his critical eye, see all the weakness of construction, my ignorance of space, an overworking of the canvas until the colours had gone dead, or an unresolvable beginning. It had been like this for years: the gulf between the marvellous powers I felt latent in myself and

160

my expression of them. My painter friend would say something perfectly innocent, such as, "You seem to like cerulean blue" (though this could be a weapon, as when Kuniyoshi at the Art Students' League, said angrily, "Why do you always use raw umber? Raw umber is an *old-maid colour!*") and everything inside me would turn to dust and ashes. "How long have you been painting?" "Have you ever looked at Cézanne's watercolours?" Questions like these, which were asked hesitantly, which were often all the friend had to say, contained awful implications: that I had just started painting or that I knew nothing about painting watercolours. I was just as tortured, if not more so, by total silence in which the implications were limitless. The only acceptable reaction, I would think, as I nursed my hurt feelings afterwards, was unmitigated praise. But unmitigated praise provoked a perverse disbelief. Once Edmund, looking at a painting of dried autumn flowers I had been fighting with, suddenly said, "You're a great painter!" But Edmund knew nothing about painting after 1900 and enjoyed saying that he couldn't stand Cézanne and Matisse. I took his liking of my work to be sentimental, but I was pleased when he bought a little landscape in one of my shows. When he got the bill, he summoned me to his house. The bill was twice as much as he expected, he said angrily, and all my pleasure dissolved in my humiliation. I wondered what he expected me to do about it; if he thought, perhaps, that I should offer to pay half, but I said nothing, feeling scared and stubborn. Years later, I saw my painting stuck in a dark corner of the study of his ancestral house and I felt ashamed of it. He was right, I thought, it wasn't worth what he paid for it. When I see my paintings in people's houses, I sometimes feel a surprising little current of pleasure, though, more often, I want to rip them off the wall and either take them home to make a needed change or destroy them on the spot. It gives me some comfort to read that Soutine was the same way and that his friends had to hide his paintings before he came to visit them, for fear that he'd make off with them.

There had been enough truth in what Sandy Gray said about Dolly Lamb's paintings to make me shrink into one of my states of shame, though I balked at the words "her work was sick." I had studied with Leonid, whose palette was a marvellous harmony of greys, light blues and greens, whose work was a serene ode in praise of sky and still water and the primitive work of fishing and farming that still goes on in the far corners of the world. He painted steadfastly through that thankless period when it was thought of as old-fashioned to be anything but abstract. The beauty of his work was more evident than ever when he died, for it was at a time when the pendulum had swung back and the gods of taste permitted a painter to paint whatever he pleased. Under Leonid's influence, I painted on a grey or brown ground—mushrooms, chestnuts, oyster and clam shells, or fruit (Mary and Bowden bought a little painting of crabapples). I painted slowly and carefully, sitting close to my easel and using fine sable brushes, so that each picture was almost a *trompe l'oeil*. I had the idea that this disciplined way of working was a preparation for something freer. My problem was that I didn't paint, *really* paint, for I was apt to yield to the temptation of seeing outline instead of volume. Even twenty years later, when I was writing to Barbara from Brittany, I still had the same problem. "Leonid came...lovely man. He helped me with the little paintings I'm doing now—not good, but I'm trying to *paint* very simply. 'Don't *draw*,' says L." I came to realize that great painters, like Cézanne or Van Gogh, painted even when they were drawing, and that their drawings, with their perfect sense of formal relationships, were paintings in one colour. My drawings were composed of lines; I realized this when I tried to translate them into colour and form. Even when I made little pencil notations all over my landscape sketches: "sky lighter than water," "darker," "brown-grey," "pink-orange," etc., I was despairingly aware of my ignorance of how colours determine form and space. Some people seem to be born painters, with an instinct for knowing which colour to put next to which, but I seem to have been born almost colour-blind. I began with the idea that painting or drawing meant to paint or draw what was in front of your eyes—in other words, to copy. (In fact, to "copy" or "to take a likeness" used to mean to "paint," at least in the novels of Jane Austen.) As a child, I made drawings and watercolours of flowers, people and landscapes, rather in the manner of my two grandmothers or any Victorian young lady who was learning one of the genteel arts. At school, no one talked about form or space, or even about old-fashioned perspective; in art class, our little exercises consisted of pasting identical tulips on identical pieces of yellow or red paper. When I was twelve or so, I copied photographs of horses, and pen and ink illustrations by Howard Pyle for *King Arthur and His Knights.* For a long time, I dreamt in black and white (I later decided that black and white films have a special meaning because they are the colours of so many dreams). Perceiving colour at last was, for me, an awakening that simultaneously released dreams, like marvellous paintings unable to make the leap into conscious life. I was under the illusion that if you put one bright colour next to another, it would work, not knowing how colours modify or kill or heighten each other, not even knowing the difference between warm and cool colours. My choices were not determined by the laws of colour, nor by what I saw (always copying) or by guesswork. I was always puzzled to see that sometimes the painting was alive, but more often than not, it was dead, since I hadn't the slightest idea of what made it live or die. Why couldn't I be like Van Gogh or Matisse or any of the other painters I loved? It still surprises me that it took me so long to learn even the rudiments of painting; that the closer I got to good painters, the less I seemed to be able to absorb of their science, that all my ecstatic looking in museums created, not the foundation for my own work, but total confusion, for there seemed to be a million directions in which to go, and I could not decide who my influences would be. If only I had known what it meant to paint, I could have taken what is fundamental from each of my gods (*i.e.,* the laws of colour and form) and still have remained myself. Even now, after thirty-five years of painting and looking at the work of other painters, I feel that the central truths of painting are still out of reach, that my hit-or-miss methods, with their relatively low percentage of real successes, are the result of insufficient understanding of a beauty just out of reach. I perceive it, but it is not accessible. It is like the garden that Alice sees through the "small passage not much larger than a rat-hole," "the loveliest garden you ever saw." When I went years ago to see the Cone

163

Collection in Baltimore and the Barnes Collection in Merion and looked with concentrated rapture at certain little Matisse landscapes, it seemed easy to paint light with warm colour, shadow with cool colour, or simply to paint with different tones of the same colour. I would go back to my studio, just as I sometimes came back from evenings at the ballet, feeling in myself the power to leap lightly into space. And just as I would fall in the midst of an attempted *entrechat* or a soaring leap, like Prince Igor, so too, I would fall out of the illusion that it was easy to paint like Matisse, having perhaps made a flying start on a canvas, and would be confronted by the same old problems and the knowledge that the lovely garden was still out of reach.

After I graduated from college, I studied cubism with Karl Knaths at the Phillips School in Washington, and, after the war, went to Hans Hoffman's school in New York for six weeks. Both were great painters who instilled the principles of positive and negative space, the push and pull necessary in every painting, abstract or not, into the heads of many painters who are now well-known. But there was something about my literal way of seeing that prevented me from understanding space, even though I won a prize—a big paintbrush—for a painting that Knaths helped me with. It was like the essays I wrote in school about Keats and Shelley, or the one about Chekhov that won a prize at college; I wrote these papers with a surface intelligence that had not penetrated the mystery of Keats, Shelley or Chekhov, any more than my painting showed any real understanding of cubism. I remember when I was a senior at college, I was asked to take over a class in English literature when the professor was sick, and how, shaking in every limb, I babbled on about Yeats without hearing a word I was saying. On the strength of this somnabulist's performance, I was asked to come back and teach, and it was only then that, hungrily re-reading Yeats, I had a sense of the difference between seeming to understand and really understanding. Over and over again during my life, I have experienced understanding in this sudden and marvellous way after a period when my mind has seemed to be as deaf, dumb and blind as Helen Keller was before she grasped the meaning of the letters "w-a-t-e-r" traced in her hand. These awakenings to Yeats,

Rilke, Gerard Manley Hopkins (who had been an enigma to me); to Bach; to a whole series of painters whose work had left me cold (Mondrian, for example) filled me with manic joy.

But the concept of space in painting was harder for me to grasp than the poetry of Gerard Manley Hopkins and even when I could say I understood it, I could not put my understanding to use in my own painting. I remember a woman student in Hoffman's class, who suddenly cried out one day, "I understand space! I understand space!" and my temptation to laugh at her. Hoffman would go from student to student like a magician with a charcoal wand. He would rub out lines, dash his broad thumb over other lines; he would make lightning stabs at the paper and the drawing would begin to live in space. It would set up an energetic pushing and pulling that I could not arrive at without his magician's intervention. I think of the genius of Hoffman, which formed a whole generation of painters; I think about the energy pouring out of his big, serene body, his blue eyes and his jolly laugh which could bring the dead to life. Did I learn from him or from the other painters that I worked with and loved: Leonid, Karl Knaths, Henry Varnum Poor and Anne Poor? The first summer of my life with Barbara, I studied at the Skowhegan School, where the student and teaching body have included the best painters and sculptors in the United States. Though I had been painting for nine years, I felt like a beginner there and I wrote despairing letters to Barbara. "A criticism by Mr. Gonzalez. He said, 'It becomes monotonous when you make all your brushstrokes the same way. Later in your career you can do it, but at this stage. . . .' This depressed me so — to be always at the very beginning. It was like the first days again, but worse. There are awfully good painters here, much younger than I am, and they've been painting a much shorter time. I look at my inept little landscapes and my heart sinks." It was always this way, the sense of not belonging to the company of "awfully good painters." But, as usual, my drawings were better. "Yesterday afternoon Mr. Gonzalez took us (the landscape class) far away to a roaring river and great jagged rocks and I drew drawings full of fury about rocks and he came along and said — 'What a bee-oot-i-full drawing. But like Leonardo. But I'm excited by this

165

drawing. Really excited.' I couldn't believe my ears, having been on the verge of throwing the drawings into the river." And so it was for years that other painters praised my drawings, sometimes saying with awful finality when I showed them all my work, "I like your drawings," so that my paintings ceased to exist. There was one painter in particular, Wallace Putnam, who had the power to raise or lower my morale by a positive or negative word. *He* knew how to paint, with the lovely freshness and sureness of *real* painting. He made me feel humble—too humble, according to Barbara. He always knew exactly what he liked and why, and he would often pick out something I had discarded, something I thought was unfinished, and praise it, while the things I liked would be consigned to outer darkness. Barbara would say, "He just likes the paintings that remind him of his own work," but I bowed to his judgement, even when I could not understand it. Wally did not like a certain kind of semi-abstraction, a half-baked tribute to cubism that was à la mode in the fifties; his own work was closer to Monet in his very late paintings, when one sees the nervous calligraphy of his brush-strokes on bare patches of canvas. Sometimes I yielded to the temptation to force a canvas into one of these semi-abstractions, fiddling at it until I destroyed the last vestige of life and had to throw the whole thing away. Wally gave these paintings short shrift; that was to be expected, but he had the power, too, to pierce my uncertainties and expose my weaknesses.

I had a show in Boston in 1957 where I sold one picture and got excellent reviews. "Her compositions are spirited, expressive of the mood and her colour is peculiarly feminine, soft, lyrical, knowing," said the *Boston Globe*. "The transference of the idea is spontaneous and unimpeded," said the *Christian Science Monitor*, "as though manipulation of brush and colours were completely subordinated to direct expression." "She is a major abstract-expressionist talent who presents a glowing lyric view of nature with a wonderful economy of means and opulence of tone," said the *Boston Sunday Herald*. I was so far from being an abstract-expressionist that I wondered if this critic knew anything about painting, but for once, my intentions had coincided with what people saw and I went about for a time in a happy daze, even though Wally still looked at my work with his terrible all-seeing eyes.

As time went on, I had a modest success in Boston, but I failed dismally in New York when I had my first show there. I had begun to do big family portraits—"life-portraits," I called them—in which my parents were represented from childhood to old age, about which Wally remarked that I was not "ready" to tackle something so difficult. Despite his warning, in my heart I continued to like them, and I had daydreams about the reviews I would get for them in New York. I was back in Wellfleet when I opened up *The New York Times* and read that my paintings were "arch and efforted," though my drawings (again!) were "another matter." It was characteristic of me to swallow the bitterest criticism and let it poison my whole system, while I rejected whatever encouragement was given. I took little comfort from the review in the *Herald Tribune* which said, "So far she displays more daring than discernment in her self-assured garish and oversized family portraits and other figure compositions. However, there is promise in her loose yet precise linear characterizations and in the human warmth with which she tackles her subject." I could only hear in my mind the words, "arch and efforted," endlessly repeating themselves; to every reader of the art page of the *Times*, to all my friends, my work was now "arch and efforted," for how could they resist the persuasive power of these two insinuating words? "Efforted," I might have digested; it was "arch," this horrible word, so far from my intentions, so destructive in its mincing brevity, that made me feel naked and ashamed. But hadn't Wally expressed misgivings about the family paintings and said, like the *Times* critic, that my drawings were "another matter"? It was precisely the praise of my drawings that made the words, "arch, efforted, garish," seem so offensive. The ominous silence of my painter friends set up hollow echoes in my soul. In my state of desolation, waiting for the exhibition to end and for the final word to come that no paintings had been sold, I had the correct presentiment that I would be booted out of my New York gallery with an embarrassed explanation by my dealer (how well I knew this metamorphosis from a welcoming enthusiast to a person with shifty eyes, with a surface as smooth as a mountain made of polished glass; and my own metamorphosis from weightlessness and light-stepping at first to someone whose cells seemed to be filled with a black heavy fluid, whose tongue could scarcely utter articulate words, who shuffled along like an old woman). A note came from Alex Katz, a painter whom I respected as much as I respected Wally, saying that my work reminded him of Munch. These unexpected words were like the sudden descent of an archangel and the light touch of his wings. Wasn't it enough that one good painter should like my work? Didn't it make up for all the rest? Didn't it matter that Barbara was a tower of strength, that she knocked down every one of my self-deprecating arguments, suggesting that the *Times* critic perhaps had had a hangover or had quarrelled with his wife, that it didn't matter whether or not you sold paintings, or whether or not you had shows in New York? It *did* matter, I insisted, wishing that it didn't. Barbara's invariable words about my work were that it was "truly beautiful." But just as later I was to think that Marie-Claire praised my work because she knew nothing about painting, I thought that Barbara praised it because she loved me and wanted to get me out of my Slough of Despond. When I was wallowing in this Slough, I turned everything against myself and snapped at her or played my mournful argument: "Can't you understand that a painter's image of herself is based on a modicum of appreciation by *unknown* people?" For Barbara was always trotting out our faithful and generous friends as witnesses for the defence, and I always replied that the only reliable witnesses were strangers.

It was my first and last one-man show in New York, but I continued to exhibit in Wellfleet and Boston. The number of sales in my shows dwindled to zero and my Wellfleet dealer went through *his* metamorphosis. I found myself with no gallery at all. Until the coming of Marie-Claire, I stopped painting for a while and had an agreeable period of time making toys and little sculptures out of old shingles and beef marrow bones that I boiled and bleached. But I continued to draw, making many drawings of flowers, marshes and dunes. I decided to wait until painting would become a joyful experience for me, instead of the torment that it was. I decided that my determined attitude, working doggedly day after day at a fixed time, furious if I was interrupted, was all wrong and that it would produce nothing but "efforted" paintings. The word "efforted" was exact, I thought, when applied to all those paintings I had worked on when not in a state of grace; and grace was that seeming absence of effort that I found common to all great art. It was that mind "moving on silence," as Yeats said, like a "long-legged fly upon the stream." Wally, who was interested in Zen, aspired to the state of the Zen archer who looses his arrow without thought; Wally was always talking about the fatal effects of too much thinking and deploring my too-busy brain. And he was right, I thought, in the sense that thinking closes the door on intuition, in the artist who lies deep in our dreaming selves, whose vision is more accurate than our waking vision. Now that I know that the brain is divided into rational and dreaming halves, I reflect that my brain is much too dominated by the rational half which meddles with the dreamer and prevents me from fully existing except in dreams. I have dreamt marvellous paintings that fade to a confusion of dim colours when I wake. And even in dreams, I am bullied by my rational self, who interposes anxieties, doubts and terrors, who clamps the fetters of consciousness on the dreamer.

Chapter Eight

For years I have written down my dreams and have tried to unlock their secrets. What do they tell me about myself, about my artist's blocks? Why have I been able to remember dreams, but not make use of their extraordinary visual vocabulary, as painters such as Redon and Max Ernst did, whose rational and dreaming selves were all of a piece. I have always marvelled at the accuracy of dream symbols and the immediate translation of complex states of being into the visual. Till we analyze these spontaneous images, undistorted by reason, we have only a dim idea of those fragile aspects of ourselves which, in waking life, are in continuous peril. I have had innumerable dreams of being robbed, of being tracked or menaced, or impeded from acting. An example: "I set antiques," I wrote in my notebook, "including a blue and white pitcher, on the ground in obscurity and they instantly disappear or they have been stolen. I am furious. A man in tattered clothes comes out of a door and I tear off his clothes, thinking my things are hidden under them. Instead, I see that around his arms and legs, he is wearing tight-fitting leather straps with buckles." The images of this dream flicker with meaning: the precious pitcher (I actually own a blue and white antique pitcher), the clarity of the colours of life and their disappearance (a failure of vision, of memory, a sexual failure? — for

171

my dream images often stand for the sum of my anxieties), the man in the tattered clothes (like me, ravaged by these same anxieties), and the terrible straps, like the ones used on an electric chair.

I long to use the lessons of my dreams to feel free of anxiety and paint better. What a waste of time it seems to be reiterating the same old messages when you could be putting your imagination to better use. But wasn't it still an exercise of the imagination to think of so many ways of saying the same thing? "By the way," I said to Barbara in a letter, "I had a most interesting dream about snakes. In some strange way, I was painting with them—incorporating them as pigment into a painting. But one got loose and fastened its jaws on my wrist—hard. I could feel its teeth and became terrified and shook it off with a great jerk—and woke up." Many painters have said that painting is a sexual act and I have often felt a sensual current run through me when I attack a painting with particular vigour. Obviously, this dream expressed my fear, both of sex and of letting my sexual energies express themselves in painting. I have had many dreams of this kind in which sex was intermingled with painting, or associated with violence, which had to do with the loss of my virginity or the loss of my inspiration—I hardly know which. "In dark streets, no pocketbook, I am looking for the Museum of Modern Art. Two black youths start to pursue me. I run. They knock me down. They take a sort of Indian cape (sari?) that I have in my hand and I get away." In the waking life of my painting, I was unable to find the "Museum of Modern Art" and what inspiration I had (the sari) seems constantly to have been snatched away from me. In my dreams, Wallace Putnam, the painter who, in waking life, would throw me into torments of anxiety, takes the role of kindly mentor, and my anxiety is personified by someone else. "At an exhibition, lots of people; on the wall, a drawing of mine and a self-portrait in colour—both very good. Wally and Miss McCantz are there; Wally tries to tell me how much he likes the drawing and Miss McCantz drowns him out. He goes away furious." Miss McCantz was a refined and virtuous lady from Charlestown, South Carolina, who wore a black velvet ribbon around her neck and not only had a plural "can't" in her name, but also exuded "can't"s as a flower exudes perfume; she was a friend of our mother's who had been chosen to be our chaperone when, at seventeen, my sister and I went to Switzerland to learn French. In this dream, all my feelings about Wally and my own work were concentrated in a little psychodrama: Wally's praise of my drawings (but not the self-portrait, be it noted); my negative reaction, in the form of Miss McCantz; and my fury, for the fury was really in *me*. All the things that constrained or threatened me—the leather straps, the biting snake, the black youths, the multiple CAN'Ts—all these things set up a fearful oscillation between my conscious and unconscious selves. I dreamt repeatedly about giving recitals (I used to play the flute): "I give a solo recital, playing either the flute or the violin (interesting that I can't remember which). In the second half of the dream, I fall asleep and wake up to see people leaving the hall. I have taken off my skirt and am putting it on again. Someone says, 'You played beautifully,' but I know the whole thing has been a disaster." This is a dream not only about my ambiguous sexual identity (am I playing a male flute or a female violin?), but also about every kind of failure that I have had, including the failure of old age with its awful mental lapses.

The dreamer in me also dramatizes my alternating feelings of arrogance and inferiority. In my dreams, Mary McCarthy often plays the part of the person who makes me feel inferior. I sit at her feet, am silenced by her, am in a play with her in which I forget my lines and have to go to the bathroom. In another dream, she kisses me passionately on the mouth and I think with pleasure that we love each other and that people will talk about "the two Mary's." Mary, in dreams, plays not herself, but her power to reduce my sense of worth and remind me that happiness is shortlived. In the same way, when I dream about Pierre Elliott Trudeau, he gives me a "quick little French kiss," but he is irritated when I say to him, "Have a good Prime Minister's day!" Oddly enough, my dreams about John F. Kennedy and Robert Kennedy are unspoiled by any reprimand; I used to converse with them like brothers and they would even ask my political advice. No doubt, these were dreams about my real brothers and the relationship I longed to have with them.

173

I am ready to take on anyone who insists that all dreams are an effort by the subconscious to make unpleasant truths palatable, that they are disguises for what the conscious mind won't admit. In my opinion, dreams make unpleasant truths much *more* unpleasant; in fact, the dreamer takes such sadistic pleasure in torturing me that my dreams often cast a shadow over my waking self. If I am really the person my dreams tell me I am, it is a wonder that I get through a single day. The dreamer is supercharged, like bottled gas, and one should control dreams, let them escape in a benign form. Otherwise, like a gas stove, they explode in your face and singe your hair and eyebrows. I told one of my flute dreams to a professor friend of mine who was steeped in Freud — a dream in which the end piece of my flute was lost and I could not play. To my friend, it was simply a dream about penis envy and about being a frustrated Lesbian (she thinks that all Lesbians are frustrated); to me, it was a direct translation of every kind of fear that I have about failure, including the familiar experience of not being able to play the flute. The flute, like the pocketbook, which, depending on the dream, contains my keys, glasses, passport, registration or *carte de séjour*, was a portmanteau image that could carry many meanings. I think of dream imagery in general as a concentrated visual and psychological shorthand, a language which, in its most primitive form, makes no use of words at all. The eyelids of foetuses in the womb are fluttered by dreams and I believe that unborn minds are already stocked with millions of inherited images, ready to attach themselves after birth to physical and mental states.

There is another state, akin to dreaming, but still conscious, the state of hallucinating, which, if harnessed, could enrich waking life. Before I go to sleep, I am often able to summon up a parade of images which tumble over one another: grotesque faces, sliding one into the next, like the faces in Leonardo's notebooks (not, I believe, because I have seen them in Leonardo, but because they are part, as Jung said, of the collective unconscious), brightly-lit figures in costumes, marvellous old cities that speed by before I can capture any image and remember it precisely. Henry Miller speaks in *Sexus* of this state of hallucinating, "before sleep, just as the eyelids close down over the retina and the unbidden images begin their nocturnal parade." I have read that both human beings and monkeys stretch out their hands to try to catch an invisible something if a certain part of the brain is stimulated and I believe that images crowd animal as well as human minds. I think that creativity is innate, even in invertebrates, and that the same subconscious forces inspire a seashell to invent its pattern as inspire a painter to paint abstractly, or a member of a primitive tribe to paint his face with geometrical zigzags. In human beings and perhaps in many animals, the power to create images is contained in those semiconscious and unconscious states which are not censored by reason. Dream imagery has inspired art, religion, myth, science and psychology, and cannot be shrunk, as Freud shrinks it, to the confines of one subject, sex, which merely inspires a part of its rich vocabulary. Freud believed that the censor lies in the unconscious and is responsible for dream disguises; I believe that the censor is the conscious refusal to understand the dazzling symbols of one's dreams. Indeed, I become aggressive in the defence of this idea, and, five or six years ago, having read a volume of Simone de Beauvoir's autobiography, a chapter of which was devoted to dreams she professed not to understand, I wrote a five page analysis of them and sent it to her. She wrote me a note in reply, amused but not at all convinced. To her, a dream, for instance, in which Sartre was piloting a plane and she was hanging on to the wing, meant nothing and was merely amusing; to me, her non-analysis was a good example of the exercise of conscious censorship.

The dreamer in me is able to play with the subject of myself like a juggler who keeps twenty balls in the air at once, who has used all the so-called Freudian imagery—knives, flutes, pocketbooks, pistols, towers, arrows, goblets, flying—who dreams, too, about danger, guilt, painting, women, inferiority, my parents, my brothers and sister, in order to say: "This is I." The enormous symbolic vocabulary of dreams does not disguise; it simply gives other forms to the whole of life, forms which can be translated directly or indirectly, for there are the symbols of fear and there is real fear; there are sex symbols and real sex, which may be pleasurable or frightening. I have dreamt frequently, not about flutes, pistols, knives, etc., but about actual penises and these dreams have been almost invariably an undisguised reflection of my fears.

What is wonderful about dreams is not that they are tricky and Protean, always eluding hard truths, but that they are so uncompromising. In conscious life, you might perhaps not know or you might deny (as Freud pointed out) the extent of various fears and guilts, but dreams never lie. Once you realize that they allow you to slip in and out of the skins of other people, or allow the use of masks, puns, etc., once you realize that all these things are part of their vocabulary, you have only to learn to read them and make a game of it, for sometimes the dreamer is in a sprightly and puckish mood, as much as to say, try to figure this one out. I have had comic dreams as well as those that said get wise to yourself. March 3, 1974: "I am sitting at a table (there are many tables in my dreams and they always seem to be connected with judgement) with my mother, my sister-in-law and my older brother, and I say, 'I'm everything you think I am!' They look shocked and I say, 'I don't drink, but if I did, I wouldn't say so.' Silence. I say, 'I'm not a Christian!' My mother says, 'Do you speak Spanish?' I begin haltingly, 'No tengo la opportunidad de hablar y he olvidado,' and wake up." As I thought about this dream, it seemed to me a concentrated description of my relationship with my family (my mother had long been dead, but she continued to live on in my brother and sister and their spouses); it seemed to represent the alternation in my thoughts between audacity and the inability to talk about myself—even in a language they cannot understand, for I have kept silent for so long about myself that I have forgotten how to talk. It was so like my mother to change the subject, unable to bear the news that I was not a Christian. She was like this in life and after her death, she kept turning up in dreams with the same ability to put a distance between herself and me. Just as long ago, she had silenced me when I spoke of my friend's illegitimate child, now she silenced me in dreams when something crucial was about to be discussed. November 18, 1973: "I dream that my sister is engaged to be married to my younger brother. In the dream, I tell my mother that I have dreamt this and my mother says,

'Mary, I don't want to hear about it!' I reply, 'But it was a dream!'" A Freudian would say that I was in love with my brother and that my mother's voice is my own, but I, who quarreled with this brother all through my childhood, who envied his boy's prerogatives, and who, even now, behave with him like a bird defending its territorial rights, doubt that this was ever so. The dream tells me more about my Kafkaesque relation with my family: seeing the mirror image of myself in the series of mirrors that is a dream within a dream. My dreaming self would invent marvellous images for the distance that I kept between myself and my family and for the bond of fear that kept me tightly linked to them. In actuality, in my waking life, I was getting close to the time when I gathered my courage and wrote a long letter to my sister about being a Lesbian.

"The art of dreaming when wide awake will be in the power of every man one day," says Henry Miller. He achieved that unity of conscious and unconscious, the tidal pouring back and forth of all experience, dreaming and waking. As for me, reading the reiterated messages of dreams or watching the pell-mell passing of images called hallucinations, I could never quite rid myself of the rational and physical prison of waking life. I wanted to use my dream images directly, without the distortion they suffered when, like Alice, they passed through the looking glass into the reality of the living room, where the Red and White Queens were transformed into kittens. There were times when the "seen" was somehow free to be itself, to be more than itself, by the substratum of dreams defining it. I am far more afraid of snakes in my dreams than in real life. When I see a snake, perhaps with a little tremor if it appears from nowhere, I take a kind of affectionate interest in it. It fascinates me that strong men have a mortal fear of snakes. Yvon, a carpenter, huge and powerful, with a wife and children, killed an entire family of snakes in my manure pile, striking them (he told me) with a heavy stick and leaving their mangled bodies for me to mourn over. "Je n'aime pas ça," he said when I remonstrated, saying that snakes did much good. I wanted to say that they were *my* snakes and that he had no right to kill them, but I knew how futile that would be. People are afraid of snakes, beetles, bats, cats, birds, mice or anything that moves unexpectedly and seems to threaten them. But in what way? Is it a sexual threat?

A few days after writing in my journal, "I want to shed my irritability like a snakeskin and start a fresh life," I saw a newly-shed snakeskin near the same manure pile where the family of snakes was later to be murdered by Yvon. The snakeskin was shining in the sun, translucent, reticulated like a honeycomb, a magic ribbon unwound in the coarse long grass that had been nurtured with manure. The snake had split the first quarter of its skin and had eased out, leaving the rest intact, like a stocking. What a wonderful thing it would be, to be able to break out of the old self every year, feeling it too tight, and find oneself in a lithe new skin! I think of all those creatures who shed their skins or their shells to accommodate their growing bodies. I was surprised to learn that all birds moult and every year endure a vulnerable period of flightlessness. This came to mind again, though, I thought, my own moulting periods were so total that I hugged the ground like a reptilian bird-ancestor. Still, in dreams, I flew, as every dreamer does. And birds have always occupied first place in my hierarchy of dream images and have always played a visionary and prophetic role in my life.

Dreams and half-dreams, words and images that slip through the looking glass as though it were clear water. "Transparency." I once heard this word on the edge of sleep and knew that it meant the relationship between trying to understand and the moment of understanding, the open eyes of real attention. In my dreams about birds, I often cry out to people to look with a kind of desperation that coincides with my own feeling about inattention. In one of these dreams, I am with a group of women who are "talking and talking." "I look at a treetop and see three bluebirds; they fly up, their wings spread like a section of umbrella, and the wind bears them away. I cry out, 'You didn't look, you didn't look! You did it on purpose!' To one woman, I say, 'They flew up and the wind caught them; their wings were transparent and I could see their bones!' I hide my face and shake with sobs, and the woman laughs, thinking that I am laughing." This dream deals, I think, with my joys and beliefs, my dislike of empty talk, my horror of the malady of inattention that poisons my own life, my longing to believe in the transparent relation between life and death, and with birds as messengers of freedom, flying in a sky empty even of the impalpable barrier of clouds.

Chapter Nine

The fear of being enclosed is, I think, in the psyche of every human being and living creature. I have seen my cats look anxiously around them when they know they are going to be imprisoned in the house and I have seen chickens pushing against the fence of a huge field or dogs making the rounds of even the biggest enclosure to find a way of escape. My fear of prisons is an extension of my instinct to be free of any enclosing situation. I remember in the sixties taking part in a mass non-violent demonstration in New York which consisted of refusing to enter air raid shelters when a siren sounded. This demonstration was held in a downtown park, full, at the fateful moment, of demonstrators and police. A siren sounded and the police began moving among the demonstrators, making sporadic arrests, and I found myself propelled away from the police, as if by the force of my wildly beating heart. Some of my friends stood still and were arrested; some were disappointed because they were not arrested, and I understood then that the difference between us could never be overcome, that I could be counted on forever to suffer the sickness of my terror and fail in courage at crucial times. The camaraderie of courageous beings, the call to pride, that devil-may-care euphoria that possesses every revolutionary, were signals for me to start my slide to safety.

Analyzing my terror of prisons, trying to sort out the elements of cowardice and claustrophobia, I have decided that at its source is my intimate acquaintance with psychic states in which my mind, my will or my heart are in solitary confinement. These states take the form in my dreams of policemen, Nazis, thieves and bullies and have all the paraphernalia of torture and imprisonment. They live in my subconscious and in conscious life are expressed by my feeling of being trapped in situations from which there is no escape. This feeling may grip me in the middle of a conversation; it can be triggered by a landscape, a person, or by suddenly seeing the boundaries of life (birth and death) like prison walls. I tried to talk about this feeling of being trapped to Edmund; about the prison of ourselves, about our lives and our death sentences that seem to have been shaken out of some impersonal lottery machine, and he answered me with one of his impatient, yes yeses, as much as to say that my idea was a cliché. It didn't matter; that was the way I felt that winter. The landscape, clamped between the ocean and the bay, was myself enlarged, extended, drawn with a draughting instrument; just as the wintry fields of Québec, even in early May, seem to spread out endlessly from my wintry centre.

In petty circumstances that other people accept cheerfully, I can almost hear the clanging of a barred door and sense myself in an empty cell. This can happen in certain houses where everything seems to be a different shade of brown, where pieces of cut glass are placed on dark buffets and forbidding chairs with carved backs and legs are set, like priests praying, around a blackish dining room table, where even the pictures on the wall are colourless, where a huge television set sits alert and Cyclopean in a brown living room. Or equally, it can happen in houses where everything has been chosen and arranged by an interior decorator, where there are photographs in silver frames, wedding pictures, family pictures, pictures of children with carefully combed hair who are smiling studio smiles, where all the scrapbaskets, china, travelling clocks, leatherbound blotters, painted trays, wine glasses, engravings of sailing ships or coaches and fours, porcelain birds on the mantlepiece, ashtrays, cigarette boxes, linen napkins and tablecloths have been wedding presents, selected at one of many shops where everything can be counted on to be impersonal, where mothers and daughters go before the wedding to select the pattern of the daughter's choice, for plates, silver and glasses, so that nothing can intrude on the perfect impersonality of the future house. To me, an impersonal choice is a sin and to live with choices imposed by other people is one of my many ideas of imprisonment, the outward and visible kind. I think of Blake and his "mind-forged manacles." Blake's cry was for freedom now (though not for women); women, who put on mind-forged manacles almost as soon as they are born, are thought not to feel the weight of convention as much as men. Convention lay heavily on my mother, who wished to impose it on my father and on her children and to some extent succeeded. We all groaned under its invisible and oppressive weight. My rebellion came by slow degrees and took the form less of active resistance than of gloom and bad-temper. People in the invisible prisons of class and respectability, indoctrinated by their own rules, taboos and tastes, like creatures that fill some evolutionary niche, become dependent on their environment. They become, in fact, a species. My parents could perhaps have lived without money, but they could not have lived without their belief in the social hierarchy, without their views of what was right and wrong, proper and improper, and of who belonged to the elect. Looking back, I see as a tragedy the warping and shrinking of my mother into a person who cared so fiercely about her position in society. She was the product of humiliation and of Mater's snobbishness. I remember how she used to describe her father's iron works, the process of feeding molten iron into the fiery furnace to emerge as ingots, how her face would light with the memory of this. I remember that instead of encouraging her to dig up memories of her childhood, we teased her. Even in this innocent sharing of her life, we failed to be receptive. The barriers between mother and children had already gone up, and I, at least, did not recognize that these precious memories of my mother's bore witness to a real family life much more natural, freer and more affectionate than our own. My mother was the youngest of three daughters, and, as the family pet, had that sense of being loved that belongs to the youngest child. I ache to think of her childish heart and the work of changing it out of all recognition to the heart of a white, Anglo-Saxon, Episcopalian, prosperous wife and mother, who believed that her comfortable prison was the best place to be. My father died, I think, not of tuberculosis, but of prison life. He could have been cured, but he did not want to go on living and could only repeat, "I'm a sick man." Wasn't it not only the frost-heavy weight of custom that oppressed him, but also the unimaginable weight of all the life that lay outside his prison, inaccessible and dreadful? He died in 1940 when the Nazis were marching over Europe. He had believed with Woodrow Wilson that World War I was the "war to end all wars"; he was bitterly disappointed when the United States failed to join the League of Nations. All his beliefs were crumbling and in his melancholy, he ceased, too, to believe in himself. For years he worked in the Department of Agriculture; he discovered the cause of mastitis in cows and wrote a paper about his findings which was published after his death. A herd of prize Holsteins was under his observation, some of which contracted mastitis from the over-use of milking machines—this was my father's discovery. He would make a daily trip to a huge experimental farm at Beltsville, Maryland, about which I felt no curiosity—I, who now gaze with wonder at the beautiful dark eyes of Holsteins, at their smooth black and white flanks with massive udders. We (the twins) shared this almost secret life of our father no more than we shared our mother's childhood memories. Our parents' outward lives, unlike those that made their hearts beat with their own rhythm, were lived in service to false gods: a falsified and prudish Christianity, a stifling view of sex, rigid ideas about right and wrong. My brothers, so truly good and kind, are still confined within the moral boundaries that kept my parents from living freely. They are trapped by rules; they suffer under the threat of punishment; and I, ground between their moral millstones, become, when I see them, the self of my childhood and youth—anxious, gloomy, resisting.

It is the work of a lifetime to recognize life's prisons. I am lucky in having had the means to escape from the prison of a hateful job, to pull up roots and change lives and countries. Billions of people haven't these means and seem as inescapably congealed in their lives as flies in amber. Finally, I can only speak authoritatively of myself: of the prisons of self, constructed with the materials of doubt and failure; of shattered dreams and unhappy loves, jealousy, hate, envy and the deadly sins of lovelessness and indifference. These inner states are echoed by outer perceptions of lifelessness; of all the ways there are of killing life. I judge myself harshly for the role that I played in the vicious circle of family life in which each of us punished the other or pruned back whatever was spontaneous and irrepressible. I seek out those memories of my father reciting poetry with sparkling eyes; all the subdued evidence that there was of passion which sometimes bubbled secretly in him, for he never drank, never shouted with rage, never, even when joyful, overstepped the boundary of perfect gentlemanliness. Were the six of us ever completely relaxed, without the sense in one or the other of us that the vigilant eye of conscience was fixed upon us? On picnics, perhaps, when we were stretched out on the warm sand under the blazing sun; or on one of those calm, cloudless days, like the outward expression of the bliss in us that for a brief time inhabited our bodies and stilled our thoughts. These were vacations from conscience, vacations from guilt; they were as peaceful as our early sojourn in the womb. I felt alive in these suspended states and I knew from an early age what made me feel alive and what made me feel dead. Gradually, I learned that my inner sun took its energy from love, from creativity, and my subconscious began inventing symbols that stood for death and rebirth. How many times when I have felt lifeless and loveless have I dreamt of leaves sprouting from dead branches or of seeing green grass and flowers in January; how many times have birds in my dreams come as messengers of life? It is as though these things stand for the persistent impulse in me to beat my wings in some kind of flight or escape from some self-imposed cage.

185

Chapter Ten

"CHEE-uh, CHEE-uh, TSWEE-ur, TSWEE-ur, pirrih, tur-rah, suwee, suwee, wooh, chik, chik, chik, wheat-*chee*-ur, whir-yuh, hoory, hoory, hoory, suweet, suweet, suweet," with sun-dry trills impossible to reproduce—a very imperfect rendition of the mockingbird's song that I am listening to, the first mock-ingbird I have ever heard in this chilly region of Canada. The old familiar joy fills me to the brim. I think of birds in poetry and how they are almost invariably associated with joy: "the first fine careless rapture" of Browning's thrush; Hopkins' windhover, "in his ecstasy"; Keats' nightingale, "too happy in thine happiness"; Shelley's skylark, panting "forth a flood of rapture"; and the "mighty singing" of Marianne Moore's caged bird, who (even he) says, "how pure a thing is joy." It is the same for me. I am possessed by a kind of delirium, no matter in what spiritual dumps I have been floundering, when I hear the eagerness, the energy of any birdsong, or watch a hawk practicing his marvellous routine. It's useless to tell me that birds do not feel joyful, but aggressive, when they are singing; I have heard birds singing in late August when there is no longer any need for asser-tion of territorial rights. Birds practice, add to and perfect their repertoires. I believe that some birds (like some people) have more pronounced musical gifts than others and enjoy elaborating on the song that is theirs by inheritance, and that they sing, apart from the instinct that insists on the musical definition of their rights, with the same pleasure that human beings sing. And *why* do human beings sing? Are they not impelled, like wolves, whales and birds, to amplify the inaudible music of the beating heart, of blood whispering through the veins; to discover all the uses of their vocal cords? I know by some powerful certainty that belongs to my cell structure that I am part of the animal kingdom and that animals and birds can suffer despair, boredom, pain, joy and love.

Birds have become so important to me, so much a necessary part of my life, that I feel sick today (May 1, 1978) because it has snowed for twenty-four hours, the ground has frozen, and the barn and tree swallows, who were scouting around for nesting places two days ago in the warm sun, have disappeared. They will come back, I suppose; probably they know this treacherous climate better than I, who suffer for them through all their vicissitudes, who went into a decline a year ago for their sake when a hailstorm in early August stripped the leaves off the trees, crushed bird nests to smithereens and flattened out the fields like a host of myrmidons. Then, I saw a bewildered flock of bobolinks fluttering over the wintry grass and a female hummingbird, who had somehow hidden from the murderous hailstones, vainly looking for marigolds and phlox to drink from, and I felt their troubles in my whole being. "You like animals and birds better than people," said a friend not long ago, and I bridled a bit, though it was not, the friend said, an accusation. I feel something indefinable for birds and animals, sorrow or joy that partly has to do with their being perpetual victims and partly because of my conviction that they are becoming scarcer and scarcer. Once, when a bourgeois Frenchman on a train began to tell me about the joy of flashing a mirror to befuddle a skylark, so that the bird would come tumbling down from the sky, and the joy of gathering the birds by the dozen to be cooked and eaten, I wanted to shout my rage at him. Had he ever listened to a skylark singing his endless sonata, so high in the air that you could scarcely see him? (The Indians say that there are thirty-two kinds of talas or time measures in the song of a lark.) If he had heard a lark sing or had seen it vibrating against the blue sky, how could he have deliberately flashed a mirror and brought it down to earth? And how could people shoot geese after hearing them barking overhead? Birds and animals are defenceless against human beings, whereas human beings can speak and reason, as well as scream out their pain.

For me, birds are the embodiment of colour, joy, music and freedom. I have learned their songs, their arrivals and their departures, and I mourn their disappearance. It is obvious to me that both birds and animals are able to identify so totally with human beings that there is an interchange of souls and that this interchange is irreversible, unlike the interchange of human love. In love, one is always slipping back into the shell of oneself, each "opaque and ultimately unknowable" to the other, as Iris Murdoch so depressingly says. But love relationships between people and animals or between people and birds hold implicit in them thousands of years of myth and fairytale in which they have taken each other's forms. They had amazing powers, those mythical creatures, like the birds of Rhiannon in the Celtic legend, who woke the dead and put the living to sleep, whose effect on human beings was that they lost their sense of time and their memory of pain. Birds have this effect on me. They make me lose my memory of pain. Sometimes my friends are birds in dreams. I dreamt, for instance, of a bird with a long neck that turned out to be a tiny baby peacock. Its name was Barbara and it talked in a low voice. In the dream, I lose the bird and I rush into a theatre crying, "Where is Barbara?" The little peacock answers from somewhere, "Here I am," and I feel profound relief and a quickening of my love for Barbara.

To rescue a bird has always been the acknowledgement of a being which had rescued me by calling on me to pay attention. Many of the poets I love have looked at birds in this way and certain women poets have allowed nature to enter their brains and bloodstreams as a kind of sacrament. With their relatively limited experience of life, they have, like blind people or illiterates, developed extrasensory senses. One thinks of Emily Dickinson in the little world, finally, of her own room and the cosmos of her poetry made from joys and pains so intense that she had to invent a new language to contain them. Re-reading her poems, I see that the smallness of her experience, far from being a handicap, enabled her to compose her own extraordinary music; she needed only a small vision, a pencil and a piece of torn paper. She saw a bird as a creature who "shouts for joy to nobody / But his seraphic self!" and was dazzled by hummingbirds and took them to be wheeled messengers from an exotic land. And for me, too, hummingbirds are magic beings. Once, I rescued one that had flown into the kitchen at Wellfleet and was dashing itself against the walls and ceiling with anguished chirps. Later, when I met Marie-Claire, I identified her with my wounded hummingbird and with Emily Dickinson's "route of evanescence / With a revolving wheel." It was as though fate, having battered Marie-Claire, had entrusted her to me and she rested in my hand until she was strong enough to fly away.

Birds symbolize my metamorphoses and my flights and fallings to earth; they waken my imagination and strike down the barrier between dreaming and waking. Birds have the power to give grace to a whole day; summers have been consecrated by them. I think now of the heronry on Sutton Island in Maine and my sense of having entered a sacred grove when, one foggy day, I found myself among the tall pines hung with moss, where a colony of great blue herons nested. I saw the ghostly shapes of the birds overhead, their slowly-beating wings, fog-shrouded, becoming more precise as they settled on their nests, saw, ringing the base of every tree, the bones of generations of fallen nestlings. I picked up some of their feather-light vertebrae and fine skulls and kept them for years to remind myself of the mortality of blue herons and the mystery of their grove of trees.

The heronry was at the furthest end of Sutton Island. Its secret had been imparted to me by "Pa" Paine, who was among those Bostonians who have the sublime features of Ralph Waldo Emerson: the great nose, the clear blue eyes and silver hair, and, in Pa Paine's case, the attenuated body that made him look like a great blue heron himself. He was a friend of Hortense Flexner, the poet, and her husband, Wyncie King, the caricaturist, with whom I stayed on the island and who communicated to me their awe of every living creature, of the waves that struck the shaggy, kelp-clad rocks, the fog, the blue-beating sky, even the chipmunk that chattered on their porch. Both these friends are dead: Wyncie and little Miss Horti (translated into French by Marguerite Yourcenar) whose eyes, behind steel-rimmed glasses, were light blue, who wore a wig because she had suddenly been struck with baldness (she took off her wig to show me hair sprouting on her head like the down of a newborn chick). She spent as much time in the hospital as most people spend in bed sleeping. She was felled by sciatica, arthritis, cancer, and rose, each time, like a phoenix—one that can laugh at itself, if such a bird exists. Out of her pain, she distilled her crystalline poems and it was only by reading them that you knew what she had suffered. She was half as tall as I was, but her hands and arms were amazingly powerful, like those of many people who walk with difficulty, and I can feel Miss Horti gripping my hand and dragging me off to look at something, for she looked at everything with the intensity of an eagle. Miss Horti, Wyncie and I spent much of our time laughing. Miss Horti would say something in a certain way and this would set us off. "That's a nice dress," I said one day at lunch and when Miss Horti replied, "I got it at Miss Titcomb's," we all began to laugh helplessly. Wyncie (who died first, in the Greece of their dreams, where they had gone, at last, for a holiday and whence Miss Horti returned with Wyncie's body) took a dim view of the world. He sent out his own Christmas cards which became more and more melancholy as the years went by, until the final one, written in white letters on a black background, said: WHOLLY NIGHT. Miss Horti gave the advanced poetry course at Bryn Mawr College, and, with a host of other students, I used to go to their house in the evening, where we drank sherry and felt extraordinarily happy. I always felt happy with them; they were givers of life and very humble about their own gifts.

My friendship with Miss Horti and with Marianne Moore, another great poet who had the same humility as Miss Horti— these two friendships were like a great and undeserved showering of gifts. Whatever our experience of life had been, all three of us were old maids, with the scrupulous fineness of conscience, fussiness and sensibility of old maids of yesteryear, from a time

191

(did it ever exist?) before it was obligatory to spend your whole time thinking and talking about sex. Marianne Moore, the most adorable old maid who ever existed, reminded one of an intricate illuminated manuscript with birds and animals surrounded by the fine tendrils of flowering vines, in short, she was exactly like one of her poems about which she was so modest. One did not ask oneself, is she this? Is she that? Has she been in love with a man or a woman—or both? She loved her mother and her brother, everybody knew that; and her loves had an angelic quality, just as she did swathed in light sweaters and shawls, wearing big hats that looked like dark haloes. There is passion in her work, but it is disembodied and unsensual. She was less physical than Miss Horti, who hugged me quite fiercely and kissed me firmly on the mouth. Neither of them, in their poetry, talks about sex; neither, as far as I know, wrote love poems, and yet, all their poems were love poems, if you think of love as intense attention.

Marianne Moore had dark blue eyes, such as I had never seen before, and it was surprising to see that those eyes, looking almost black sometimes in her pale, roundish, lightly-freckled face, were really the blue of a swallow's back. I held Marianne Moore in such awe that the fact that we were friends made me tremble with fear, for her sense of me, whose work she praised with her extravagant stylistic involutions, seemed to me like a bubble that might burst at any moment. Both these poets had graduated from Bryn Mawr, but they did not know each other there and having decided that they should meet, in an agony of apprehension, I invited them to lunch in my apartment in New York. Would they like each other? With my senses alert, I was aware of an invisible, inaudible ruffling of feathers and a circling of one around the other, of unspoken disagreements as fine as cobwebs, and I suddenly felt the powerful presence of each, so self-effacing alone, assert itself. One tunes in on the milliwatts of aggressiveness or acceptance that leap between friends, particularly when one is anxious for them to like each other. I suffer because of the changes in emotional climate I perceive in others, but my suffering is often useless, for the sensor in me magnifies impulses that people are unaware of, or won't admit, and I am frequently surprised after one of these encounters when my friends express delight at having been introduced to one another. Such was the case with Miss Horti and Marianne Moore, and yet as far as I know, they never saw each other again — and we three were never together again.

A real flowing of attention into another being is like a transfusion of life. Birds and animals remind us more simply than human beings of the meaning of another presence that we somehow take into ourselves in its entirety, but without self-consciousness. Martin Buber tells the story of his relationship when he was a child with an enormous horse, whose silky nose he stroked, into whose dark, intelligent eyes he gazed; how each seemed to become the other. But, one day, he saw himself stroking the horse's nose and the horse was immediately aware of this new element of their relationship and he turned his head away. When I read this, I thought sadly, there's no hope for me, for I am almost always conscious of myself doing something, try as I will not to be. In 1962, under Barbara's influence, I was trying to be "good." I was having my old trouble with "the oppression of bad temper and self." I read Martin Buber and was moved by him, feeling that he spoke directly to the so-familiar "status of the dully-tempered disagreeableness, obstinacy and contrariness" which had to be broken through into the "tiny strictness and grace of every day." No one better than Buber has defined what it is to be present and what it is to be absent. "If I am not really there I am guilty. When I answer the call of present being, 'Where art thou?' with 'Here am I,' but am not really there, that is, not with the truth of my whole life, then I am guilty. Original guilt consists in remaining with oneself." These words rejoiced my soul. I suppose that Buber meant that one feels guilty *because* one remains with oneself and that one is delivered from this guilt by answering "the call of present being"; this is a kind of guilt that can be isolated and treated and from which one can recover. I preferred to think the kind of selfishness that consisted in remaining with oneself created its own pain, sufficient unto itself. There was much about Buber with his patriarchal beard, his infinite, relentless patience and his wisdom and sense of always being right, that suggested God the Father, and while I was reading him, I spent my time arguing with him in my mind, much as I argued with Barbara about God. I would think of willing my life into the hummingbird that I rescued as an instance of being "really there"; this was the tiny grace of that day. I wanted to say, "Please, Dr. Buber, don't make me decide whether I was there 'with the truth of my whole life,' for my whole life seemed like an alternation between states of awareness and blindness.

On the page of my journal facing this dream, I had copied out a poem by Denise Levertov in which a blind cuckoo is beating his wings at her window, singing of the fear of death—"timor mortis conturbat me." "I want to move deeper into today," says the poet, "He keeps me from that work." The cuckoo sings of a time that is never *now* and his wings "spread at the window make it dark." This image is like a negative of my dream image of the bluebirds with outspread wings, an image that transmitted both light and the suggestion of death, not death to come, but the presence of death in life. I ponder over Levertov's cuckoo which evidently represents the blind repetition of an obsession. What prevents us from moving "deeper into today" (another way of answering Buber's call of present being) is this same kind of taking over by a creature that demands to be fed: a fear, a grievance, a guilt that destroys the present and darkens the future. The blind cuckoo, finally, is whatever stifles life. For Denise Levertov, it was the deadly interference of future with present; for me, the blind cuckoo is named guilt. The doctrine of original sin is repulsive to me, for I rage against my sense of guilt and think of original sin as all those untamed impulses and spontaneous strivings in which Christian society has to rub people's noses. Having been thoroughly indoctrinated with a Christian upbringing, I believe in sin (not original, however), but I hate the darkness of confession and contrition, the sharp definition that society and religion give to right and wrong. To me, the Ten Commandments are a completely negative force and Jesus' simple idea that you should love your neighbour as yourself is much more persuasive than his harsh treatment of the sterile fig tree or the parables in which punishment is meted out. You can't think about loving your neighbour as yourself without wondering whether the hate you sometimes feel for yourself is mirrored in the hate you sometimes feel for your neighbour; if so, you have to discover what it means to love yourself in a way that makes it easier for you to love your neighbour. The great paradox of Jesus' sayings, it seems to me, is the part that judgement plays in them, though Jesus said, "Judge not, lest ye be not judged." The parables are full of threats and terrors and dire punishment of people who are enjoined to forgive, but who are not forgiven. And sometimes the punishment seems to dwarf the crime, such as the casting into outer darkness of the man who came to the wedding "which had not on a wedding garment," a crime which I myself have committed. You will say that Jesus is not talking about wedding garments, but about one's readiness to enter the Kingdom of Heaven, but in the eyes of devout Christians, it all boils down to the same thing, namely, proper behaviour. In His name, Christians have become as narrow-minded and bigoted as the Pharisees were; and since they are born, if not with original sin, but with an original desire to force themselves into unnatural shapes like topiary, it is not surprising that they choose words suitable to that instinct. And haven't Saint Paul and many others blighted women's lives for almost two thousand years by their choice of Jesus' words?

Chapter Eleven

A woman's Christian duty has always been to fit into the space men consider suitable for women, whereas a man can grow in any direction. I have observed this freedom in the men whom I have admired and I am interested to see that it often goes with a freedom from guilt, or at least from the petty kind of guilt that torments me. Edmund, Karl Knaths, Leonid, Henry Poor—all had the indefinable ease of male animals conscious of their power; the power of men with women, contentedly or otherwise, in their orbit. Of the four, I felt closest to Henry Poor and longed to learn from him how to be strong, how not to care what other people think, how to go steadily forward with my life as a painter without being deflected in one way or another. I loved what he loved: the same flowers, landscapes, birds, houses; and hated what he hated. We agreed about everything except obligations; why was I torn by my sense of obligation, why did I let this weaken and paralyze me and make me guilty? Unlike me, Henry was "bien dans sa peau," had always been comfortable in his strong solid body, as huggable as a teddy bear; he looked like a blond bear, in fact, with curly close-cut grey hair on his square head, pink, healthy skin, and blue eyes, behind glasses. His voice was surprisingly high and gentle; he sometimes said sharp, teasing things with a little chuckle that was intended to mitigate their sharpness, but I never heard him raise his voice or bellow with rage like Edmund. He might, by example, have taught me more lessons than anyone in my life. I would have liked to turn into Henry, but remained myself, with my changeless limitations. I think of the way he did everything with patient grace, using his sensitive bear hands to make a surpassingly beautiful cup or plate, or paint a still-life, or plant the petunias and nicotianas that perfumed the air around his house in Maine. I look at a small painting of Henry's in front of me—of asters, white berries and petunias, and two little pale yellow apples, one with fresh green leaves, all on a warm grey ground flecked with apple green, with light surrounding the darker flowers; I look at the delicate energy of the brushstrokes, the gentle golden light falling on the apples and the berries airborne like bubbles or tiny balloons, painted in one sitting by a master who knew the secrets of light and shade and volume and had a lyrical and happy soul. Even his signature seemed to be taking off, flying with its "V," like a bird's wings, with the pennant of the "P" blowing in the wind.

Henry as a painter (like Leonid) was not threatening to me because he belonged to the school that persisted in believing that there was meaning in the visible world. To paint was to look with love at the landscape, the fruit or flowers, or the person in front of you, and to make your own translation into form and colour. I do not think he tormented himself with theories of what painting should be or suffered from what avant-garde painters were doing, but simply felt sure of his own way, which had been prepared by the painters of the past whom he loved. There were other younger painters who hung on to their own vision, but Henry and Anne and Leonid were close to me and I longed to draw strength from them. They never pushed me beyond my capabilities and they spotted any concessions I made to ways of painting that I had not really assimilated. Both Henry and Anne knew instantly what was true and what was false and pretentious in painting, and this made them both extraordinary teachers.

There was a time when I was troubled by my love for Henry and for the first time in my life, I was obsessed by the wish to have a child—ours—a beautiful child, of course, that would combine the best features of both of us. Henry inspired this kind of love in other Lesbians, in Carson McCullers, for instance, and in both Barbara and me, perhaps because his body held no threat (unlike Edmund's), but was fatherly and tender. I had first met him in Truro, Massachusetts, and we had immediately embraced, as though we had known each other for a long time, while his little wife, Bessie, beamed in approval, like an amiable owl. From then on, the sight of him made me tremble with happiness, which he seemed to catch and give back to me like a benign contagion. There was a series of cloudless early October days and the three of us lived the kind of honeymoon that is only possible when the weather and circumstances combine to fill people to the brim with what seems always like imperishable love. Later that autumn, I went to see the three Poors in the brownstone house that Henry had built in New City, New York, surrounded by huge trees and green lawn, with a rushing stream at the back, beautiful and full of imminent sadness, the leaves hanging listlessly on the trees and the still, damp air heavy with autumn smells. I was dressed in grey flannel pants and a surplus jacket I had bought at an Army and Navy store, and suffered from one of my states of self-consciousness and malaise. "You look as if you were ready for a trip on the Ramapo River," said Henry with his little laugh. He no longer had his exclusive and loving relation with me, but had resumed his role in the Poor trio. It was obvious that they had been quarrelling before I came; I sensed anger still suspended in the air and Henry's concealed irritation. With my love-awakened sensibility, I knew suddenly that his irritation could now be directed at me as easily as anywhere else, that the sight of me looking like a Lesbian was perhaps part of it. I knew that from then on, he would be careful to keep me at the right distance, that, to him, I was just another of the countless women who worshipped him. How many times had I heard a woman say (and felt a pang of jealousy), "I just adore Henry." I wanted him to love me most, that first insatiable requirement of love, and I would comb his letters for signs of specialness. One of them ended: ". . . and be glad for some people who love me and whom I love"; I smiled at the carefulness of the "some people," which can be either singular or plural, but I take these words to me as though I were once again embracing the real Henry.

Henry, in harmony with himself, lived with two tortured and extraordinary women: his wife, Bessie Breuer, the writer; and his stepdaughter, Anne, the painter. It was one of the strangest and most tightly-bound triangles I had ever seen, resolved, in part, by the departure every summer of Henry and Anne to Maine where they taught at the Skowhegan School, leaving Bessie to work alone in Truro. They were three great stars, burningly close to each other and locked into the permanency of their constellation. Impossible to know the three of them without falling in love with at least one; I was simultaneously in love with Henry and Anne, now the last living star of the constellation. My relation with Bessie, the most volatile, ferocious and vulnerable of the three, tossed like a ship in a storm and ended calmly, but I long for Henry and Bessie to be alive again and to speak the words of love that you can only pour out to friends who are dead.

Henry was always surrounded by women, adoring or resisting or scolding. "My harem," he called us, with his unconscious male superiority. "I know that I'm pretty hard to take," he wrote me, "because I make a sort of half-principle of being rough shod with tender feelings—female especially—I want to drag them all out and put them under full light to see how logical they are. But none of the females that I love *are* logical and I suppose I love them because they are not, so the end result is just a form of torture that I half enjoy. But it's all calculated to keep the air clear with little explosions instead of letting a dark cold front settle over the land." Re-reading this, I am again ruffled because I was lumped together with the illogical females Henry loved. It seemed to me that I was more logical than either Bessie or Anne and as logical as Henry, but that, in our conflicts of will, his was the stronger. It was true that he was "rough shod with tender feelings"; in fact, he made me feel stupid for having so many. But I thought this was as much to protect himself as to expose those feelings to the light of day. "In our family we scream at each other," Bessie said in a letter to me, and indeed, the air in their house often crackled with electricity, with spent passion and storms that were constantly breaking or passing overhead. In spite of Henry's pacific nature, big explosions and "dark cold fronts" did settle over the land. Bessie, Anne and I had this in common: that our exacerbation broke against Henry's calm and made us angrier. Henry did not let tender feelings, that is to say, the intuitions and scruples and inferiorities that make the lives of sensitive women miserable, deflect him from his monolithic sense of himself. And this was primarily the lesson he had to teach others. He refused to be distracted by what to him were unimportant emotions, unhealthy even, or by great events that sucked people into their vortices.

It worried Henry to see me following in Barbara's wake and suffering from guilt because I never did enough during the long period when the Poors, Barbara and I could never be together without the conversation turning to the subject of pacifism, or nuclear testing, or civil rights; and later, the Vietnam war. In 1961, Henry wrote me, "Please let painting be enough and keep that stern conscience from caring too much about setting the crazy world straight. Forgive me for trying to tell you what to do—but mind me just the same. Be contented and relax—into paint." I see before my eyes his worried frown and hear the note of exasperation in his voice; his harem was screaming at him and Barbara was forcing him into discussions which made him feel like a baited bear. "I have so little a life of the mind and so entirely one of the eyes and hands and nose," he wrote me. He had his life of the mind (he wrote beautiful books about Alaska and about making ceramics); it was just that his mind was detached from everything that seemed irrelevant. In another letter of 1962, he wrote, "Let's you and me remain calm as possible. What do you say?! And not worry about being too selfish." But at the heart of my moral dilemma was my worry about "being too selfish," and the definition of the word "too." It seemed to me that a great artist was not selfish when he or she concentrated on his work; the high quality of his work gave him the right to think of nothing else. But how good does your work have to be to give you this right? Many women artists have the sense that they have neither the right to devote themselves exclusively to their work, nor to succeed too well. I have a gifted niece who, when she begins to do something really well—to paint, to weave, to play the violin—is seized with panic and stops; and another niece, a journalist, who looks at her published articles with misgivings—will they perhaps lead to her becoming well-known?—a thought that horrifies her. For centuries it was not thought seemly for women to write well or paint well ("Women can't write; women can't paint," says Mr. Tansley to Lily Briscoe in *To the Lighthouse*). Men think that this is no longer so, that a beneficent society now encourages women to express themselves in every possible way and praises them for it. I do not propose to refute this on a grand scale, only observe that almost all the women artists I have known have suffered from the sense of what society expects from them as women, whether it is to be "normal" (*i.e.,* to marry and have children) or to do good; that is to say, to have a social conscience. Women are supposed to be the consciences of the whole world and to inject merciful and altruistic feelings into the men close to them. They do much of the charitable work of every community in the United States, and in Wellfleet, I was constantly being asked to serve on this or that committee, all of which invitations I refused with awful pangs of conscience.

In the great period of protest between the first civil rights marches in the sixties to the end of the Vietnam war, it was as though the consciences of half the citizens of the United States were fanned to flame. A host of writers and painters took part in the March on Washington, the March on the Pentagon, went to jail and diverted the attention of their work to the crime of Vietnam. I compromised, not taking part in the great marches, not getting myself arrested. Of all my friends, Henry remained most steadfastly true to his own life and I was dragged between his pole, to which I was secretly attracted, and Barbara's, which was an appeal to my conscience. I hated to be scolded by Henry for doing something that assuaged my sense of guilt; it took all the pleasure out of my gestures, which, depending on which of the two was looking at them, were either too much or too little. Barbara mourned over the liberal (almost as bad as being conservative) views of Henry and of various members of her family and tackled them so convincingly that I was elevated to the Olympian plane of her viewpoint. But life is full of the necessity to choose sides between the people one loves best, or to veer back and forth in alternations of loyalty and disloyalty. As I have already said, Barbara was incapable of the small betrayals represented by these shifts in point of view, but for me, they were another facet of my perpetually uneasy conscience. To think Henry was wrong was to betray him, but how could you accept Barbara's radical orthodoxy *without* thinking he was wrong? But I felt bruised by my choice to mourn with Barbara over Henry's pigheadedness in political matters, bruised by all the choices I have made in my life to believe one person at the expense of another.

I was forever wanting to detach Henry from his harem and have him all to myself, like a sun warming me, who would give me the strength not to give a damn about trivial matters of conscience, to live as he lived, waving away bothersome thoughts like a giant percheron swishing its tail against the flies. But *his* loyalties lay with Bessie and Anne and they acted as body and soul guards, just as my life with Barbara fixed me as one half of a couple. On the rare times when I saw Henry alone, he wore his little frown and I felt that my whole life was wrong in his eyes and could never be righted, that he could not possibly know how I longed to set it in harmony with his because I felt compelled to defend it, to argue with him, and this set the uneasy pattern of our times together. One summer when I was living with Barbara in Maine, I went to Boothbay Harbor with Henry. It was lost in a sunny and dazzling fog and we wandered along the street to an antique shop where I bought a heavy polished pulley made of *lignum vitae*, the kind you can still see at the tops of the masts of big schooners that sit in their grey old dignity in certain New England harbours. Its three holes, elongated and smoothed by years of big ropes sliding over them, are worn in the direction of the pull, so that the two sides look like an anxious two-faced skull. Henry explained how these pulleys were always made of the hardest of hard woods, and I am struck now by the weight of mine, like iron or stone. We were drawn together by our love of "natural" things ("We both have a deep love for soft-tanned leather," Henry said, for instance, in a letter of thanks for a deer-skin bag I had given him). We took a picnic lunch to the end of a dock where, at a distance in the fog, we could see a hoary schooner with two pulleys still on its mast-tops—and Henry talked very gently and patiently to me. I said that I had to go back to Wellfleet because various members of Barbara's family were coming to visit, and Henry said, "Let them come. You don't have to be there." Explaining all the reasons why I had to be there and complaining at the same time that I didn't want to be there, I felt the old tug of war and saw the warning signal flying. I was being disloyal to Barbara, for I heard myself trying to win Henry's sympathy for my plight, and yet, I really wished he would say, "Yes, I understand," instead of saying almost angrily, "You should do *what you want to do*." He thought that I was weak. He wanted me to follow him, but I couldn't follow him for he had his own loyalties that bound him hand and foot. There was a kind of concealed jealousy I felt in him (and in Edmund too) that made him want to exercise much more power over me than circumstances permitted, that made him nag possessively at me in his mind. I felt this as soon as I began my life with Barbara, which meant a relinquishment of Henry's power, even though Barbara was linked indissolubly to the Poors. It was like a chess game in which the position of the pieces prevents certain moves from being made. And perhaps chess is fascinating, partly because it is so much like the game played between human beings with their forward, backward or oblique moves, their little hops, like pawns, and their eternal and inexorable checkmates. Marriages are held together by blocking actions and cunning strategies that immobilize both players and pieces. Barbara was like a powerful queen who blocked my move toward the king opposite, already flanked by two queens of his own.

When Marie-Claire came to live with Barbara and me, my distance from Henry became greater, for this new love was impossible to understand, though I felt him kindly trying and failing to accept it. The Poors' love for Barbara set them against Marie-Claire; I had a falling-out with Bessie and broke off our friendship with bitter and futile words. Barbara left, Andrée appeared on the scene, and I drifted in my determined secrecy from all the Poors. I was in Wellfleet when Anne called to say that Henry had died, standing against his bed with a smile on his face. Lost in my quarrel with Bessie, I felt incapable of going to his funeral and I cannot forgive myself for this sin against love.

Chapter Twelve

I find it easy to imagine Henry here, standing in his rumpled pants, belted around the big girth of his waist, wearing his blue denim jacket. He would have been happy here today, for the weather has changed as it almost always does at the beginning of June from summer heat to the coolness brought by a north wind. The landscape that burned yesterday in the sun is a uniform green, except for the tall cedars and spruces rising above the other trees. The cedars look dead and the spruces are spotted with red-brown, as though a flock of brown thrashers had settled in them, where the hailstones struck them last August. This was just a gratuitous piece of summer mischief, but it was more deadly than the worst winter, from which trees and plants awake like risen gods. Winter is an endless but predictable ordeal from which you emerge stir crazy and with a prisoner's pallor. My hatred for snow has increased as the years have gone by and I was glad to find a letter from Henry in which he said, "I'm past the age when I think snow beautiful any more. I just resent it for blotting out all the warm earth colours." In winter, I welcome those damp days, detested by good Québécois, that come from the south, like messengers, and seem to revive my skin and hair, and my nose, freeze-dried, begins to breathe again.

Yesterday, a thunderstorm hovered tantalizingly over the

hills; one saw rain far away and angry clouds came quietly and disappeared without releasing a drop of rain. The rain never came, but the wind changed during the night and began to blow through my north window. I had a childhood memory, of lying in bed at Woods Hole on Cape Cod on a warm summer night, listening to the faint lapping of waves on the beach. When the wind changed to northeast or northwest, the waves would begin to slap the shore with sudden energy until the noise increased to a steady roar and the frame house shuddered in the wind. The next morning, the little bay behind our house would be lashed with friendly waves that came rolling up the beach and went hissing out again and there was a commotion of white clouds and blue sky that made my sister and me jump around with crazy joy. Here in Canada, there are no waves to announce a change of wind, just the movement of the curtain and the sounds of early morning borne into my room: the neighbour's rooster, a meadowlark, a bobolink and a song sparrow. When I went downstairs, I saw the greenness and greyness so like a cool Maine day, with a long white line lying along the distant hills and a bright explosion of cloud bursting from the hill due east. The fields were speckled with dandelions and their smoky seed-bubbles, and a goldfinch was bowing a blade of long grass, betrayed by its black wings and the butter-yellow of its back.

During those long periods of hot weather without rain, I feel the thirst of the trees and flowers and of the wilting lettuce in my garden in my own heart, and I am unloving and cranky. When it rains or the wind changes, it is as though a fresh spring bubbles up inside me. I think of all the great friendships of my life in terms of their changing seasons, their storms and sere periods, during which nothing would grow. I think of all my quarrels and reconciliations and wonder how necessary quarrels are to friendship, whether they are a kind of negative mortar that holds the whole structure together. Do some people get through life without quarrelling? I know many people who abhor quarrels, who take alarm when voices are raised, who curl up like hedgehogs or shut up like clams. Henry's technique was to act as a lightning rod or a lighthouse against whose base furious storms raged; Barbara's was to argue patiently or to keep broodingly silent, for she was undone by harsh words that for another person would have set off a good quarrel. Some people bottle up their rage and then let it out after several days, months, or even years; some never speak, but water their resentment, as Blake waters his wrath in *A Poison Tree*, for both the wrath and its object can sprout poisonous growths. "I was angry with a friend," says Blake, "I told my wrath, my wrath did end." One wonders if the friend's wrath ended, or whether it didn't perhaps begin, since such efforts of honesty often, if not always, backfire.

Sometimes I provoke gratuitous quarrels, responding, like the Caterpillar in *Alice in Wonderland*, impatiently or rudely to every word the other person says until there is either an explosion or an ominous silence. I feel myself in a state of nervous clarity in which every word uttered is a provocation to which my uncontrollable tongue responds with lightning speed. I can find no force in myself to stop being hateful. I remember how, when I was in Europe with my mother, I was often in a sick state of overpowering irritation with her whole being, while she, with the humility of dependence, was preternaturally patient. We were in Tréguier, the lovely little town in Brittany where Renan was born, lived and wrote. Renan, I was to discover, was one of many great French writers behind whom stood the person of an adoring and adored mother. In me, groundless hate for my mother had been building until I felt I would be glad if she died. We strolled into a beautiful little church and were walking back toward the entrance when my mother stumbled over a low step and fell headlong on her face, while her umbrella flew out of her hand and lay beside her like a dead bird. Terror-stricken, I rushed to help her; she sat up slowly and a few drops of blood fell from her nose onto the worn granite of the church floor. I can see those drops now, red against the grey stone, and see my mother's dazed face, trying to smile, and feel the turmoil of shame, fright and tenderness I felt then. I began to cry, while my mother actually managed to laugh and get to her feet. She was bruised and her nose was scraped and seemed slightly out of kilter, but she was not seriously hurt, and, that evening, we ate big bowls of lentil soup at our ancient hotel and were in a state of harmony that lasted for the rest of the trip. From the day of this terrible lesson until now, I have only to think of the scene in the church to feel tears coming to my eyes. It was not the first time in my life that a shock had worked the alchemy of changing hate to love; it seems to me that whenever I am inhabited by my blackest self, something happens to make me ashamed. But my mother's accident seemed the direct result of my deathwish and I was terrified by this proof of the violence of will, as hard as the church floor which rose up to strike her.

I try now to analyze the life cycles of the blacknesses, quarrels and misunderstandings that have come between me and my friends. I think of the kind of quarrel which is based on supposed grievances: the jockeying for position, the clash of wills, the preparation of accusations, the necessity to be right. Most essential, the conviction of rightness and the moral force this gives. I have had ample time to study the art of quarrelling in my life with Marie-Claire, who puts the same creative passion into a quarrel as she does into her writing. An alarming light begins to burn in her yellow-brown eyes as she launches an irrational accusation, invented as dreams are instantly invented to suit the occasion, with Mephistophelean suitability, as if the other person had to be contained and transformed the way dreams transform disagreeable facts. The master-quarreller can take the matter of her victim and turn it to the poison of self-hate; she can make good qualities despicable and change strength into weakness. It is a relief to me when Marie-Claire seizes on something that can be legitimately complained about, such as my gratuitous bad temper. Our quarrels have become so ritualized that they begin to peter out before their climax and turn into amiable conversations, but they can flare up the next day like imperfectly extinguished brushfires and rage for several hours. I used to feel that love was eroded by quarrels, but now I think them preferable to the exhaustion of not quarrelling. I no longer feel sorry about the unjust things I have said which are part of the unreal rhetoric of quarrels. Marie-Claire has never felt sorry and I get the impression not only that she is proud of her own artistry, but also that she is perfecting secret new weapons.

People's anger takes many forms: Edmund's, like a charging bull; Henry's, contained, unresentful and impervious to assault;

Anne's and Bessie's, much like that of my mother, who nursed the little cloud until it grew to a thunderhead. There is anger that is there, like God's anger, without cause and without resolution. Or, if you discover the cause, it is something so odd and unlikely that there is no way to grapple with it. I used to attempt to argue with Bessie; I wrote long logical letters and got replies full of bewilderment, hurt and indignation, like the flight-pattern made by a half-crazed bird shut into a cage. Bessie looked like a quail; she wore soft browns and greys, like feathers, and I now understand her furious need to expel Marie-Claire, that other brown bird, from her territory. They were alike in many ways, each charged with love, anger and the torment of brains that gave them no peace. Each had a mighty writer's will that reconstructs the lives of others.

Bessie knew so well what other people were thinking that she did not need to listen. She would talk as though ears had been invented to receive her words, keeping watch on her listeners, however, like a lion-tamer, to see if the lions are attentive and subdued. I listened to her enthusiasms, to her outpourings of fury that constituted indictments against people she disliked and whom it was impossible to defend, and as always happens to me when I am compelled to listen to someone for a long time without being able to reply, I was gradually filled with murderous rage. I wanted to yell angrily, insultingly, to burst into tears. I had ceased to exist, except as a pair of ears and a clamouring ego. The talker, oblivious of all this, drunk with power, is furious if she is interrupted. "Let me talk!" she is likely to cry, or, "Stop interrupting me!" if the listener tries to insert a word into the monologue, and is hurt if accused of talking too much. "I won't say another word," she says, closing her mouth grimly. But the listener is unable to speak, for a silent non-listener does not listen either; she is too busy feeling hurt and preparing her next speech. However, I never shouted at Bessie as I longed to. I shout at Marie-Claire, who compels attention sometimes, much as Bessie did, who even provokes answers and arguments that can be immediately disposed of, who sets up an irrational case for the sole purpose of defending it against all comers. As Bessie did, she sets a prisoner (in absentia) in the dock,

211

and with an audience of one or more, presents the damning evidence. It is like a one-person quarrel, but preferable, for not only is the other person absent, but also one has a captive audience whose slightest rebellion can be instantly quelled. Bessie would release her wrath indirectly, as if her pent-up suffering could only take the form of anger against others. I think I have never known anyone so destroyed by her own anger as Bessie or so childishly joyful and loving when it had subsided. After one of our black periods, she would appear at my kitchen door with a jar of peach-plum jam, or a cake, or part of a chicken, stretch up her arms like a little girl and we would hug each other and laugh joyfully. In her heart of hearts, Bessie was humble and generous; she had to go through the process of expulsion of Marie-Claire before she could acknowledge her large existence. Too apt to react violently against direct assault, I forgot for a while the extraordinary and complicated essence of Bessie's being, how much a victim she was of her uncertainty and self-hate. "Henry says pain is good and necessary to be an artist," she said in a letter to me at the beginning of our friendship when there was nothing but love between us, "and loneliness, and fear and uncertainty, and that through all these instruments we see form, life. But you know all that. I have always to be told this, and each day to surmount the pain and the loneliness and the fear *and* the love. This is my constant lesson for the day, and is the only process of religion an artist can ever afford himself." Since I believe I know better than anyone else what is best for me, I began to quarrel with Bessie when she, with her writer's zeal, tried, so to speak, to write my life. And isn't this kind of possessiveness, of no less than the other's life, the genesis of almost all quarrels; isn't a quarrel the striking together of two invisible wills? In the midst of one of my silent quarrels with Bessie, words could not even get out and I was aware of a darkness that had engulfed the two of us and in which the black formless creatures of our wills lunged at each other, fell and bled to death, and others rushed in to take their places.

What explains the amazing aggressiveness of this being in each of us, ready to leap to battle, endlessly to assert our unique possession of all truth? Does it come from the violent disappointment of being born, the shock of leaving the womb where one has reigned supreme? I had not reigned supreme in the womb; I had been crowded in with my twin sister and even had to wait ten minutes to be born. I wonder if this explains my impatience, my need for solitude, and worst of all, my instinct to make a distance, sooner or later, between myself and every being who is close to me. Does my infancy explain my competitiveness and jealousy, my hatred of noise, for my twin was always there competing for our mother's attention, claiming one of her breasts or yelling close to my sensitive ears? But non-twins are jealous, too, I have noticed, and afflicted with the same imperious yammerings of ego. Original sin comes from the intolerable discovery that you are not alone in the world ("Not the only pebble on the beach," as Miss Balfour used to say), and worse still, that every other ego is as insatiable as your own; and your reaction—of rage. For this rage seems to be in everybody, even if they do not admit it, and it feeds on whatever material is at hand. Even at the beginning of a great love, it begins gathering the material of judgement and stashing it away, the essence of it consisting of the differences between the lovers. Perhaps I have been hunting for an identical twin to love, so upset am I by lapses in the other from my way of seeing and doing things, from proper ways of housekeeping to an appreciation of the artists I love. There must be something wonderfully gratifying in living with yourself, or so many identical twins would not stick together and marry other identical twins. Would I have felt such impatience with an alter ego or tried to expel her from the womb? My father, so different from my mother, used to say to me that they complemented each other and this was supposed to be the basis for their love, but it did not prevent them from quarrelling. On the other hand, I have heard it said of two quarrellers (most often a parent and a child), "They quarrel because they're so much alike." Perhaps if they had been *exactly* alike, they would not have quarrelled and the quarrel was because of those differences that they hated in each other?

I think of the identical twins, Tweedledum and Tweedledee, who quarrelled with ritual fury because their destiny, in the form of a poem, compelled them to. Lewis Carroll seems to say that each of us is the subject of a life-poem written before we are even born. Tweedledum and Tweedledee, identical twins who adore each other, are programmed by destiny to expiate their "original" rage. But since they are identical, they go about their quarrel (after Tweedledum's first explosion and Tweedledee's terrified attempt to fold himself into their umbrella) amiably, observing only the outward forms: the armour, the weapons ("'There's only one sword, you know,' Tweedledum said to his brother, 'but *you* can have the umbrella—it's quite as sharp.'"). We know in advance, looking in the crystal ball of the old nursery rhyme, that the quarrel will never take place, that just as they reach the moment of combat, the monstrous crow will have the paradoxical effect of uniting them in fear. And isn't it often the case, that something much more terrible than the grounds for the quarrel intervenes and unites the quarrellers?

Unlike Tweedledum and Tweedledee, I am programmed to allow a quarrel to go so far that the monstrous crow comes in the form of remorse. I envy them the sweetness of their love for each other, which is destined to be reborn as fresh as ever, after every battle. I admire the extraordinary patience of Alice, who is the puzzled victim of their irascibility and gratuitous rudeness. Lewis Carroll wrote as profoundly about bad temper as other writers have written about love; he had obviously made a detached study of his own crankiness. One can open to almost any page of *Alice* and find creatures snapping at each other or at Alice. There are tempers within tempers: the Caterpillar (with whom I tend to identify myself), after being both rude and contemptuous to Alice, ends by counselling her, 'Keep your temper.' The Duchess' cook, the Duchess, the Queen are possessed by irrational fury; the Mad Hatter, the March Hare and the Mock Turtle, by an irritable sense of superiority. Bad temper enters into the whole fabric of existence: into time, which won't stand beating; into objects, like the White Queen's shawl—'It's out of temper, I think. I've pinned it here and I've pinned it there, but there's no pleasing it!'; into words—'They've a temper, some of them—particularly verbs,' says Humpty-Dumpty. Lewis Carroll understood the utter perversity of bad temper, how it permeates everything like a poison that has entered ground water and spreads

214

invisibly into people's wells.

To me, the two *Alices* are a series of parables, as accurate as Kafka's, about the nature of waking life as it is governed by the subconscious; and they represent as well a life-portrait of Charles Dodgson—Lewis Carroll. Charles Dodgson, "a puttering, fussy, fastidious, didactic bachelor," says Alexander Wollcott, "who was almost painfully humourless in his relations with the grown-up world around him," through the agency of a little girl is able to live fully as the artist, Lewis Carroll. Little girls represented his ideal of chastity and innocence, an ideal which perhaps kept him sane. They stood for *what was permitted* (*i.e.*, the degree of sexuality that Dodgson permitted himself). It was permitted for a clergyman-don of his time to make friends of little girls, to be alone with them and to tell them stories. The irony is that the stories told to these personifications of Dodgson's ideal contain, in the form of a hilarious mockery of the permitted, everything that was forbidden: the anger, violence, punishment, craziness and arbitrary judgements that dwell in the shadows and leap out or take open and licensed forms in religion, law and social conventions. Alice is that little area in ourselves and in society where innocence can be said to be still intact, like an old-fashioned garden somehow preserved in the middle of a jungle.

The *Alices*, in their dream-indiscretion, are full of sexual images, as is pointed out in various essays by psychoanalysts in *Aspects of Alice*: her growing and shrinking, the immensity of her neck in Carroll's original illustration, her falling down the rabbit hole, the sneezing baby, the flamingos which refuse to keep their heads down. A.M.E. Goldschmidt comes to the conclusion that *Alice* is "perhaps to be explained by the desire for complete virility." Lewis Carroll, continues Dr. Goldschmidt, "is described in middle and old age, as morose, irritable, intractable, and subject to fits of depression. Had he lived today he might have undergone analysis, discovered the cause of his neurosis, and lived a more contented life. But in that case, he might not have written *Alice in Wonderland*." I think that if Dodgson-Carroll had not found his own key to the garden of his imagination, he might well have gone mad, and that the *Alices* are, like many works of art, a form of subconscious self-analysis. I recall that

Rilke refused to be analyzed, fearing that analysis would derange his poetic universe, and that Marie-Claire is angry at the thought of analytical formulas that squeeze the cosmic complication of her being into their Procrustes' bed. Dr. Goldschmidt, not giving us his own opinion, allows us to decide which is more important: *Alice in Wonderland* or the hypothesis of a "more contented life," for it is impossible to have both. I infinitely prefer the morose and irritable Dodgson, whose genius could only be released by living out his neurosis, to one who has been analyzed, and who, knowing now that Alice represents his own penis, has come to abhor his love for little girls, and in his contented state of complete virility, dreams no longer.

Chapter Thirteen

I have been thinking about the ambiguous character of primitive emotions—those that are thought of as negative: anger, hate, jealousy—prompted by our so-called animal instincts (love, generosity, etc., supposedly belonging to man and womankind alone) and how even these take on a justified grandeur in the eyes of the ego. Who has not heard a man relate with modest pride how he collared so-and-so and punched him in the nose? As for women who have traditionally been ashamed of the rage secretly boiling in them, they are now being enjoined by the women's movement to let it out, to enjoy it, to think of it as healthy. The volume of their anger, so surprising to men, is the volcanic result of thousands of years of keeping it pent up; it is the kind of benign steam that powers all revolutions.

For me, the dignity of anger depends on its cause. I am invariably ashamed of my childish outbursts of rage when I feel my eyes staring wildly, hear my voice mounting to a roar, when I slam doors or throw things on the floor, being careful, however, not to throw things that will break. Marie-Claire, whose anger does not take the form of childish tantrums, who, when angry, is more like a swarm of hornets, now reminds me that I look around hastily to find something non-breakable, and we both laugh at this evidence of my ever-watchful respect for objects.

217

My most violent outburst with Marie-Claire was caused by a rage of jealousy. I had been reading, as I always did, the pages she had written that day of her book, *Les Nuits de l'Underground*, reading the lyrical description of Lali, a loving portrait, the details of which began to sting me with intolerable pain, even though Marie-Claire no longer loved the real Lali. It was a good example of the pain of seeing or hearing something which you have only imagined. I looked through Marie-Claire's magnifying lens and realized that what I had seen in fancy was in fact infinitely more beautiful, that Marie-Claire's love for Lali was infinitely more profound. It was as if I, who had suffered from jealousy and loneliness during the period of this love, were now the prey of a magnified suffering, like the magnified portrait. "Je suis jalouse," I said. "Jalouse?" But it was a book; it was all over; I didn't have the *right* to be jealous (nor had I ever had it). I stood up, rumpled the manuscript pages and threw them on the floor while Marie-Claire's pale face registered alarm and disgust. A few seconds later, alarmed myself, I picked up the pages and smoothed them out. I was ashamed of the destructive and uncontrollable monster in me that was, I thought, unworthy of me, that came from God knew where and forced me to do hateful things.

Jealousy is an unworthy emotion and yet it, too, commands respect. People have a sneaking affection for their own jealousy, though they are irritated by that of others. A sign of possessiveness, they say sagely, and no one has the right to be possessive of another person. So says Marie-Claire when I am jealous, but when *she* is jealous, she says that no one is capable of understanding that her emotion is much more profound than jealousy. Many women, particularly Lesbians, having explored the nature and eternal presence of jealousy in their relationships, have attempted to eliminate it by sharing in a free exchange of love. But is it possible to release your rage and suppress your jealousy? I am convinced in the rational half of my brain that no one has the right to be jealous; I practice an exercise of letting-go, which consists of seeing my friends as autonomous beings like myself, on whom I have no hold, reminding myself of how my hackles rise if they are possessive of *me*. But since jealousy was born in our infant egos, since it has to do finally with our sense of worth, since, for some reason, our sense of worth is fatally in-jured if the person we love ceases to love us, and worse still, loves someone else (we can be loved by ten other people, but it is only this *one* person who can reduce us to nothingness by preferring someone else), it is an illusion to think it is dead.

There were periods of weeks and months during my life when I was sick with jealousy. Another memory of Woods Hole comes back to me. I am lying in bed and wake up before dawn; the fog-laden air comes through the open window and encloses me in a damp, sticky embrace, black as the gloom that possesses me. I have been in love with Caleb, my sister-in-law's brother, who looked like Praxiteles' Hermes, with a hawk nose, a round-ed chin, chiselled lips and the body of a Greek athlete. Everything about him pleased me (I was twenty-one): his masculine cruelty and heroism (one of his gestures was to put out a cigarette on his arm), the battered black Stetson he wore, pants low on his hips, his thick curly hair, his grey eyes squinting at the sun. If he liked you, you were taken into his world, as if it were a secret society. His attention was briefly fixed on me, like a brother's attention, I think now, for it was playful and unsen-sual. Not that that prevented me from falling sick with jealousy when I came back from a trip and found that he had a new friend (a college friend of mine), shy and inarticulate, with straight yellow hair and blue eyes. I saw them together at the end of a dock, standing shoulder to shoulder, swaying slightly. I saw Caleb's big sneakered foot move over and place itself against Mathilda's smaller one, and the eloquence of those two feet together sent a shaft of pain through me. I had to pretend to re-joice at their wedding, but for months was enclosed in my dark fog of jealousy. I knew myself so imperfectly that I thought I *might* have married Caleb; it was before my first real love for a woman and it was as if he represented my conviction that I could and did love men — and my sense of the finality of my failure.

A year ago, at my niece's wedding party, my eyes were riveted on one of Caleb's sons, a replica of his father, but smaller, who had joined in a square dance. His eyes (behind glasses) squinted like Caleb's, his chin was round with a dimple in it, his pants were low on his hips; he danced with a kind of awkward grace, leaping energetically about without knowing the steps. In my self-consciousness, I always envied the fine unconsciousness of handsome young men and beautiful animals who moved in perfect possession of their bodies and looked through you as if you weren't there. Caleb's son did not see me staring at him, and if he had, he would have seen a woman his mother's age, to whom he was supposed to be polite. He would not have guessed at the complicated emotions tumbling about in my head: the desire to go on watching him for hours, to discover why this replica of Caleb had the power to produce in me envy and nostalgia for something I had never really wanted, for, at the same time, I felt far from him, from all of them, dancing so cheerfully, from their good, sensible and "normal" lives. There would be generations of Calebs, all with those recognizable features like the Kennedys', which I admired and envied, just as Tonio Krüger in Thomas Mann's story of that name envies the handsome young people. I even looked like one of them, like my sister and brothers, but I was different inside. What would he think, Caleb's son, and all the rest of them, if they knew that when the minister asked if there was any impediment to the marriage of Pauline and Simon, I had a crazy impulse to get up and say, "I don't think Simon's family knows that Pauline's aunt is a Lesbian." Of the hundred or so people there, of all the sons and daughters of all my friends and relations, there was not a single Lesbian or homosexual. I was back in my secret world of silence, pretending with that power to charm that belonged to my family, composed of polite attention and interest in one's fellow-person, that I was *one of them*. As I thought about the power of Caleb's son to make me feel nostalgic, I realized that the comfortable state of being one of them, of developing those aspects of myself that would make me belong to their world, would have kept me from finding a more difficult self. And that it was a good fate that made Caleb lose interest in me, for it made it easier for me to go my own way.

Perhaps my envy had to do, too, with the spectacle of all those happy marriages, of couples who gave no sign of ever having been unfaithful to each other. A heterosexual marriage legitimized jealousy and possessiveness (aren't all excessive emotions and acts legitimized by society: murder, rape and theft by war; prejudice by religion; greed by ritual feasts, etc.?) whereas they somehow became ugly and impermissible in a relation between women. Lesbian couples, no matter how loving, are inherently less stable than heterosexual couples; other women are always temptingly present and there is no restraining convention, only the fury of jealousy to prevent the couple from becoming a triangle. It is true that the mechanism of expulsion of a third person that would be automatic in a heterosexual marriage works, too, with a Lesbian couple, but in my case, as we know, there has frequently been an effort to live as a triangle, a subsequent changing around of partners and a horrid explosion that has wounded all three. Thus it was with Julia, myself and the real Lali (whose name Marie-Claire borrowed for her novel), a triangle grown from the couple Julia-Mary. Julia had been my friend when I went to live in New York after the war; we had known each other as children in Woods Hole, but our friendship took years to germinate. It was because Julia was a friend of Marianne Moore, e.e. cummings and his wife, Marian, Loren MacIver, Elizabeth Bishop, Sylvia Marlowe and Leonid, Eleanor Clark and Jane Bowles, that I became their friend, too. Julia was, and is, a person one can only describe as in a state of permanent innocence and candour. That she should have chosen to love me was surprising, for we were incapable of understanding each other. I loved the outward Julia: her oval face and startlingly blue eyes that reminded me of my father's, her plumpish, comfortable body and white skin that never browned in the sun, and the qualities that still make her irresistible to all her friends. She spends her life helping people: artists, writers, musicians, with self-deprecating generosity. I see her now and then, waving her hands like the White Rabbit in *Alice,* teetering on high heels, her eyes as blue as ever in her plump pink face, presiding over the apartment full of treasures where her mother used to invite everybody who was important in the cultural life of New York.

I spent winters in my own apartment and summers with Julia in the Berkshires, in Guatemala, and a painful summer in Europe where we formed a triangle with Julia's mother, justifiably

221

hostile to my threatening presence, as any good mother would be. I hardly knew how it happened that Lali was suddenly present in Julia's life and in my own. Lali's husband had been a German diplomat, who, insufficiently loyal to the Nazis, had been taken away for questioning one day and never returned. I tried to imagine their pre-war life, the great dinner parties for which Lali's husband chose all the flowers and china and crystal and supervised the arrangement of the table, while Lali, even then, perhaps, a ghost in their big house, read poetry and dreamed in her own room. She had a chalky pallor and jet black hair, never laughed and smiled small painful smiles. She wrote a book about the war and its aftermath, when her house was looted and she hid from the Russians who were raping every woman they could find. At night, she would creep out and dig up rotting potatoes and carrots out of the vegetable garden, for there was nothing else to eat. But the fact about her life that fascinated me the most was that, at nineteen, she had tuberculosis and had gone to the same sanatorium where Rilke was and had made friends with him.

Lali's life was composed of tragedies, yet this and her quietness, her fragility, her delicate perceptions (she was like a night-blooming flower)—none of this spared her from the punishing brutality of my jealousy. I remember with shame how rude I was to her when the three of us were together on Sutton Island; I remember Julia's indignant blue eyes and protective manner and Lali's passivity. She was frightened by my sharp tongue and drew further into herself, like others who have been my victims in the game of love.

And then, as always seemed to happen, my feeling of hate turned inside-out, my soul was flooded with peaceful feelings and I realized that I was in love with Lali, whose ghostly presence, her trim body dressed in grey, white and black, her dark, fathomless eyes and musical voice with its little accent, now enchanted me. We went for a walk and I told Lali that I loved her. "Is it easy for you to fall in love?" asked Lali. It was hard for *her*, she said. Julia was the only woman she had ever loved. When I was in love, I forgot that it was easy for me both to fall in love and to fall out of it. I was convinced, as everybody is, no doubt, that every love was unique and eternal, and I never learned from experience.

That autumn, I found myself in New York for a few days, while Julia stayed on in the Berkshires. Lali had returned to New York and we had dinner together, and afterwards, we mounted in the elevator to her apartment. It had been raining and water ran off the tip of my umbrella and formed a little pool on the elevator floor, with which I traced the words, "I love you." I looked at Lali, who was smiling an embarrassed little smile. When, in the apartment, I asked her if I could spend the night, she said no, very gently, like a mother talking to a stubborn child.

It was the first time I had felt the imperious instinct to make a triangle equilateral — and, in addition, to punish Julia by making love with Lali, and bringing her the triumphant news, "Lali loves me, too." But Lali was much too sensible and kind to permit this, and my attempt at vengeance only made me weep uncontrollably while I described it to the furious Julia. Julia and Lali went off together for a month to New Orleans, and not wanting to share my humiliation with my New York friends, I spent the month with my mother in Washington. I could not tell her the reasons for this surprising and welcome attention to her, but I felt strangely happy with her, as though her ignorance of my life made it invisible, as though a spell had been cast over me that made my New York self cease to exist. I would drive down to the Potomac River and sit on a bench in the tranquil sunshine, while the arms of the weeping willows swayed lazily behind me and the grey-brown river lapped along the retaining wall. There, I struggled against surges of violent feelings and had the false impression of having won victories. At the end of the month, I got a telegram from Julia saying they were going to stay four more days. It was as though I had suddenly gone mad, as though there were no trace of goodness, patience, generosity left in me; it had all been replaced by murderous rage and hate against the two of them. I wrote them both savage letters. Lali opened hers on the ship that was to take her back to Europe; she read it silently in the presence of her son-in-law (a friend of mine), looked agitated and said, "She should get married," an example of her forbearance and discretion. Hearing this, I wrote a letter of apology, for, though I was less careful with people than with objects, I always tried to put the pieces back together again. Several years later, I heard that Lali had died mysteriously somewhere in South America, felt her ghostly presence and thought with regret about my own insensitivity. As for Julia, my letter killed our love once and for all and it was followed by stormy quarrels, and finally, by an affectionate but distant friendship. It is almost as if we had never loved each other, the impersonality of this friendship and our polite conversations about our animals and our mutual friends.

Jealousy to me is proof of the amazing instability of the self, which seems positively eager both to be hurt and to believe the worst about another self. One would think that Othello, a man who was respected by everyone, would have been strong enough to resist Iago, that he would have chosen rather to believe Desdemona whom he loved and who loved him. There is nothing in *Othello* to suggest that he was particularly vulnerable because he was a Moor; no, his vulnerability is something that lies at the bottom of every human and animal heart, the suspicion that one is not loved, that one has been abandoned. In the case of Othello, or of any man with a wife, the suspicion is enforced by the sense of possession; a man *owns* an infallible source of love in the form of his wife. She is there, as his mother was there, to allow his ego to flourish properly. She is grafted onto his ego and nourished by it, having learned to keep hers secondary to his. When a man really loves his wife, as Othello loved Desdemona, it is as if the vulnerable secret part of himself were embodied in the beloved, as if, when he feels betrayed, he feels more humiliated because he has allowed the secret part of himself to be visible to others. The wife who betrays her husband must be punished, or better still, killed, so that she can no longer remind him that he is not omnipotent, that he cannot enforce love, that he cannot control what is *his*. The idea that husbands have the right to be jealous is an acknowledgement of their right to control. If Desdemona *had* been guilty, Emilia would not have raged at Othello; she would have thought, it serves her right. The punishment of Desdemona is all the more terrible when one

224

thinks that her life consisted only of loving Othello, that she was a "perfect" wife. In general, wives, like public servants, who, when appointed, give up their fortunes, give up whatever is dear to them, their singing (fortunately, Desdemona went on singing, at least in the opera), painting or writing, their passion for this or that which might distract them from total attention to the husband. If a woman writer marries a writer, she is expected to sublimate her own ambition in his. And in case men's desire for omnipotence is still unfulfilled, society has gone further — it allows them to beat their wives, their dogs, their horses, their children. I think of a poem by D.H. Lawrence called "Bibbles," about his "little black snub-nosed bitch with a shoved-out jaw," a hilarious poem from which one learns that even a little dog can play the role of an unfaithful wife. It is intolerable to Lawrence that Bibbles loves everybody, that she goes chasing after an old Mexican woman in the plaza:

> *...your black little body bouncing and wriggling*
> *With indiscriminate love, Bibbles;*
> *I had a moment's pure detestation of you.*

Bibbles further enrages Lawrence by eating dung and throwing it up. But he has his revenge. It comes when Bibbles, in heat and pursued by "the great ranch dogs," comes to him cringing and rolling her eyes with fear. "All right, my little bitch," says Lawrence, "You learn loyalty rather than loving. / And I'll protect you."

It is intolerable to Lawrence that Bibbles not only does not love him alone, but also that other people have the illusion of being loved by her:

> *And even the dirtiest scallywag is taken in,*
> *Thinking: This dog sure has taken a fancy to me.*

And who among us has not suffered a pang when one of our dogs appears to adore a friend, when a cat makes a beeline for a friend's lap, and the friend says complacently, "She likes me!" One of my minor problems in Wellfleet was that old Gillou barked furiously at Edmund and even snapped at his ankles when he trudged up the hill to our house, and that Edmund was genuinely hurt every time this happened. "She doesn't like men," he once said in exasperation, taking a swipe both at Gillou and at Barbara and me. To explain that Gillou liked men with soft voices only made matters worse. Edmund tried to bribe Gillou by bringing a piece of meat and holding it out to her, but she would snatch it out of his hand and remain in her state of hostility. It was a relief when Maidie, an emaciated spaniel rescued from a dog concentration camp, who, like Bibbles, ate excrement, would sit mournfully at Edmund's feet and rest her head on his thigh, while he smiled complacently and stroked the high silky dome of her head.

It is interesting that an animal's attitude is always taken personally, though there is no reason why one should be automatically liked by a dog or a cat. But in our paranoia or our self-satisfaction, we think either that there is something likeable in us that the animal has immediately perceived or something *not* likeable. I have seen grown-ups making frantic efforts to win the affection of cats or dogs, and, once won, showing a very special kind of vanity, or if the cat flees, being crestfallen in a special way. But how hard it is to control the octopus in one's heart that shoots out a tentacle almost without our knowing it and fastens on something, or someone, saying, "Mine, mine"; the creature which is jealous, even of ideas, saying, "That was my idea," or saying, "Agree with me, but look out!" Sometimes Marie-Claire takes possession, as it were, of a writer, a painter, a landscape that I love, as if to say, "Look what *I* can do with this subject," elaborating on the most minute details of a painting by Munch or of the Breton landscape, details that I have forgotten. "Do you remember?" she says. "No, I don't," I say, becoming more and more gloomy. "Yes, you *do* remember!" And she piles up detail on forgotten detail until I think, the subject is yours, and I have no more claim to it. A game, you will say, but like all games, deadly serious. In this way, painters possess their landscapes or their gimmick; and writers, their territory. I remember Rothko once saying, half in jest, "Some of my imitators are better than I am." The danger of the theft of oneself is everywhere. Even gifted or beautiful children pose a threat to their parents, whose pride contains the secret anxiety that they will be surpassed.

Possessiveness is a primal emotion, like the fear of falling. At the centre of it sits the ego, for which no reassurance is ever enough, which learns to share only by loving and is always suspicious of the lessons learned through love. It is so finely tuned to the possibility of diminishment that there is almost nothing another person can say or do that is not processed subconsciously. "Does this diminish me?" We do not feel ourselves doing this, but there is something in us that *knows* instantly and touchily reacts; something we call touchiness or vanity in others and sensitivity or pride in ourselves. I recall Morley Callaghan's *That Summer in Paris,* in which several extraordinary stories about Hemingway and Fitzgerald reveal the primitive nature of male pride. Callaghan has friendly boxing matches with Hemingway, and, in the middle of one of them, when he has just planted one of his surprising punches square on Hemingway's mouth, Hemingway spits a mouthful of blood in his face. "That's what the bullfighters do when they're wounded," he explains. "It's a way of showing contempt." He suddenly becomes good-tempered, even amiable, and Callaghan, too shocked at first to have reacted violently, forgives him and they go on being friends. It is obvious that Hemingway's fantasy of spitting blood at a bull was a lightning excuse for his explosion of rage and wounded vanity, a cover-up, which Callaghan, in the generosity of his heart, accepts. Or, one can't help wondering, was Hemingway *really* pleased with himself? For the mechanisms of defence can whitewash and transform the most repellant behaviour, and his sudden identification of himself with a bullfighter and subsequent good humour were strokes of defensive genius that excused him in his own eyes. He never apologized, since an apology would have suggested that he felt badly. On the contrary, he seemed to think that his "cut and swollen mouth" was in itself a kind of payment for his brutality, that it cancelled it out and gave him the right to be particularly cheerful.

Morley Callaghan reminds one of Alice among the "mad" people of Wonderland, and of her conversation with the Cheshire Cat, who tries to convince her that she, too, is mad. "We're all mad here," the Cat says. "I'm mad. You're mad." "How do you know I'm mad?" says Alice. "You must be," says the Cat, "or you wouldn't have come here." But Alice (like Callaghan) does not think she is mad. In a conversation between Callaghan and his wife, Loretto, she observes that all the friends they have made in Paris: Sinclair Lewis, McAlmon, Joyce, Hemingway and Fitzgerald, have behaved in some crazy way. "Do you know you have the craziest friends?" she says. And Callaghan ends by saying, "Aren't you lucky?. . . I'm the only one who is calm, objective and rational."

But the Cheshire Cat is right. We're all mad and the irrationality of Wonderland is perfectly normal. In the case of Fitzgerald and Hemingway, Callaghan is a witness to the quivering vulnerability that makes people behave crazily (*i.e.*, in inexplicably childish, brutal or violent ways). Elena Wilson once said to me that evil is the absence of good. All evil is alike, she said; it is good that is different and individual. But didn't this idea spring from the wish to disassociate oneself from the crazy violence in oneself and to claim the good as if it were one's real nature? A few years ago, I wrote a poem called "Alter Ego," in which I tried to analyze my seemingly dual nature, the coming and going of "the beast" who insists on his identity with me:

> *Paralyzed by my poison*
> *You make your feeble excuses,*
> *Say you are possessed*
> *By the devil or a beast,*
> *But once and for all, you should know*
> *That you are I and I am you*
> *And that I come and go as I please.*

Human beings have devised the most ingenious ways of dealing with "the beast," sometimes denying its existence, sometimes shaking their heads and saying, "It's human nature," just as they say of a cat with a bird in its mouth, "A cat is a cat." I used to argue with Barbara about aggression. Are you born with it, as Robert Ardrey thinks? Barbara thinks that violence is learned; I think that it does not need to be learned if you are born

228

with the conviction of being at the centre of the universe, of being infinitely important and infinitely fragile. There are wonderful times in our lives when our need for love and attention is satisfied, times of harmonious equilibrium when it seems as though giving and receiving are one and the same thing. And then, the unity of love is somehow fractured, the lovers or friends (for the same process can destroy friendships, as it destroyed the one between Hemingway and Fitzgerald) split into two people at war with each other, watching and punishing and judging.

Chapter Fourteen

Thinking about the morphology of violence and the wish to punish, I wonder how much of my own inner violence comes from my childhood and the fact that judgement was ever-present. Children, it is said, imitate their parents' behaviour, scold and spank their dolls, and if they have been beaten, beat their own children. My adult self nags at my beloved friends in much the same way that Miss Balfour nagged at me, and my imperious need for a scheduled day perhaps comes from her insistent sense of time. I still remember elements of our childhood schedule — for instance, the hour of bedtime for my sister and me was exactly twenty to eight. No lingering was ever permitted. We were allowed to stay in the water during our summer holiday for seven minutes, and then, Miss Balfour began shouting and waving her arms. To this day, I am forever looking at my wrist watch and cannot imagine how some people live without watches or how they have acquired their total indifference to the passage of time. Part of my irritability is the result of having an inexorable clock ticking away inside me, like the clock in the crocodile in *Peter Pan,* and sounding its regular alarms. I measure the probable length of my future, the number of years during which I can still depend on the working of my brain, hands, eyes, etc., and I am obsessed by the conviction that I must not waste a minute of this time, which I see suddenly as the last few grains of sand racing through an hourglass.

My impatience is linked to a sense of what must be done, with an exaggerated mustness: we must leave; we must get there at such and such a time. I remember how, travelling in Italy with my Argentine friends, Patricio and his sister, Estela, they would linger over meals in restaurants, or sit in a sunny piazza, as if there were nothing more important in life than drinking a glass of vermouth, while I would become desperate about seeing the cathedral, the museum (like Barbara, they belonged to that race of tourists who abhorred guidebooks and saw a cathedral only if it was directly in their path), about how the precious hours had to be filled in what I thought of as good and positive ways, and how surprised they were at my asperity when I interrupted one of their endless dialogues. I grow literally sick with impatience in situations like this, as though I were being suffocated, with the steam of irritability building up its fatal pressure. My grandmother and my uncle were like this too; so is one of my brothers, and I think that perhaps irritability is a hereditary disease (I can feel it invading my body, my nervous system) rather than the legacy of my strict upbringing.

It is distressing to me that I never seem to learn from experience and that, at sixty-one, my character is as difficult and unpredictable as it has always been. I am able with great lucidity to see what I am doing while I am doing it, but have learned no mechanism for controlling the alternations of love and hate, happiness and misery, jealousy and acceptance that fight it out in my depths. I can see that my ruthless judgement of myself has something to do with my judgement of others, and yet, we are never as ruthless with ourselves as we are with others. If it weren't so awful, there would be something comical about the solemnity of our judgements, our certainty of being in possession of the truth about someone's flaws or the direction their lives should take, the severity with which a long-winded person says that so-and-so talks too much, or a selfish person condemns someone else's selfishness. Judgements are constantly in our heads or on our lips and even positive statements about people inspire us to challenge them.

Even love, by its intensity, contains the seeds of judgement and destructiveness, and just as my dislike for someone would suddenly change to love, the opposite would happen and the beloved would have to be pierced with my destructive arrows. Or I myself would be subjected to the process, as I was by Patricio after our brief love affair. Patricio went about the work of destruction as though he were doing an autopsy, opening up innocent events or traits of character, like blood vessels, to the light of day and discovering diseased cells within. He did this with an earnest passion, for he wished to convince me that his view of me was correct and that my view of myself was false, but he only succeeded in making me shout with rage. Patricio's art was not so much in diminishing me, as in transforming me into an authentic monster; and his reconstruction had a certain grand negativity.

It seems to be a human need to be totally for or totally against. In politics, one side is thought to be all good and the other all bad, and this view seems to be the secret of keeping love and allegiance intact. The first critical thought one has about a lover is as insidious as a splinter that works its way all the way to the heart. In the merging process of love, lovers actually exchange identities and, thus, may be false to their true selves in a way that they may later resent. So it was that Marie-Claire, who claimed that she loved her austere and barless life with Barbara and me, and the sensible hours we kept, who did this for six years in the name of love, now talks angrily of the sacrifice of her youth, as though it had been imposed on her by her pitiless friends. We are strangely acquiescent in the hypnotic state of love, and afterwards, blame not ourselves, but the person who bewitched us. I think with disgust of my submissiveness to the blandishments of Andrée, of the zombie-state that paralyzed my will, and wonder at the memory of Marie-Claire dancing like a marionette when Andrée twitched the strings.

The first appearance of resentment in a relationship means that one has begun to take back the portion of oneself that has been freely given, to take it back with ominous tightness, locking the pieces of oneself together, and suddenly seeing the other as an outsider. I can feel myself toughening as I return to my own shape and am irritated if the ex-beloved, now an outsider, has the illusion of still owning little pieces of me. Indeed, it becomes dangerous, the possession of parts of one's self by someone else, and not only have all the pieces to be taken back, but also one has to be careful not to let any escape. I become neurotically aware of pressure that the other person exerts by retaining the sense of our old relationship, the closeness of it, and aware of the exercise of this pressure through innocent reminders such as, "Do you remember how?" etc. Worst is the tangible evidence — love letters that remain like statements sworn before a notary. I am glad, however, that Barbara kept all my letters and that they can still remind me of the intensity of our love for each other, and sorry that Andrée forced Marie-Claire to destroy my letters; and me, to destroy hers. I think with a sinking heart of letters I wrote Andrée, used, no doubt, when she wrote her book, and letters to other friends declaring the permanence of my love. Love letters tend to repeat themselves. But, in fact, I am less ashamed of having flowed out of myself into another person, than of having reeled myself in until I shrank to a state of penury with nothing left to give and felt myself compromised by having loved. I changed from loving to loveless, from generous to stingy; to a person who wounded by my hardness, and I was even glad to be free of the sickness of love and to be all of a piece again. It is always at this stage, I think, when one person has ceased to love and the other hasn't, that the ex-lover cannot speak or act in a way that doesn't seem intolerably cruel, that invariably falls short of what the other needs and hopes for. Need provokes cruelty, but indifference is just as bad. The person who has ceased to love becomes blind in a way that is peculiar to this state; it is, perhaps, an everyday sort of blindness, like that which keeps so many relationships polite and formal. But to the lover, it seems part of a fiendish strategy. In the vulnerable state of not being loved, one has an acute sense of what ought to be, how the beloved should behave if she were truly sensitive. Sensitivity, which comes so naturally to a lover, is sacrificed to the ex-lover's awful carefulness, her refusal to give a single crumb of encouragement, and it can be resumed only when there is a "safe" distance between the lovers.

So it was, by passing through the dark night of lovelessness, that my friendship with Barbara, permanent and unshakeable, was forged. And Barbara has just come to visit, the first time she has seen Marie-Claire and me in our own house since we left Wellfleet. She arrived at the airport dressed in a blue denim shirt, clean cream-coloured frontier pants and white canvas shoes, with a knapsack on her back. She was sunburned; her brown hair with no grey in it, exactly as it always was; her face—the lines from nose to mouth, and from mouth to small determined chin, deeper; her brown eyes seemingly a little smaller and lighter—is the same serious, anxious and kindly face; her hands still cut and shape the air, palms inwards, shape every sentence as if it were dough or clay. Her tall body is absolutely arresting in its difference from any other in the world, and was more so when she appeared in a pair of baggy dark green parachute pants—took off her shirt to reveal a navy blue undershirt edged with faded red, from the waist up, the thin torso with long muscular brown arms (she and I compared biceps), the throat where one still sees a faint scar from the tracheotomy that saved her life when her lung was punctured and her whole body fractured in an automobile accident six years ago, and beautiful hands with the knuckles widened a little by arthritis—the tall half-person, rising from the voluminous pants with white duck-like feet below, was so touching in her unselfconsciousness, her pride in her pants which she loved, that my fussy finickiness and vestigial conventionality were vanquished by this friend who dares to be wholly herself.

The three of us talked with utter frankness about our lives, our loves, our likes and dislikes, our quarrels. Barbara recognized in me the same old resistance as she talked about androgyny, her hope that women and men can be brought closer together by recognizing the man in a woman, the woman in a man. She builds her hopes on exceptions, on miracles. She knows that miracles really happen, that blood can be squeezed from stones. She lives outside the framework of conventional scepticism, has picked up folk cures: the juice from a certain cactus will cure boils (it has worked for her); the inner membrane of an egg can be used as a poultice to draw out infection; if you know what

235

spot to touch on your foot, you can help the pain in your back, or cure a headache. She seems steeped in the age-old wisdom of women—in literature by and about women—and she makes me and Marie-Claire aware of the magnitude of women's accomplishments.

Barbara and I went for a walk in the woods and heard a wood thrush, a veery and a yellowthroat; we saw a female redstart and a woodcock. She recognized Daisy Fleabane growing. "Do you remember how surprised Edmund was when I knew what Daisy Fleabane was?" It began to rain and we sheltered under a huge blue spruce, its lower boughs resting on the dark tumbled rocks of a mysterious wall that I found one day. We are bound together by the things that make us alike: the sense of ferns and ground pine seeming to grow in our own veins; the sense of birds as creatures of our inner kingdom. With all her heart and sensitivity, she wills me not to become the prey of my guilty conscience; she has five hundred reasons why my life is no more selfish than her own. Even in my most generous periods, I have always been careful to keep enough to be generous to myself, and now, in Canada, far from my old causes, I am even more careful. Listening to Barbara talk about her organization, Money for Women, and about the good it has done and intends to do, I feel something like the hand of Scrooge tightening around my heart, but I know that this will put in motion my whole mechanism of shame. Barbara, for me, is still Mary, embodying the purity of conscience, even in the smallest details of her life, and I am still the reluctant and gloomy young man who turns away when it is a question of relinquishing all his possessions.

I think of the strange mixture of heaviness and lightness in Barbara, the gravity of her voice and her words—as though every word had a volume and a weight, so that I sometimes feel myself literally sinking into the ground under the accumulated weight of her words, for each has to be held and examined with attention and cannot be tossed aside like other people's—my own exhaustion of attention, and a sense, too, of something as light as the thread a spider throws out to walk on. Like thought. I know that Barbara arrives at her words by delicate thought-processes—and what is stronger or more tenacious than these almost invisible spider lifelines that support the spider's weight? Her handwriting is tiny, shaky and faint as a sigh; it reminds me of the De Kooning drawing erased by Rauschenburg, with the title, "Erased De Kooning," the ghost of the drawing emanating the disquieting energy of the painter which is there, just as Barbara is there in her handwriting.

I think of the energy of will. "Settled by her unconquerable will / In this hard place," I say in a poem about Barbara on her Florida key. "Do I have a stronger will than either of you?" she asks Marie-Claire and me. We discuss our respective wills and how we exercise them. "Yours is a will for good; you will radical changes in society," I say to Barbara. "Marie-Claire's is used to change people, particularly people she loves; she wills people to find their best selves. And I use my will to make my own life." We are talking about the mainstream of will, not small exercises of it, such as Barbara willing me to give up salt or to drive more slowly, Marie-Claire willing me to travel more, or my willing everybody to observe my ideals of household perfection. Barbara insists that she is as egocentric as I am: "I do what I do because I like it," she says. She believes in identity. Reading what I have said about seeking an identical twin, she says that in consciousness-raising sessions, her group of women have discovered that they are all identical twins, that they share much more than they believed possible. The alarm signal flies up in both my and Marie-Claire's head, we two who are constantly afflicted by a sense of difference. In a consciousness-raising session, each woman is allowed by the others to talk without interruption and without immediate commentary for as long as she wants. After each woman has finished, after hours or days, everything is freely discussed. Listening to Barbara, I realize that meetings like this have a revolutionary force, for they infuse the participants with a patience and an attention that carry over into everyday life and that they reveal all the aspects of women's experience that bind them together. All this is so wonderful that I detest myself for harbouring the little worm of pessimism that reminds me of what is hidden, unknowable, even to oneself, and uncontrollable. I think of Iris Murdoch's words, "opaque and unknowable"—an extreme view of human relations. Has Iris

Murdoch ever been part of a consciousness-raising group? I think of the times when Barbara's differences with other women have refused to be resolved by reason; the mistakes that each of us made about the other, mistakes which grew from the impossibility of knowing our invisible selves. Barbara seems to believe that the elements of ourselves that we share with others should be merged in a kind of loving cup from which all women can drink. Her optimism lies in these expansions from units to the whole, and we disagree not about the unit of optimism, but about how much optimism it permits you to have. Barbara believes that vast numbers of women must come to see how much they suffer from the oppression of marriage and the patriarchal system; she is like a growing plant that cracks open a cement road, and though I accept with joy the evidence that this is possible, I boggle at the application of faith on a large scale. Confronted by this, she says, "It's how I keep on hoping."

Is it stinginess, this niggardly hedging, this inability to say a wholly affirmative, "Yes, yes, yes"? Why not say it and be flooded for once with the joy of one hundred percent affirmation? It seems to me that it is only when I am in my country paradise listening to bird songs, picking vegetables and flowers, that a loud "yes" sounds in me. It is a small affirmation, but it is better than the despair that invades me when I contemplate the world outside. Barbara suffers from the same horror, but she manages to remain whole and true to herself with her faith in the evidence of good. Just as I am heartened by reading, for instance, that peregrine falcons have been raised in captivity and released to form a new breeding stock, just as I look to certain areas like this to build up a little reserve of hope, so Barbara draws hope from her own sources. But my hope drains out of me when I read that deserts are marching over the face of the earth and that the gradual destruction of rain forests not only threatens innumerable species of flora and fauna, but also the very existence of human beings. "Don't you agree," asks Barbara, "that if men don't become more like women, they will destroy our planet?" "Yes, I agree," I say, for the people who are in the process of destroying our planet, who cut down the great trees of the rain forests, who hasten the march of the deserts, who slaughter whales, who kill and torture each other, who head the great businesses that ship oil all over the world (oil that spills out by millions of gallons and destroys the planet by proxy, so to speak), who are presidents, premiers and dictators of every country of the world—they are all men, yes, every one of them. "They are doing these things because they want to prove they are men," says Barbara, whereas I think they are doing them because they are caught in the inexorable momentum of habit—the habit of power, politics, industry, greed, fear and need. If every one of them said without shame, there is also a woman in me, would that change everything? If every woman said, there is also a man in me, would that change everything? It would mean, rather, that everything had already changed and that people had been able to look deep into themselves and to see the reasons for being as they are. "It's not a question of sex," says Marie-Claire, "but of conscience," meaning that only by an exercise of conscience on a vast scale will humankind save our planet. "Or by a recognition of where their self-interest lies," says one of my brothers, who, having grown less optimistic about human nature from personal experience, believes that "original sin" can be channelled into constructive paths. All three of my siblings put much of their energy into helping other people and they help with a loving concern that I greatly admire.

Chapter Fifteen

I have said little until now about my siblings and little about my twin, the one who shared with me the intimate space of our mother's womb. This tidy quartet, composed of two older brothers and the twin sisters, meets once a year in Washington, D.C., where Charles, the eldest, now sixty-six, gives a report in our lawyer's office of the state of the family finances. Charles is an expert, has studied the management of every company and its personnel practices, analyzed the ups and downs of the stock market in terms of national and world politics, and he can recommend changes—or what to hang on to. He looks into space as he talks, his brow furrowed horizontally by his raised eyebrows. Both of my brothers raise their eyebrows high and emphatically when they talk. When Julian, the younger brother, takes the floor, the lines of his forehead push high into his snow-white hair. He has our mother's imposing nose and forehead and our father's big, deep-set eyes. Charles and I are said to look alike, though he has brown eyes and our maternal grandfather's full mouth. The four of us have enough features in common: our grey or white heads, our tallness, our eager diffident politeness, our elegant hands and feet, to be instantly recognizable as siblings. There is rivalry between the brothers and a concealed determination by Charles to hold on to his subject. Julian, a professor of preventive medicine at Yale University, has been crusading for better working conditions in factories, conditions that will prevent accidents from happening. A little flame is ignited between the brothers when Charles says that union demands have made it inadvisable to invest in certain mines and Julian replies that the miners have good reason to complain. While Julian is talking about conditions in mines, and Charles, who has been interrupted, sits brooding (for he, too, cares about people's welfare and he is doubtless smarting from this exercise in one-upmanship), I mentally try to squeeze in a visit to the National Gallery before leaving Washington. Suddenly, Charles says, "What do *you* think, Mary?" As usual, I am hard put to answer, since what I really think is that it is nice to have two brothers who watch so skillfully over our inherited income that I do not need to do it myself. Charles has given up hoping that I will take an active part, read *The Wall Street Journal,* etc. I have practiced non-violent resistance in this respect since our mother's death.

I notice this year that we have all begun to look our ages (sixty-six, sixty-three and sixty-one), that we have in common an almost imperceptible slowing down. Our voices are alike, all with traces of a Philadelphia accent, all highish, slightly nasal, often inaudible (for we all murmur, except Julian), slow and articulate. Perfectly constructed sentences roll out of our mouths, as eloquent as if they had been written in advance. When my mind is working well and I am not nervous, this kind of old-fashioned (Charles and I often sound as though we had been influenced by Dickens) speech comes effortlessly out of my mouth. Charles, in his youth, was the most accomplished talker in the family, but he now tends to keep silent, except when the others are listening respectfully to his annual report. Julian, who has a speech stored up in his head about every subject on earth, only needs a little trigger to set him off; I am constantly amazed by his computer mind and almost afraid of touching certain buttons. We no longer argue about politics, communism or the war in Vietnam; we do not talk about music, books, painting or even about our lives, except where our lives deal with social problems. Hester, my twin, has set up libraries in black schools in Boston; Julian has made a study of lead poisoning and works with the black community in New Haven; Charles is head of a civic group in Washington that deals with the city's problems —and each of them talks confidently and competitively in the manner of siblings about these things they know. I feel my conscience beginning to writhe like an unhappy eel and the frustration of forbidden subjects beginning to possess me. About my subjects, painting and writing, I am apt to become first defensive and then arrogant, even though Charles loves Shakespeare and the old masters at the National Gallery; and Julian, having sung in choral groups, knows Bach and Handel more thoroughly than I do. Why am I so uptight? Why do I clutch my life and my interests to me as though they were threatened? When I show them my *Illustrations for Two Novels by Marie-Claire Blais,* they turn over the pages in silence. Charles has what I interpret as a shocked expression on his face and I injudiciously accuse them of being shocked. The blood seems to explode in my head and accusations rush out of my mouth: you are Puritan; you don't know anything about life (they, who, in their work, see much more of life than I do). Julian explains patiently when my tirade is over that it is the result of the rush of lipids to the brain, cells laid down millions of years ago, that produce instant defensiveness and then aggression. "A wolf ends one of these displays by lying down and presenting his throat," Julian says, which I already know. I throw myself on the floor in a posture of submission, and the others, startled, laugh nervously. I am alarmed both by the pressure of the feelings boiling in me and by the fact that the whole scene is my fault, that I haven't waited for their reaction, have assumed that it will be negative and have charged blindly at them. I apologize, but it makes me angry to apologize for there is something, I think, that Charles, at least, believes and will not admit—namely, that art should not deal with certain subjects; and that if it does, it is indecent, even pornographic. I remember an argument that I had with him several years ago about an illustration which showed children in an outhouse. "You do violence to my feelings," he said. His feelings of decorum and decency were exactly like our mother's, though she might have been amused by this illustration. "We're *not shocked*," say both brothers. Yet Charles seems to have created areas in his mind that should not be thought about or talked about or looked at—invariably having to do with bodily functions and sex. "Give me time to look at the book carefully and then I'll write you what I think!" he says to me the next morning, but I am still waiting for his letter.

Is there a human being who does not tend to interpret silence as disapproval? The power of silence to put me into a state either of self-doubt or judgement of the other person has not waned after repeated proof that it can come from many sources. Silence, for me, is bloated with threats and fears; there is no way of fighting it, and the fact of it, both enclosing and assailing, makes me want to rage and accuse. I have spent most of my life sealed in a self-imposed silence, affronting the silence of others. "I belong to a generation which has lived and suffered in silence," I wrote to my sister when the barrier between us finally gave way. It was because of Barbara's courage that I was able to break my silence; Barbara had sent Hester her book, *We Cannot Live Without Our Lives*, with its dedication, "To my Lesbian sisters," and then, she sent me a copy of Hester's warm and loving letter of thanks for the book. "I have to admit that I'm not brave at all," Hester said, "and the jacket made me flinch. It doesn't make any difference to my feelings about you, as to whether you're a Lesbian. You're a brave, kind, intelligent, witty, sensitive, warm person and it appalls me to think of what you've put yourself through. . . . You may find it hard to believe that I've never discussed it with Mary, but that fact may show you quite simply why your book made me tremble."

With this, I began a correspondence with my sister from which I will quote at some length, for it took the classic pattern of over-reaction (mine), indignation (Hester's), hurt, apology, an attempt by both of us to straighten things out, and finally, a great harmony between us and an entirely new and really *sisterly* relationship. My silence with my family had always been that of pure terror; I was afraid when I saw my sister of even saying that I knew she had read Barbara's book and seen the dedication. I said in my first letter, "I was ever on the verge of mentioning it, but restrained by my pounding heart and FEAR, both of which I guess are the reasons for *your* silence." At the beginning, I was at least lucid about this thing which is so hard to remember—that the other person is conceivably as afraid to speak as you are. I went on to speak of "our parents' absolute horror of 'that,' unmentionable even, firmly planted in all of us, ignorant pronouncements...on the subject...contemptuous remarks about 'fags,' etc." by other members of the family. "One gets the feeling of being both visible and invisible, visible in the sense that one's outward life is there for anyone to see, and invisible in the sense that people can express their distaste for homosexuality in one's presence as if one weren't there listening and reacting. You have no idea how it feels to have to be as wary as an animal ALL THE TIME, to feel every single person (except homosexuals) as a potential enemy who can turn against you in the twinkling of an eye. For you may think you've accepted the idea just because of what you know of my life, but to have the words fall on you like a thunderbolt, if I say, 'I am a Lesbian,' or if you hear, 'Mary is a Lesbian'—that's worse, isn't it? Words are awful and 'Lesbian' is a word I've never been able to stand, so how could you?" At this point, I began to be carried away by my sense of the injustices that Lesbians in general and myself in particular have suffered, and I began to accuse my siblings. "Naturally, I associate you, C. and J. with Mother and Father; what have you ever said or done to prove that you feel differently?...I feel that NOTHING can be talked about...and the moment I set eyes on them (my brothers) I seem to have been tied into a strait jacket. As for you, I set you somewhat apart from our brothers and truly think that you're paralyzed by the fear of offending me, making me mad, saying something that I'll misunderstand or something you don't mean, of not being able to say (before I jump on you) what you DO mean. I realize it's exceedingly hard on you, given all our millions of years of total silence...."

Why, one may ask, did I not include my brothers in this last sentence? The answer lies in the fact that we presume to know what is in other people's heads, that we make deductions from tiny, often faulty bits of evidence. My brothers may well be paralyzed still (I have not yet talked to them) by the fear of offending me; *mea culpa*, I think, if I have misjudged them and if I haven't the courage to talk to them before we die. Not only do I presume that my brothers would judge me and that any conversation with them would be intolerable, but, after my first letter, I proceeded to tumble into all the traps I myself had foreseen. Hester, who was busy with many things when my letter came, called and said, "I just wanted you to know that I still love you." Alas, Lesbians are as touchy as lovers, and Hester's "still" touched something in me that released a bellow of hurt and rage. "Why *still*?" I asked in my second letter. "Why *not*, I should say? What has changed? Do you mean that you still love me even though I've finally put a label on something you've always known? You still love me in spite of the fact that this label makes you unhappy, that 'normal' people are made unhappy and uncomfortable by the knowledge that this awful thing exists so close? And that therefore it should never be mentioned and we (the 'abnormal' ones) should go back to hiding and silence? What has happened is, in fact, that we, who have been made unhappy by *you* ALL OUR LIVES, have now caused you a teeny bit of unhappiness and embarrassment, but you are so big-hearted that you *still* love us. We are the same nice people whom you've always loved and will always be these nice people (if only we'd shut up and not make you feel uncomfortable!). But do any of you ever ask yourselves, 'Does she…*still* love me?' No, you don't, because you think that only 'normal' people have the right to give and withhold love from the people who stray from society's laws. It never occurs to you to ask yourselves, 'Are we, who have made the lives of homosexuals unbearable and humiliating, guilty in *any* way? Do we deserve always to be loved in spite of it, and forgiven, forgiven forever?' Isn't it like saying, 'Some of my best friends are Jews'? this idea that because you like a person for herself, you'll still love her, even though she's a homosexual? When you said that, I thought, 'But that's exactly what Mother would have said,' feeling very proud of herself for having overcome the immense obstacle in the way of her love — *i.e.*, that her daughter is coming out and disgracing the entire family." Obviously this bitter speech had been in my mind for a long time and I needed only the flimsiest pretext to speak it. Re-reading my letters, I am sorry that I made my sister, who, as I said by way of apology, has never "as far as I remember said anything or done anything that I could construe as disapproval or dislike of me or my life," the scapegoat for society's undeniable anti-Lesbian attitude, but I am not sorry that I was carried away by my own touchiness. Many complicated aspects of prejudice were thrashed out in our letters and one of them was precisely that Hester seemed to be avoiding an examination of her feelings about homosexuals in general by insisting on her affection for the Lesbians she knew well. In a later letter, she said, "I don't deny that many people do feel disgust for homosexuals and I do understand your reactions to their snide remarks, but I'm sure that the very same people who make snide remarks about homosexuals in general don't feel disgust for you as an individual. You will no doubt say that this is the same as saying, 'My best friend is a Jew." To this, I replied, "It's *exactly* the same as saying, 'My best friend is a Jew. . . .' You seem to think that I'm comforted by the fact that people like me as an individual, but that really isn't the point. I'm lucky in that respect. The whole battle that we're fighting is precisely about 'homosexuals in general,' just as black people are fighting against tokenism. People have to be taught that they have no right to make snide remarks about the colour of one's skin or one's sexual preference or anything else."

After my first explosive letter, Hester answered, "I wish you could concentrate on your own present and not sicken yourself with bitter thoughts about the past or about what people think of you as a Lesbian, or indeed, what they think about homosexuality in general." In effect, she had said the same thing in her letter to Barbara: "One thought that is uppermost in my mind is that you've been, for some reason, determined to punish yourself all your life, but that now you've suffered enough." To which Barbara answered, "I don't enjoy punishment *at all*. Every 'courageous' act I've ever taken has been to *protest* punishment, to try to help bring about an end to it." To Hester, Barbara was punishing herself by deliberately putting herself in the line of fire; and I was punishing myself by sickening myself "with bitter thoughts." In my answer to this, I tried to explain the genesis of my bitter thoughts. "The trouble is that at the bottom of every homosexual heart there is a sediment that's very easily stirred up—of resentment and frustration and all the rest, because we really haven't been allowed to live our lives without fear and without a sense of being disapproved of. I don't think you have any idea of the effect this can have on a person and the struggle one has to wage against being deformed or destroyed by it.... I can remember little things: for instance, C. saying with a superior little laugh about a sculptress, 'She's as queer as can be.' Multiply remarks like this by one thousand, and then add a good dose of Sodom and Gomorrah and hellfire and abnormality and perversion, the components of every society, and try to drink it down without choking."

Hester's concern about my bitter thoughts was concern for me, that I was making myself unhappy, that these thoughts were perhaps partly responsible for my headaches and backaches. To Barbara, she said, "You've suffered enough." Perhaps this concern of hers was absolutely free of the guilt feelings that homosexual bitterness and rage create in heterosexual hearts and the subsequent backlash in the form of a wish that they would hide their feelings, behave in a more dignified manner and stop airing this painful issue. But the end of silence for a homosexual, even if it is ended by the breaking loose of anger, is such an inebriating experience that it is worth the pain of being out in the open. When my correspondence with my twin had passed through violence to become a real dialogue, I had a sensation of joyful relief, of liberation from a burden I had laboured under all my adult life. I suffered for years from the distance between myself and this nearest relation, and now, we had begun not only to talk easily about the long-forbidden subject, but also to analyze our respective touchiness.

The effects of this correspondence were positive for me, but I wonder now if my sister, too, benefited from it. I was released from dread; but Hester, what was she released from? From silence? From her own fear? When I called her to ask if I could use her letters in this book, I could tell that she was afraid. That phone call made me feel as if nothing had been gained and I fell into a state of depression. It was at this time that Anne Poor came to visit, the friend whom I have known even longer than I have known Barbara, with whom I have gone through the joys and

vicissitudes of friendship, our difficult characters clashing sometimes like cymbals, with periods when each of us was enclosed in
her own life and inaccessible to the other, "opaque and
unknowable." But now we were close enough to each other, I
thought, so that I could give her my book to read and talk to her
about Hester's fear. To my surprise, she got very angry. "If she
doesn't want you to use her letters, you can't use them. It's
against the law! You can get put in jail!" We were at the dinner
table. Anne was wearing her dark glasses and her invisible eyes
seemed to be glaring at me. "You asked me what I thought!" she
said furiously. I felt the painful vulnerability of someone who expects to be defended and is, instead, attacked. Anne evidently
considered Hester to be the victim in this family controversy, at
the mercy of my indiscreet wish to present my case. "Books are a
form of witchcraft," I remarked, for hadn't I been hexed by Dolly Lamb? My book threatens everybody: family, friends, even
myself. I have opened my soul to interpretation and dragged the
others with me. And Anne feels vicariously threatened. It isn't
the first time that I have touched this fear in people — of being
seen, of letting little pieces of themselves escape and become
public property. One gives up power by sharing oneself with
others; in another sense, one gains by receiving from other people. It depends on their use of you. The fear is that the fragile
pieces of oneself will be mistreated, broken, altered beyond
recognition. Anne, like many people, lives by keeping herself
safely under lock and key, whereas my belief is that the sharing
of oneself is much less dangerous than one thinks. Still, it is seen
as an ordeal and Anne cannot endure another ordeal. She has
borne her mother's long illness and death; Henry's death; her
own almost mortal illnesses — gratuitous slings and arrows that
seem to seek her out. She has been beaten down by misfortune;
her body is a little stooped; she walks slowly on her painful foot;
her black hair has turned grey, has thinned and falls raggedly
over her forehead. She has a strong, noble head and dark eyes
that can flash fire under the menacing black of her eyebrows or
glow with tenderness; she has alternations of gaiety and sombre
darkness, when she is full of irrational anger that scares me, I who
never know the reason for it. Every visit has the same form: first

the gaiety; then, the mysterious anger; and finally, the loving feelings that mark our separation, as if the latter could not come into being without the unexplained anger of the middle period.

Of all my painter friends, Anne seems to me to be the most extraordinary. Perhaps Emily Carr was like her—ferocious in her solitude, irascible, passionate, longing to give herself in love and fearing for her life as a painter, angrily guarding that life, sure of her genius, androgynous like many great women artists, and fiercely keeping her secret-self secret, shut up in a "yourself shell," as Emily Carr put it. "You can't break through and get out; nobody can break through and get in. If there was an instrument strong enough to break the 'self shells' and let out the spirit it would be grand."

That Anne is a great painter, this is perhaps all she wants known about herself or wants to know. My love for getting everything out in the open dashes itself against her determination to hide, her flights into irrationality and anger, her ability to turn the subject upside down and backwards, so that I end by defending myself against some wholly unexpected charge. After reading a few pages of my book, she says, "I'm not going to finish this book," but she goes on to the end, almost without comment. Always destroyed by silence, I try to draw her out. I guess that Anne's anger has to do with two things: her entire dedication (another Mary!) to her work and her determination to be only a painter; and her fierce sense of privacy. I have broken two rules: I have given up painting for a whole year in order to finish this book and I have talked about myself in a way that Anne would never do. I recall scraps of conversation. I have asked Anne if she thinks the book will change people's minds about Lesbians. She flares up, tells me I shouldn't try to convert the world, says she didn't know I suffered from being a Lesbian, says people now take homosexuality for granted. I swallow my anger for once, backtrack from my crusading position and say that I wanted to write an honest portrait of *one* Lesbian—myself. Pat me on the back, I beg silently, but Anne's reply is non-committal.

Anne's life has been consecrated to the essential—to her work of seeing. She gave up playing the piano long ago in order to be more entire. When she looks at something, it is as though a burning-glass had gathered the rays of the sun into one piercing ray of attention. She sees things undistractedly, sees where I fail to look, or where I look with indifference. I have noticed the focusing power of Anne's eyes and brain many times in the course of the years; how ideas would coalesce in her mind and come out in some beautiful form. Once, in Wellfleet, we drew each other simultaneously in my studio; I still have my drawing of Anne, crouched over, like a runner or a wrestler, with an almost crazy brilliance in her eyes, her whole being concentrated on the athletic task of attention. From this powerful concentration, the strong hands, the big head with its glowing eyes, came paintings of unimaginable delicacy: flowers charged with the poetry and light of summer; light gathered into the canvas and subjected to a refining process that breathes it out as pure spirit. She paints big landscapes, the whole shimmering with pure light, like Turner's, that dissolves the hard volumes of houses or mountains and makes them one with trees, earth and sky. She has done hundreds of portrait sketches and portraits in oils, not literal likenesses, but portraits of the life in every sitter; of the soul, if you like, fragile and enduring. I think of her human portraits and one of an Afghan dog in a field, so electrically alive that the canvas seems to explode with the unclouded happiness of Everydog running in the sunshine. I feel the same awe when I look at Anne's work that I feel before all the great painters I love, before Redon and Munch, in particular, for Anne has something of each in her work—the unearthly delicacy of Redon and the piercing and tragic vision of Munch—and will be recognized like them, if the world holds together for a few more years.

I read my letters to Anne, written over a period of twenty years, nostalgic and yearning, for I never saw enough of her. I find one from Wellfleet that I wrote in April, 1969: "It's raining and gloomy; the redwinged blackbirds are shrieking and yelling in the treetops, I'm playing Brahms trios and feeling pleasantly solitary. Suddenly the thought of you came to me so strongly— with such nostalgia—that I wanted to write and say—*dearest* Annie, we'll always be friends, won't we? *Always see each other.* So many years have gone by, so many complications and people

251

obstructing our view of each other and snarling our lines of communication; so many letters written . . . so many paintings painted, so much silent pain and the impossibility of talking about any of it. And yet you're just as real and important to me as ever and I feel as if the distance between us is artificial and that the tenderest moments of our friendship are the true ones. . . . Sometimes I need terribly to talk to you about painting, what's happened to it and to us and what prevents me from painting. . . ." And I end on an apocalytic note, "I honestly don't think the world is going to last very much longer—fifty years maybe." It was a time of doom-saying in every realm, including the arts. Easel painting was said to be dead; so was the novel, and people who still painted from nature spoke of themselves as an "underground." Under the pressure of outer and inner doubts, I look to my friendships as the most solid reality of my life. "Some friendships I hope must and shall last as long as life itself," I read in one of Anne's letters to me. I am thankful always for my three closest friends: Marie-Claire, Barbara and Anne. They are all heroic, have been tested, have forged themselves out of the matter of their lives. Anne, Barbara and I are all anxious about the time that remains, how to keep to what seems essential. Marie-Claire, only thirty-nine, has years ahead of her, can hardly imagine what it is like to be able to count the years of active life that are left, if one is lucky, years that slide by now like months, like hours. I am going to watch myself die, if possible; indeed, I am already interested in the strange non-cooperation of my body when I wake up in the morning, my legs like pillars of inert matter, my back that refuses to bend, my alien hands and feet. "It's nothing to how you're going to feel in a few years," said my doctor when I complained about incipient arthritis, so I take vitamins, essence of New Zealand seaweed; read pamphlets about miraculous cures by means of massive doses of dolomite, vitamin C or vegetable soup.

Chapter Sixteen

July 31st, 1978. The bobolinks stopped singing in the middle of July and now one hears only an occasional robin, a song sparrow, goldfinches, and the chittering swallows lined up on the electric wire that runs to the barn. The latter have profited by the summer's marvellous alternation of rain and sunshine and have multiplied. Thirty or forty at a time slip out of the high windows in the barn and join in an ecstatic aerial dance. The young, still unsure of their wings, sit timidly on posts or on the swaying ends of dead willow branches, waiting their turn to be fed. The forking feathers of their tails have not yet grown. The parents rise and fall on air currents so close to the east windows that I get a good look at the transparent white of their tails when they bank and turn. Today is almost cold. The western sky is a dazzling blue, and, in the east, a long curtain of fog is hugging the mountains, while in the foreground, the grass is bright in the sun. The fog curtain narrows, trees emerge; two crows are perched on the tip of a big dead spruce down the hill; a song sparrow sings close to the house. The wind is from the northwest. My heart begins to ache when the birds stop singing; just as the bobolinks have come to herald summer, their silence heralds autumn. At night, the stars are brilliant in the moonless sky, and I see the familiar constellations, as I used to in Woods

Hole, Wellfleet, Maine and Brittany, and think of the combinations of names that have always seemed beautiful to me: Antares in Scorpio, Spica in Virgo, Regulus in Leo, Aldebaran in Taurus. In early July, there was a celebration of fireflies and an enormous toad sat motionless just outside the garage door; now they have gone and the frogs and tree toads, like the birds, have stopped singing. The days have begun to get shorter and summer is slipping into autumn.

August 12th. Solitude induces contemplation of one's life, nostalgia and creeping melancholy. I reflect on the millions of things I have seen, heard, smelled, tasted and touched that are unrecorded in this book, for it is not a book about my life's events, of which I hardly speak, but an attempt, rather, to define myself through its inscape. I look at myself in the mirror and see a cap of pale hair, neither grey nor white, but greenish-blue, falling from the crown of my head over my grey eyebrows, with two wrinkles like long vertical commas that rise at each inner end. I see eyes the colour of faded blue jeans, close-fitting eyelids descending at a wide angle toward the nose instead of forming a classical crescent. Something like a stain in the corner of each eye seems to set them further behind a smallish straight nose with prominent nostrils; the mouth, a broad turned-down bow with wrinkles at the corners leading from the nose; erstwhile dimples; good strong teeth apparently, but much mended on the inside; a wide smile, a potential grim look when the mouth turns down; a square jaw; two folds leading into a skinny neck. My sunburned face makes me look younger than I am. My wrists are thin and brown; my hands almost square in their broadness, veined, with long tapering fingers, the knuckles expanded by arthritis; the index finger of my right hand, humped and thick, the result of a basketball that landed directly on it years ago. They are artistic and serviceable hands that can draw, paint, carve, saw, hammer, sew, garden, type, etc.; in winter, when the sunburn has faded, they are covered with freckles, as my mother's hands used to be, the freckles of age. My thin body with square shoulders, bony shoulder blades, small virginal breasts, narrow hips and straight legs with thickish ankles and well-preserved, high-arched feet, is dressed in jeans and a green turtleneck. I have shrunk to a little under five feet eight inches. I wear horn-rimmed glasses for reading, but I can see a bird at a great distance without glasses. I look unmistakably Anglo-Saxon, so that, in foreign countries, people always answer me in English, even when I speak their language, and I remember myself and Barbara in Japan, two tall thin women with brown bangs, towering above the sea of black heads, whose strangeness provoked giggles or fixed stares wherever we went. In photographs, my hair looks silvery and my face very pink; one gets the impression of a woman sweeter, younger and more graceful than I feel inside. Sometimes Marie-Claire and I look alike in photographs because of our high foreheads which we keep hidden, nervously patting into place hair that is blown back by the wind; and because of our strong jaws. Her hands and feet are like narrowed reductions of mine, but pale, almost bloodless, whereas my blood seems to lie just under the surface, ready to rush to my extremities and to turn my face peony-red.

I do not wish to pronounce judgement on this person I see in the mirror who at least has the virtue of being more visually interesting as she grows older. For years I have fought in self-portraits with the intractable facts of my face, wanting to show something profound and succeeding only in painting a face either too pretty or too severe. Looking in a mirror at my painted image (a way of seeing everything one has done wrong), I would see that one eye was perhaps higher than the other, or that the mouth had a Calvinist dourness. If I had the obscure wish to torture myself on a certain day, I would start a self-portrait. Almost nothing remains of these exercises in masochism, and yet, I continue to hope that some day a self-portrait will appear that will seem to be myself. The lines around my mouth, my anxious eyes, my boyish body with its muscular arms and powerful hands—these are the elements of a portrait of a Lesbian; my life with its mixture of shame and pride must be visible in my face like those ambiguous features that are neither masculine nor feminine.

"I have had my vision," thinks Lily Briscoe at the end of *To the Lighthouse*. All through the book, she has been working on a landscape, with alternations of hope and despair. When she draws a line "there, in the centre," she has the sense that the picture, an "attempt at something," whose fate, she thinks, is to be hung in the attic or destroyed, is finished. A moment before, she and old Mr. Carmichael somehow know that Mr. Ramsay and the children, Cam and James (now grown-up), have landed at the lighthouse, "'He has landed,' she said aloud. 'It is finished.'" It is as though Lily Briscoe, the artist, has succeeded in arresting time, as though only art can arrest time, the continuum which, in the book, has dissolved insubstantial memory, grief and love; and the substantial bodies of Mrs. Ramsay, Prue and Andrew. Mr. Ramsay has withstood time almost by the exercise of his ego, it seems, and so has James, by the force of his rebellion against his father. These are held in the present by Lily's vision, as the book makes an eternal present out of the continuous flow of time—and death. Lily is the channel through which time flows and she suffers throughout the book from her inability to arrest it long enough even to speak the words of love that she wants to speak. She longs to speak of Mrs. Ramsay, about her death, and can only feel the unexpressed want of her heart, and, at the centre of what she sees with her eyes, "complete emptiness."

In the course of *To the Lighthouse*, Lily Briscoe becomes middle-aged. Writing this book, I have become four years older. A life is so enormous, a single day so infinitely long! The inexorable flow of time is braked by visions like Lily Briscoe's, by any effort to make time yield the fullness of its meaning. To write about one's life is an attempt to arrest time, as art does; to order it, just as Lily Briscoe ordered the elements: light, colour and form, of her landscape; to see it rather than just submit to the flow of dissolving minutes. Already, today has its composition and is filling with details: the hummingbird inspecting my head as I picked snowpeas; the sparrow the cat caught and I managed to set free; the gentle rain in my face as I walked down the hill with the three dogs, saw a female marsh hawk cruising over the field, heard the twittering of a goldfinch rising and falling, saw a new wildflower growing on the other side of the ditch that runs the length of the road. I slid into the ditch in order to cut a spray of the flower and had a hard time getting out, saw myself, grey-headed, clambering up the bank under the barbed wire, bearing home the flower and making it into one of my instant images. It was an Everlasting Pea (*Lathyrus Latifolius*), "Alien," it says in the flower guide. What is it doing here? Life in Canada has reduced the size of the flower and elongated its leaves. I, an alien, like the Everlasting Pea, have also jumped to Canada. I feel the familiar ache induced by the sweetness of my life here, the sight of the grand and subtle landscape and the feel of its small rhythms; and those other terrible images of the "real" world superimposed on my peaceful ones. I hear the monotonous voice of a friend who lives on the West Side in New York City, where gratuitous acts of violence, beatings, rape, murder, theft are committed every day by people who have nothing better to do. She has seen three teenagers set upon an old man and beat him senseless. She rushed to her apartment to get her dog, but it was too late, they had disappeared. "There is nothing to do but round them up and exterminate them," she said. This was the mood of people on the West Side who had been beaten and robbed and who were watching the city slowly go to rot. I thought of Edmund. "Exterminate them," were his words, too, though he had not suffered like my friend in New York. Barbara would have something to say to this woman who wanted to take a gun and exact a life for a life, who could see no reason not to, and to whom I could give no reason that would change her mind. After all, what do I know about it? Don't I grow savage when people abuse my precious property rights, kill birds, ride motorcycles on *my* land?

What would I be like if my landscape were a hot street littered with garbage and broken glass, if I had never received nor given love in my life, and if the future held only the prospect of more of the same? Wouldn't I turn on people, the more helpless the better, with murderous rage or with careless indifference, and punish them for the way I'd been punished? As it is, living my privileged life, I punish in my mind what hurts me and struggle with the inexplicable anguish beating dully at the heart of every second, existential anguish, my small share of the pain and fear that is the heartbeat of life. Even as I fix my eyes on the glimmering green back of the hummingbird below me as she hovers over a flower, as I admire the delicate scimitar of her beak, I feel anguish squeezing my heart. Is it the accumulation of great remembered tragedies or those too tiny even to be recorded that scatter their mute evidence like the scattered feathers of the cat's victims on the garage floor? Or is it the thought of friends, each bound like Lazarus in his shroud, to whom one wants to say, "Yes, in this, we are identical twins, all of us, our identical caged selves, beating our wings and crying for help or huddled in miserable silence."

It is 10:30 a.m. I am thinking of Barbara and her pain, which she fears is cancer. I close my eyes and touch her long body in imagination, under her ribs where the pain is, and my hands draw it out, finer and finer, until it has all flowed from her body and she says, "It has gone!" One can only share the physical suffering of others by the transfusion of love which flows from life into life, despite the barriers that our pain and our selves erect. A letter has come from Sylvia Marlowe, who speaks of a "Job-like suffering." She has been chosen by the usual obscure forces to be tortured with burning scars on her face, eyes, neck; she is drugged and miserable, her eyebrows and eyelashes gone, her eyes half-closed; she is tormented by loneliness, by the fear of death and by unremitting pain. Barbara, who felt peace entering her body and steadying her soul when we all thought about her, agreed with me to think of Sylvia in the same way; Barbara and Marie-Claire and I intend to concentrate together. Again, I close my eyes, hold Sylvia's hand and stroke her face. I tell her repeatedly in my mind that she is not alone, that we are there with her, that the scars will fall off and her skin be smooth again, that she will feel the peace of our love entering into her, will sleep and feel better when she wakes up. A series of pictures of our long friendship crowd into my head, like dreams. I hear her practicing her harpsichord in the house in Newport. The notes fly out from under her strong fingers, her artist's hands, rain, like sunlit drops in a fountain, or are compressed in emphatic chords. She is practicing Bach's Italian concerto with its ringing two-chord opening followed by notes tumbling over each other in their ardent haste, bound by the decisive rhythm. I hear this beginning repeated and then rushing like a waterfall along its course. And I see her magnificent self, clad in a full white satin dress, like a queen, her blonde hair piled high on her head, at a concert, bent over the harpsichord, plucking out the shimmering or quick-beating notes with the marvellous machinery of her hands. Sylvia, brusque, tough and tender, with her deep laugh, and abrupt, sometimes biting response, whom I feared in my hopeless timidity—and loved. She was capable of knocking me flat with some verbal swipe and then picking me up anxiously like a mother bear. Tough and tender, even with the gentle Leonid, who sulked a little, but who was never outwardly angry. She has a passionate respect for everything great in art and a profound knowledge of music, the mysteries of which I would be unable to grasp in several lifetimes. She is a vessel for the mystery of art and holds in her brain and hands: Bach, Rameau, Vivaldi, Mozart, Handel, Rieti, de Falla—all those millions of notes with their hundreds of precise structures. All this, I think about now, willing her to know that she is not alone, wishing that the body that has betrayed her artist's mind will again become the sun-loving, sensual body I used to see stretched out in a black bathing suit on the Newport rocks, that her voice on the telephone, heavy with pain, will have the old playful brusqueness. "It didn't do any good, but thank you," she tells me when I ask about our concentration on her. She is suffering as much as ever from the aftermath of shingles, but her voice on the telephone sounds better and she says she has at least begun to believe she may get well.

In our isolation, our only hope is to try to be "members, one of another." I try to tune out my doubts, the knowledge that we can look so often on our fellow human beings as members of an alien race. We are so sure that we could never behave like the murderers, the torturers, the human monsters who seem to have multiplied in the world. We scarcely know the dark places of ourselves and cannot foresee the *reductios ad absurdum* that old age is preparing for us. Each of my annual visits to Wellfleet is an ordeal of acceptance of the changes in old friends, the ghostly maps that age seems suddenly to have made of unlined faces, the departures and disappearances: the senile to rest homes; the dead to their graves.

We like to think that death, the brutal metamorphosis that takes life's matter and makes it unrecognizable and stills the wild music in the brain and heart once and for all, is powerless to kill the energy of all those impulses that have been emitted from the living individual, have entered into the air, and into other minds. The death of friends has only this comfort to give us. I think of all the friends to whom I never said goodbye: Edmund, Miss Horti and Wyncie, Henry, Bessie, Leonid. Indeed, I have only said goodbye in a literal sense to one person, my mother, as she slipped from sleep to death. Whatever our closeness or distance from the dead, from the almost careless way in which our brains register the megadeaths of our time, to the burning reproaches we make ourselves after the death of someone we love, the thought of death, with its certain and imminent coming, should be a call to shake off the fetters that keep us from being alive; a call to refuse to accept those pernicious and recurrent deaths of our most living selves that kill as surely as any disease. Among these deaths is the refusal to "thoroughly live" in the presence of others, really to greet, really to say goodbye, which is a long process of simultaneous attention and letting-go. Growing old does not always make people better at this; reason can speak its words of wisdom and make its resolves, which the body then betrays. But as I grow older in the body that keeps me ignorant of my own future, I draw up a defiant master plan — promises to myself that will require many years to fulfill — and I propose to keep as many as possible.